Introduction to
Local Area
Networks

GET THE BEST CONNECTIONS FROM
NETWORK PRESS™

You CAN judge a book by its cover.

This Network Press™ title is part of a new, expanded series replacing Sybex's acclaimed Novell Press® book series. With Network Press, you'll find the same dedication to quality from a truly independent and unbiased point of view. Our unique perspective guarantees you full coverage of Novell, Microsoft, and the other network environments.

Building on 20 years of technical and publishing excellence, Network Press provides you the broadest range of networking books published today. Our well-known commitment to quality, content, and timeliness continues to guarantee your satisfaction.

Network Press books offer you:

- winning certification test preparation strategies
- respected authors in the field of networking
- all new titles in a wide variety of topics
- up-to-date, revised editions of familiar best-sellers

Look for the distinctive black-and-white Network Press cover as your guarantee of quality. A comprehensive selection of Network Press books is available now at your local bookstore.

For more information about Network Press, please contact:

Network Press
1151 Marina Village Parkway
Alameda, CA 94501
Tel: (510)523-8233 Toll Free: (800) 227-2346
Fax: (510)523-2373 E-mail: info@sybex.com

Introduction to Local Area Networks

Robert M. Thomas

NETWORK PRESS ®
SYBEX

San Francisco ■ Paris ■ Düsseldorf ■ Soest

Acquisitions Manager: Kristine Plachy
Developmental Editor: Guy Hart-Davis
Editor: James A. Compton
Technical Editor: Denise Martineau
Book Design: Seventeenth Street Studio
Technical Illustrator: Cuong Le
Desktop Publisher: Printed Page Productions, Berkeley, CA
Proofreader/Production Assistant: Renée Avalos
Indexer: Nancy Guenther
Cover Design: Archer Design
Cover Photographer: Michael Orton

Library of Congress Card Number: 95-71248
ISBN: 0-7821-1814-3

Manufactured in the United States of America
10 9 8 7 6 5 4 3

To
Tully Bascomb,
with admiration

Acknowledgments

I AM DEEPLY GRATEFUL to Jim Compton at SYBEX books, first for his editing—he transformed my inchoate and often murky manuscript into something more coherent and clear than I ever could have written on my own. I am also deeply appreciative of his support for the book's point of view, and patience with me while the project was coming together.

Many thanks as well to Guy Hart-Davis, developmental editor at SYBEX, for the time he took to make many useful suggestions, most of which found their way into the final product in some form, and have improved it a great deal.

I am grateful as well to the many people who work behind the scenes to make a book out of a simple manuscript: Thanks to Cuong Le, who took what amounted to some "chalkboard sketches" and produced book illustrations; Renée Avalos, proofreader and production assistant; also thanks to Seventeenth Street Studio for their book design, Marla Wilson at Printed Page Productions, who handled the desktop publishing, and Nancy Guenther, who produced the index. My thanks as well to Denise Martineau for her technical editing.

A bit closer to home, many thanks to Rich Teich and Francia Friendlich of Aquarian Age Computers in San Francisco, who generously supplied printed documentation and other research materials, then cheerfully and thoroughly answered my many questions. I am grateful once again to my wife, Krista, for her patience while I obsessed over the manuscript. And finally, as always, my thanks to Roscoe and Elaine, who've been networking quite successfully for some time now.

— BT

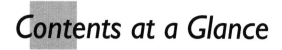

Contents at a Glance

Table of Contents

Introduction

THE GOAL OF *Introduction to Local Area Networks* is to offer a bird's-eye view of the computer networking landscape to people who are approaching the subject for the first time. This book intends to demystify the networking process, and describe it in general, as nontechnically as the subject matter will allow. The book will succeed if, after reading it, you are comfortable with the networking process and can talk knowledgeably with colleagues, consultants, and system vendors about installing or upgrading a computer network for your business.

Who Should Read This Book

If you do everyday business tasks using a desktop computer, you have all the necessary background you need to read and understand this book. This book was written for you if you are a manager or executive in a small to medium-sized business, and:

- You believe that your business could do better by connecting computers that currently reside on desktops, allowing your users to share information electronically;

- You have a network, but don't understand enough about how it works to decide whether it's working at peak efficiency;

- You are not certain how to begin moving from stand-alone desktop computers to an integrated, networked system;

- You believe that computers are business tools whose purpose is to save or make money for your business, and you want to find out if a computer network will do that.

How This Book Is Organized

The book has fourteen chapters grouped into five parts, plus two appendices:

- **Part I**, Making Computers Communicate, gives a general overview of what networks do, how they go about doing it, and who benefits from them.

- **Part II,** Network Hardware, introduces the hardware components of a networked computer system: cabling, network interface cards, workstations, servers, and the like.

- **Part III,** Network Software, describes the types of software that networks use: network operating system software and application software that is especially designed for networks: databases, e-mail, and groupware.

- **Part IV,** Network Design and Management, ties the hardware and software concepts together, showing you how to design and manage a local area network.

- **Part V,** Networking the Database—and Beyond, looks at databases, because they are integral to so many networks; it suggests strategies for designing and maintaining databases, and it offers a brief look at SQL, the standard language for managing databases on a network. The last chapter pulls together the book's most important tips for getting started in networking your business, and it offers some suggestions for further study.

- **Appendix A** offers advice on selecting and hiring a networking consultant; Appendix B is a handy glossary of network-related acronyms and jargon.

A second purpose of this book is to convey a specific attitude toward networking and business computing in general: Computers are tools, nothing more. They are tools in the same way that hammers, saws, and paintbrushes are tools used to construct a dwelling. Construction tools operate on raw data (wood, nails, plaster, paint) to make it useful. Their use is not an end in itself, nor a substitute for the goal of the construction process, which is to produce a worthwhile end result.

Likewise, computers are not ends in themselves, they are tools for facilitating what it is that makes business worthwhile: forming fulfilling relationships between people, and making some money along the way.

But how to begin? If you wanted to build your dream home but did not know where to begin, you might start by learning about various tools that are available for getting the job done. With that first step in mind, you could go to your local bookstore and pick out a book that shows you home-construction tools and describes how they work.

This book shows you hardware and software tools that you use to construct a network and describes how they work. The descriptions in this book won't turn you into a networking consultant overnight, but when you are finished, you will be a lot more comfortable with the subject, and you'll have a solid basis for going forward into the details of designing and constructing your own "dream network." Have fun, take your time, and above all, enjoy the process!

Making Computers Communicate

PART

Networks in the Workplace

THIS CHAPTER PRESENTS a brief overview of computer networks—their power and their limitations. It will help you decide whether your business is well suited for implementing a network, and what choices you have regarding the type of computer network you should consider.

Why Networks Exist

IN THE EARLY 1980s, when desktop computers began to proliferate in the business world, the intent of their designers was to create machines that would operate independently of each other. The computing ideal was summed up with the phrase, "One User, One Computer," which meant that individuals were free to manage information on their own desktop any way they liked.

This attitude was a reaction to the business-information environment of the time, based on large mainframe computers controlled by technical specialists and programmers. If you wanted information—a report on the aging of your accounts receivable, for example—you made a request to the Information Services (IS) Department, who would program the computer to provide the report for you. The report could take any length of time to produce, depending on its complexity, and your only choice was to wait while IS massaged your report out of the mainframe. Once you got the report, if you didn't like its format or if the information in it wasn't clear for any reason, you would make another request to IS, wait some more, and hope the revised report was useful.

Desktop computers changed that. With a computer on your desktop, you could enter the information yourself, manipulate it to your heart's content, and produce the report you really wanted. (Of course, information stored on the mainframe would have to be re-entered at the desktop, but this was often considered a worthwhile trade-off for the freedom to manipulate the data at will.)

IS departments were slow to realize the value of the desktop computers, and through the early 1980s regarded them as toys rather than worthwhile business information machines. By the time IS realized something serious was afoot, desktop computers had become more powerful, and applications for desktop computers included simple spreadsheets, databases, and word processors.

The market for desktop computers exploded, and dozens of hardware and software vendors joined in fierce competition to exploit the open opportunity for vast profits. The competition spurred intense technological development, which led to increased power on the desktop and lower prices. Desktop computers were soon performing what appeared to be miracles in comparison to mainframe applications: desktop publishing, graphics, computer-aided drafting, more powerful databases, and sophisticated user interfaces. Small businesses in particular were able to benefit from information management services that, a few years earlier, had been available only to wealthy corporations.

Something interesting happened as the desktop computer took over the way the world conducted its business: the ideal of "One User, One Computer" became an obsolete handicap rather than the liberating idea it was intended to be. Marketplace competition created large numbers of computers from different manufacturers and vendors, large numbers of applications, and the unimaginably vast amount of information stored in desktop systems.

Businesses soon rediscovered an old axiom: Business information is useful only when it is communicated between human beings. They also discovered a frustrating bottleneck: The process of distributing and communicating information among individuals, each with an independent desktop computer, is slow and prone to error.

Because of the large volume of information now being handled, it was impossible to pass along paper copies of information and ask each user to reenter it into their own computer. Copying files onto floppy disks and passing them around was a little better, but still took too long, and was impractical when individuals were separated by great distances. And you could never know for sure that the copy you received on a floppy disk was the most current version of the information—the other person might have updated it on their computer after the floppy was made.

For all the speed and power of the desktop computing environment, it was sadly lacking in the most important element: communication among members of the business team.

The obvious solution was to link the desktop computers together, and link the group to a shared central repository of information. Desktop computers were not designed with this capacity in mind, and there were now thousands of these machines in the marketplace representing billions of dollars in business assets. No one was willing to scrap their desktop machines altogether and replace them with new machines (and new software) designed for the sort of communication people now realized was necessary.

Besides, computer manufacturers were quite clever, and they were able to create additional components that users could attach to their desktop computers, which would allow them to share data among themselves and access centrally located sources of information. Unfortunately, the early designs for these networks were slow and tended to break down at critical moments.

Still, the desktop computer continued to evolve. As it became more powerful, capable of accessing larger and larger amounts of information, communications between desktop computers gradually became more reliable, and the idea of a Local Area Network (LAN) became a practical reality for businesses.

Computer networks, with all their promise and power, are more complicated to maintain than simple stand-alone machines. They require consistent attention from managers whose job it is to oversee the network and keep it running smoothly. Ironically, this concept looked a lot like the old mainframe paradigm, where a specialized cadre of technical insiders has power to make information available. In some ways, it appears as if business computing has come full circle, from IS to desktop and back to IS again.

But IS departments look a lot different today than they did ten years ago. Users are more sophisticated, or at least more demanding. They want the same instant access, flexibility, and independence they became used to with their stand-alone desktop machines, plus access security and data accuracy throughout the business enterprise.

Add to this the fact that the whole idea of networking has evolved as well. Computer networks can exist within a single room, an entire building, a city, a country, the world. There are networks of networks, and networks that access each other at will, or at the whim of individual users who contact them any time over telephone lines.

IS personnel have evolved from "high priests" with exclusive access to sensitive business information, to "manager/mechanics," whose chief function is to keep the data flowing smoothly among users. They also function as "security guards," who keep data safe from accidental (and sometimes deliberate) damage and loss. In some cases, the entire IS department has been replaced by a *network administrator*, a single person with responsibility for training, problem-solving and technical support throughout the enterprise.

The proliferation of manufacturers and vendors, each vying for the loyalty of the hardware and software consumers, makes the new IS manager's job more difficult. The intense competition is in some ways beneficial, because it keeps prices low and fosters technical innovation; but it also has its drawbacks. There are conflicting technical standards for exactly how all these billions of bits of electronic data are to be transferred quickly and accurately between dozens of different types of machines. Each type handles data in its own unique way, and the technical standards must define how to avoid typical network problems: electronic collisions along the data pathways, corruption of the data into meaningless electronic gibberish, lost data, or misdirection of data to unintended destinations.

For the time being, the world of networking looks like a Tower of Babel, at least until certain manufacturers and vendors, who do the best job of filling the information and communication needs of the business marketplace, emerge and narrow the spectrum of choices.

Is it worthwhile simply to wait? The answer depends on your own circumstances, and how profitable your business can remain in the advancing information age. In the computer world, waiting while the technology evolves has always been rewarded: prices tend to come down, technology to become more powerful. But waiting can be punished as well: Businesses with access to modern information technology enjoy a significant competitive advantage over their more technologically limited counterparts.

Networks allow more efficient management of resources. For example, multiple users can share a single top-quality printer, rather than putting duplicate, possibly lesser-quality printers on individual desktops. Also, network software licenses can be less costly than separate, stand-alone licenses for the same number of users.

Networks help keep information reliable and up-to-date. A well managed, centralized data storage system allows multiple users to access data from different locations, and limit access to data while it is being processed.

Networks help speed up data sharing. Transferring files across a network is almost always faster than other, non-network means of sharing files.

Networks allow workgroups to communicate more efficiently. Electronic mail and messaging is a staple of most network systems, in addition to scheduling systems, project monitoring, on-line conferencing and groupware, all of which help work teams be more productive.

Networks help businesses service their clients more effectively. Remote access to centralized data allows employees to service clients in the field, and clients to communicate directly with suppliers.

Wait as long as you can, so that you can take advantage of falling prices, but jump in too soon rather than too late. Too much delay can cost you your opportunity to compete altogether.

Who Needs to Network?

A LONG WITH ALL the overheated competition in the computer business comes a deluge of hype. Vendors, with a sharp eye out for your limited technology budget, are shouting over each other about how you cannot possibly survive without their system, and how their system will transform your business from a plodding, unprofitable tin box into a fast, impregnable money machine.

Will it? If you are the leader or IS manager of a business considering the switch to a networked computing environment, you may be wondering if all the trouble and expense will be worth it. Here are some questions to ask yourself, which will help you decide if your business can benefit from a networked environment, or if your current networked environment is living up to its promises:

Are you spending money on redundant hardware upgrades for each desktop machine? For example, modern software packages require immense storage space; the typical package uses 20–50 megabytes, plus the space required to store the associated data. It seems wasteful to buy larger and larger hard disks and redundant peripheral upgrades for each machine throughout your enterprise. Networks can reduce the cost of hardware by sharing resources and reducing redundancy. (Bear in mind, however, that you will make a trade-off eventually, between saving money by using shared software and saving money by optimizing your network's performance. Some of your applications will remain on workstation hard disks because the system runs faster that way.)

Are employees unable to share data because of software incompatibilities? While application data is frequently transferable from an earlier version to a later one, it often doesn't work the other way around. For example, an employee who develops a document on the latest version of a page-formatting program may not be able to pass that document along to another employee who has not chosen to make the upgrade. And if employees have become used to different applications from different vendors, the data may not be sharable at all. Networks provide the opportunity to create application standards and centralize the upgrade process.

Are support and training costs on the rise? The trend among software vendors is to charge for support. Training has always been costly, and frequently not as effective as a manager would hope. Networks can reduce the cost of training and support by centralizing and reducing the number of applications used throughout the enterprise.

Are a great many vendors servicing your information management needs in a piecemeal fashion? A networked environment can reduce administrative overhead by streamlining the supply process. For example, you can use a network to pass ordering information to a central database of approved vendors, and combine or time requests to take advantage of discounts.

Are business bottlenecks created because people must wait for information before they can act? For example, do your customer service representatives have immediate access to customer account histories, payment information, ordering trends, and the like, or must they place customers on hold or call them back after combing other departments for answers to questions or solutions to problems?

Finally, there are some everyday signs that networking would help your business function more efficiently:

- Lost data because some individuals don't make backups as well as others;

- An increasing number of files being transferred via floppy disks (often called "sneaker net," referring to individuals wearing sneakers, carting disks around a building);

- Routine business communication being conducted in an ad-hoc, haphazard fashion, or by arranging formal meetings to discuss everyday issues;

- Important messages being passed via adhesive note pad, report margins, or scraps of paper, being lost or simply not noticed until it is too late.

If you recognize your own business in the above questions and scenarios, you could benefit from establishing a networked system (or seriously redesigning your current system). Later chapters in this book will give you the information you need to choose the best system for your business from among the most common systems available, or to develop a strategy for making your existing system work as intended.

Networks in the Workplace

WHILE COMPUTER NETWORKS can make a business more productive and efficient, they are hardly a panacea. Despite the vendors' hype, and claims that computers are miracle machines capable of transforming businesses, computers can only optimize existing systems, they cannot turn bad systems into good ones.

In stand-alone computer environments, each individual user is responsible for the performance of his or her machine. Each user devises a personal method for getting results from the machine. Some users are simply more talented or enthusiastic than others, and these users tend to be called on for support when things break down. As valuable as talent and enthusiasm are, they are no substitute for hard information. In a stand-alone computer environment, inefficiency and underutilization of resources become a part of everyday routine simply because people are able to get by, and expertise is more difficult to share.

A networked environment, on the other hand, is only as good as its administrator. A network administrator must have good training, and be able to draw on a deep store of factual, detailed information about every aspect of the system. Talent and enthusiasm alone will not suffice. A computer network requires daily maintenance and supervision if it is to function as advertised and keep its vast data stores secure. The network administrator is by far the most critical component in any system, getting the most out of a system that may be less than state-of-the-art, or bringing the most advanced system in the world to its knees.

If you are now making the switch from a stand-alone to a networked environment, the best place to begin is with the hiring of your network administrator. The administrator should be brought on board first, and become involved in every aspect of the system's design, selection, and implementation. The search for a suitable administrator should be done slowly and carefully. Interview fully, check references carefully, and hire only that candidate with a proven track record and credentials.

Alternatively, you can make an investment in training an existing employee who has demonstrated serious aptitude. Such an employee demonstrates a focus on achieving real-world results, looks for ways to maximize results from existing technology, avoids money-wasting, impulsive acquisition of leading-edge technologies, and understands the difference between the tool and the task.

A top network administrator can command an annual salary of fifty thousand dollars or more, depending on the complexity of the system and its location. The system administrator's salary could easily be the most expensive single aspect of your system. You do not want to waste this large an investment on dilettantes, part-timers, or hobbyists-turned-"consultants." Seek recommendations from other network professionals who have credibility and track records of their own. Insist that candidates speak plainly and avoid a litany of jargon. The time and trouble you take at this stage of the process is trivial compared to the time and trouble you will save once your system is up and running.

The Tool and the Task

The "tool" is the machine, and also the style by which the machine achieves its ends. The "task" is the process of achieving an intended purpose as efficiently as possible. An employee who spends hours making a report look pretty is wasting company time if the task is merely to transmit some necessary information to its destination. On the other hand, if the purpose of the report is both to impart information and to impress the receiver (for example, an advertising flyer), then the extra time spent may be worth it.

Some computer enthusiasts spend more time teaching their computer new tricks than getting real jobs done. They may appear to be experts or "computer wizards" to those who find the world of computers daunting. In reality, the "Wiz" can often be someone who has merely confused the tool with the task. The "Wiz" can be useful on occasion, but can break down in situations where substance is favored over style, when the mundane necessity of getting real work done interferes with computer experimentation, exploration, and playtime. Beware!

Depending on the complexity of your network, you may require additional personnel, who also must be chosen with great care:

Database administrator. Responsible for programming and maintaining a large multirelational database in a networked environment, and facilitating direct access to the database by individuals on the network.

Workgroup manager. Responsible for problem-solving, implementing standards and solutions, reviewing performance, facilitating the efficiency of a specific group of individuals who are connected, as a group, to a larger network environment.

Support staff. Responsible for technical assistance to the system administrator in large, complex network environments. Provides routine problem-solving and spot training to end users.

Maintenance contractor. Responsible for hardware repairs and upgrades; often this position is filled by contracting with a third-party service provider, or with the vendor.

Later chapters in this book will help you learn the basics of the network world and speak its language. This information will enable you to work with your network system administrator to implement a cost-effective network system; one that justifies your investment of time, trouble, and money with measurable increases in productivity, efficiency, communication, competitive advantage, and profitability.

In the next chapter, we will move on to more technical information: how networks connect desktops, what those connections look like in the real world, and what options are available to you for making the best connections for your business.

How to Become a Network Guru

So you have decided that your next career move is into the exciting world of computer network support. You believe you have the necessary aptitude. You understand the fundamentals of desktop computing, operating systems, and hardware. Your intention is to use technology to increase your business's productivity. You have extraordinary patience, can cope with high levels of stress, and work well with other people. You still need two more things: an understanding of the technical aspects of networking and experience using them.

You must undergo training to acquire the necessary understanding. Network training is becoming more and more formal. Novell, for example, has set up authorized training centers that teach the technical details to beginners. A Novell training center can certify you for two levels of networking expertise: a Certified Network Administrator (CNA) can provide day-to-day support to users on a Novell network; a Certified Network Engineer (CNE) has more detailed knowledge of the hardware and software, and is qualified to design and install complex network systems. Local colleges and universities may offer classes and degree programs in data communications. Local dealers and vendors may offer training in the products they sell. If you have the required aptitude, it can take about a year to acquire enough training to qualify you for hands-on experience.

You acquire the necessary experience the old-fashioned way: hunting for a low-end job, working for less pay than you would like, and slowly working your way up. The field is already a crowded one, full of people who believe that the future of technology is built around networking, so expect competition. Your job is to impress all potential employers and keep your eyes open for opportunities to advance—just like any other job. Good luck!

Network
Topologies

CHAPTER

2

THIS CHAPTER TAKES a "bird's-eye" view of the landscape of the networked environment. It discusses how networks go about the business of connecting computers and transferring data between them. It also defines some basic terms used to describe networks and how they work.

If you are new to networking, it is important to understand the different ways computers can be connected to one another. They are connected physically, via cables, phone lines, or wireless microwave transmission; and they are connected logically, using software to manage the flow of data across the physical connections. In both the physical and logical realms, different types of connections are suitable for different types of businesses and budgets. This chapter explores the fundamental options that are available.

Making the Connection

THE PROCESS OF SETTING up network hardware is relatively straightforward, at least when compared to the process of setting up the software. Although there are different types of networks, they do have certain hardware characteristics in common. (Technical details regarding individual network hardware components are discussed in Chapter 4.) Following is a general overview of the workings of network hardware.

Network Interface Cards

A *network interface card* (NIC) must be installed in each computer on the network. This card is inserted into a slot inside the computer. There are several types of cards manufactured by different vendors, but they all perform the same fundamental operation: They manage the flow of network information to and from the computer in which they reside. Figure 2.1 shows a typical NIC. As you

FIGURE 2.1

A network interface card.

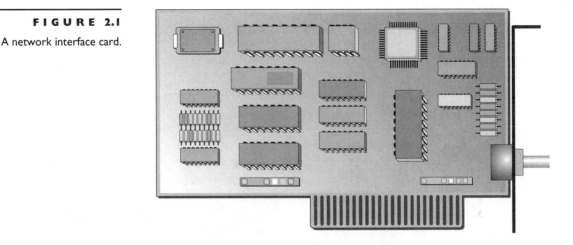

can see, it looks pretty much like any other plug-in computer card, except for one item—the jack for a cable connection. (We'll get to that in a moment.)

The differences between various NICs are based first on the type of computer with which they are designed to work. For example, IBM-compatibles require one type of card, and Macintosh computers require another. NICs also differ in the speed and efficiency with which they manage the information flow. For more details on network interface cards, see Chapter 4.

Cables and Connections

A user-accessible computer on a network is called a *workstation*. A connection to the network made by any type of device (including workstations, shared printers, modems, and the like) is called a *node*. Each node on the network must be able to communicate in some fashion with the others. Most networks whose nodes reside within a reasonable distance of each other (say, for example, on the same floor of an office building, or perhaps between a few adjacent floors) make this connection using *cables*.

A cable is an insulated wire that is attached to each NIC in the network and thus becomes the pathway along which the network data traffic travels. Figure 2.2 shows how a NIC is installed in a workstation and how a cable is attached to it.

There are, as you might already suspect, different types of cables that can handle the flow of information at varying speeds, and with greater or lesser efficiency depending on the physical environment in which they are used. See Chapter 5 for more technical information on different types of cable.

FIGURE 2.2

A NIC installed in a
workstation, with
cabling attached.

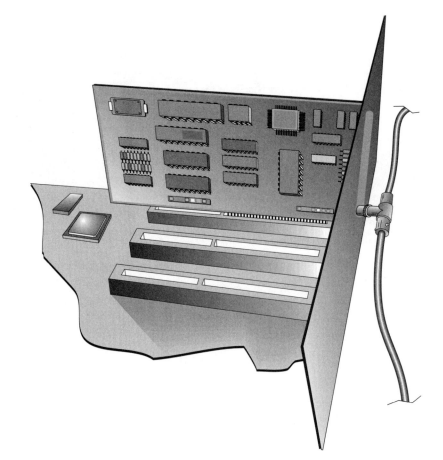

If the network is spread out over an extremely wide area (for example, between different government office buildings in a town or state), cabling becomes impractical. These wide-area networks may use existing telephone lines to establish the connection. If the wide-area network is handling especially large volumes of information or requires exceptional speed, it may require its own dedicated telephone system cables (called T1 or T3 lines) to handle the traffic.

A third alternative for establishing the connection is called *wireless transport services*. This technology consists of hardware that manages the connection using radio or infrared signaling devices, eliminating the need for cables altogether. Wireless networks are expensive and require additional support services to insure reliable communications; they are usually operated by large corporations with compelling needs for them and the budgetary resources to afford them. A wireless network may be required in areas where cabling is extremely difficult or impossible. Some cable-based networks may use a wireless connection for temporary connections from remote locations (see Chapter 7 for more information on remote access). A wireless network can make use of existing cellular telephone technology, satellite communication systems, or commercial paging systems.

Topologies

*T*opology IS A TERM used to describe the way in which computers are connected in a network. The *physical topology* describes the actual layout of the network hardware; the *logical topology* describes the behavior of the computers on the network, from the perspective of its human operators.

Physical Topologies

Most networks use one of two types of physical topology:

Linear Bus (See Figure 2.3): This is a common layout. A single main cable connects each node, in what amounts to a single line of computers accessing it from end to end. Each node is connected to two others, except the

How Big Is Big?

Some networking terms can be loosely applied. A local area network, for example, is generally defined as a network that is entirely contained within a specified fixed location—but how specified is that location, or how fixed? Certainly a five-node network in a single room would be local; likewise, a 20-node network on a single floor of an office building. What about a network between two buildings a city block from each other? Does a wide-area network stretch across town or across the country?

And how big is a big network? If you are used to working with networks that have 1,000 nodes, 100 nodes could look small. If you are used to a network with 5 nodes, 50 nodes can look pretty big.

In the end, if you can maintain the network and keep all the users happy, you've earned the right to call it what you want.

FIGURE 2.3

A linear bus topology.
Computers are connec-
ted to a single cable,
end-to-end.

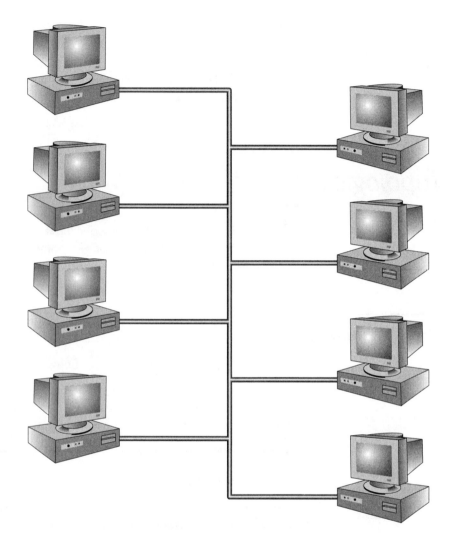

machines at either end of the cable, which are each connected only to one
other node. The network operating system keeps track of a unique electronic address for each node, and manages the flow of information based on this
addressing scheme. (See Chapter 8 for more information on network operating systems.) This topology has the advantage of not requiring that every
computer be up and running in order for the network to function. But because a single cable is dedicated to all the information traffic, performance
can be slow at times. This topology is often found in client/server systems,
where one of the machines on the network is designated as a *file server*,
meaning that it is dedicated solely to the distribution of data files, and is not
usually used for information processing.

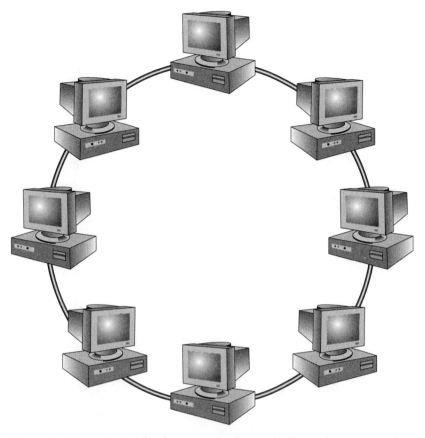

Ring (See Figure 2.4): This layout is similar to the linear bus, except that the nodes are connected in a circle using cable segments. In this layout, each node is physically connected only to two others. Each node passes information along to the next, until it arrives at its intended destination. Performance can be faster on this system because each portion of the cabling system is handling only the data flow between two machines. This type of topology can be found in *peer-to-peer* networks, in which each machine manages both information processing and the distribution of data files.

There are two other less common (but nonetheless fairly widespread) physical topologies:

Star (See Figure 2.5): Each node is connected to a single, centrally located file server, using its own dedicated segment of cable. This topology has the advantage of minimum data traffic along the cables (node-to-server only), for optimum performance. But because a single machine must coordinate all the data communication, this topology requires an extremely powerful (and expensive) file server, plus additional cable.

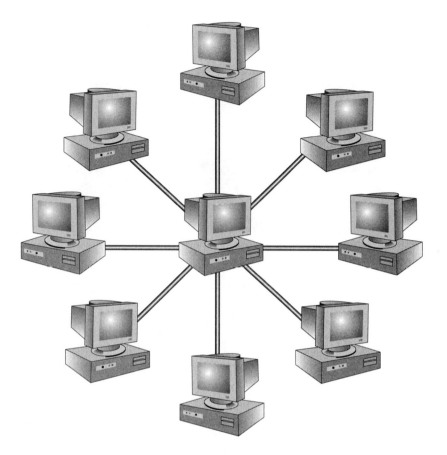

Daisy-Chain (See Figure 2.6): This topology is like a cross between linear bus and ring topologies. That is, each node is connected directly to two others by segments of cable, but the segments form a line instead of a complete circle. The network operating system passes the information up or down the chain until it reaches its destination. This type of layout is less common because, although it is less expensive to install and maintain, it is the least reliable over time.

Logical Topologies

Logical topology is a term used to describe a scheme used by the network's operating system to manage the flow of information between nodes. The operating system's communication scheme influences how persons using the workstations visualize the way their computers are communicating with each other.

A daisy-chain topology. Computers are connected with cable segments, end-to-end.

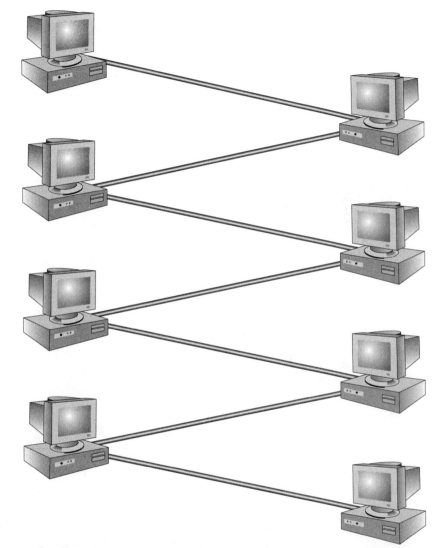

Most network operating systems use one of two basic kinds of logical topology:

Linear (See Figure 2.7): This communication scheme functions like the linear bus topology and is common in Ethernet-based systems. Each node has a unique address, and the addresses are accessed sequentially. Information is passed up and down the list until the right destination address is found.

Token Ring (See Figure 2.7): This scheme can be found on both linear bus and ring topologies. Each node has a unique address, and the addresses are accessed in a circular fashion. Notice that there isn't necessarily a correspondence between the logical addresses and the physical location of the computers relative to each other.

Choosing Your Network Topology

When you first set up a network, you need to choose the type of hardware, software, and network operating system to be used, and the physical and logical topologies. These choices are interdependent upon each other and

FIGURE 2.7

The difference between physical and logical topologies. In the Ethernet system, the logical addresses correspond to the physical location of the computers. In the token ring system, the logical addresses do not have the same correspondence to the linear bus layout.

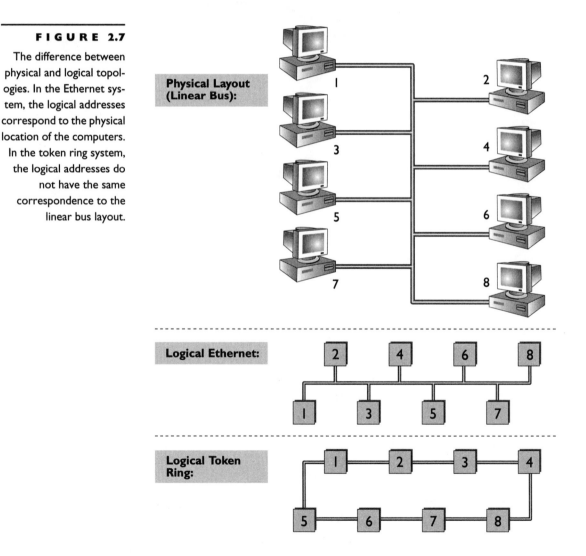

together make up the *network configuration*. You can make these choices by weighing together such factors as:

Cost: What is the most efficient system your business can afford?

Speed: How fast does the system need to be?

Environment: Are there environmental factors (for example, the presence of electrical fields) that will influence the kind of hardware required?

Size: How big will the network be? Will it require a dedicated file server or servers?

Connectivity: Will other users (for example, field representatives using laptop machines) need to access the network from various remote locations?

In some circumstances, your choices regarding certain kinds of hardware and standards will be constrained by other choices you've made. For example, if you elect to use an ARCnet system, you must use wiring concentrators to make the network connections. These concentrators (also called *hubs*), are required by ARCnet to condition the electrical signal and thus maintain the electrical standards ARCnet needs in order to work.

You will find that your decisions tend to revolve around money: the cost of the number of nodes on your network, distances involved, and whatever future plans you envision for your business.

From an information-management standpoint, nearly every business has certain unique characteristics. Each business must take the time to design a suitable information-management system. An experienced network design consultant or responsible vendor can help you analyze your business needs and explain your options in detail, showing you which options are most suitable for your particular business. Above all, proceed slowly in these early stages. Don't hesitate to get a variety of viewpoints from different vendors. Take your time so as to fully understand the systems you are offered; in this way you will save time and money in the long run, and be assured of getting the solution your business really needs.

Clients and Servers

THE TERMS *server* and *client* are used somewhat loosely when discussing networks. In general, any machine that sends out data along the network can be called a server, whereas a machine that receives data can be a client.

More specifically, the term *file server* refers to a computer whose sole purpose on the network is to send out and receive data files. It does not process or make changes to the data it sends out. It may not even have any intelligence regarding what kinds of data it sends; in other words, the server doesn't have to know whether a file is a text document, a graphic picture, or a financial spreadsheet. Instead, it busies itself answering requests from client machines for files that it keeps stored, and leaves it to the software on the client machine to know what the file is, what kind of data it contains, and what to do with it. Figure 2.8 compares a file server and a workstation.

In this system, clients are usually computers on the network that are operated by human beings, making changes to the data files they receive and, when those changes are complete, sending the data back to the file server for storage.

This arrangement has the virtue of processing efficiency, especially on large networks with dozens or even hundreds of machines. With the full processing power of a very powerful computer allocated solely to sending and storing files, individual clients are not kept waiting for data, and they can process different files with different software independently of each other.

A single file server may be made even faster and more efficient if it contains more than one central processing chip, so that complex requests for data from dozens of different clients can be allocated to different processors running concurrently. These servers are called *symmetric multiprocessor units* (or SMU for short).

FIGURE 2.8

A file server. Notice the absence of keyboard and monitor. Some file servers can be accessed directly using a keyboard and monitor, but this server is accessed only from client nodes across the network.

Workstation Client

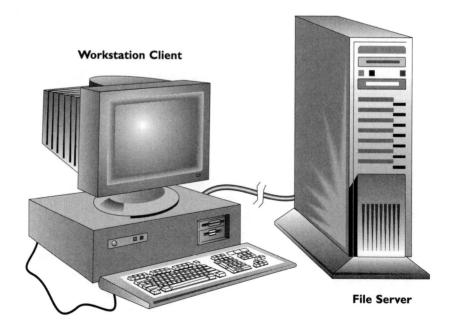

File Server

If the network is extremely large, it may employ more than one file server, each server handling specialized requests for specific types of files. For example, one file server may handle requests for customer database records, and another for company budget information. Figure 2.9 shows the layout of a basic file server system.

Clients on a network don't have to be other computers. The server also can direct data to and from other automated devices, such as printers (in which case the server is called a *print server*), pen plotters, scanners, and modems. Most file servers handle security issues such as limiting access to certain kinds of data or devices, or access to data by select users, or at specific times of the day.

FIGURE 2.9

A fundamental client/server system. One computer is dedicated to sending, receiving, and storing data files, also managing the system. Notice that, although the system is physically connected as a linear bus, most of the network data traffic passes to and from the server.

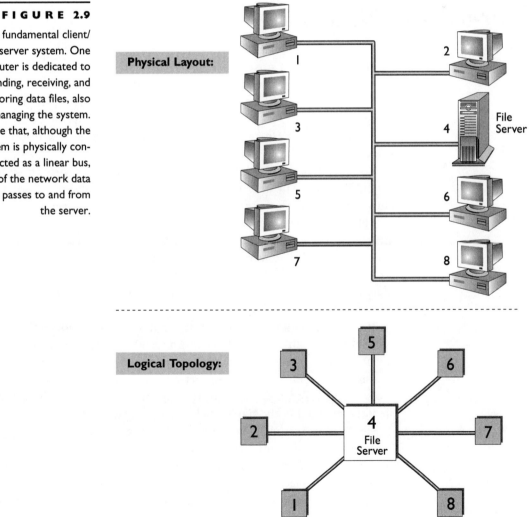

Systems like these are called *client/server* systems and they are distinguished by a high degree of data centralization. This creates the need for a system administrator or specialized group of support staff who understand the system as a whole, and take responsibility for the safety, accuracy, and availability of the data stored on the server.

Networks like these are suitable for large organizations with large budgets who require that many users have access to the same general data, and that current, updated information be available to all users at any given time. For details regarding client/server operating systems, see Chapter 8.

Peer-to-Peer Networks

NOT EVERY BUSINESS needs the power of a complex client/server system. Many smaller companies can do well using a network of computers in which each machine sends and receives data files, and processes data using those files. Since each computer has the same poten-tial to access and process data, these types of networks are called *peer-to-peer* networks.

A peer-to-peer network (as shown in Figure 2.10) has the virtue of simplicity in both design and maintenance. It is usually less expensive to set up as well. However, it is also slower and less secure than the client/server network. It is suitable for smaller organizations with limited budgets where security is less of an issue, and where the number of computers on the network is limited (usually twenty or less). With fewer computers on the network, performance and speed are not noticeably degraded. This type of network is also well suited for groups of users who must freely access data and processing abilities that reside on other computers across the network.

Maintenance of a peer-to-peer system can be tricky. Although this type of system can be configured to offer some measure of security and limited access to data, it cannot offer the robust security features of a client/server system. Because all individual peer-to-peer network users are capable of storing and accessing data files, they share greater responsibility for maintaining both the smooth operation of the system and the integrity of the data.

Peer-to-peer technology is improving, because the market for it is growing among smaller companies with smaller budgets. Peer-to-peer systems are connecting more and more powerful computers with larger RAM and vastly increased data storage capacity. With these advances come better and more reliable performance, and more features like intra-network communications (also

FIGURE 2.10

A peer-to-peer system. All
computers send, receive,
store, and process data
files. The absence of a
dedicated file server
lowers hardware and
maintenance costs.
Performance is slower,
especially if the network
has many nodes.

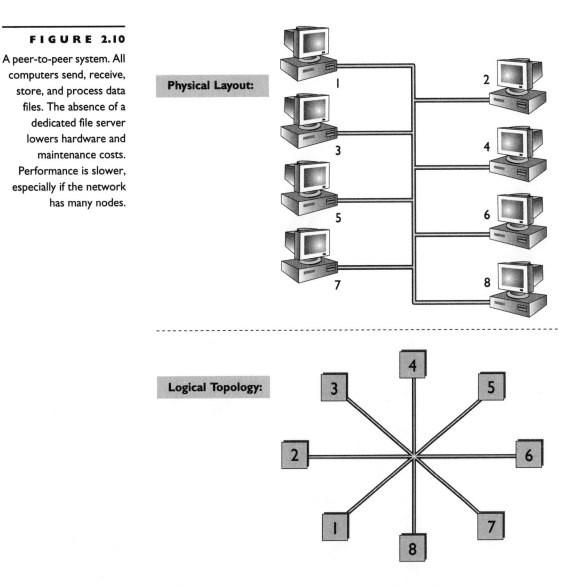

FIGURE 2.10

A peer-to-peer system. All
computers send, receive,
store, and process data
files. The absence of a
dedicated file server
lowers hardware and
maintenance costs.
Performance is slower,
especially if the network
has many nodes.

called electronic mail, or e-mail), and temporary connections from remote sites
via telephone lines. Although client/server is still the system of choice among
network power users, the peer-to-peer model can deliver quite satisfactory
results for these smaller companies, or for client workgroups that attach to
larger networks.

For details regarding peer-to-peer operating systems, see Chapter 8.

Complex Networks

NETWORKS CAN BE connected to other networks, and networks can consist of different types of machines from different vendors, each with its own unique way of handling electronic information, not directly understood by the other machines on the network. Special software and hardware can be attached to the network to handle this complicated setup. These devices, called *bridges, routers* and *gateways,* perform in different ways the task of "translating" the electronic information supplied by one machine into a format that can be understood by another. Once installed and configured, these devices can operate in a way that does not require any additional work by each machine's operator. Let's look at each device in turn.

Bridges

A *bridge* consists of a computer with two or more network interface cards, connecting two different types of network. For example, one interface card might connect to an Ethernet system, while a second card connects to a Token Ring system. These two systems speak two entirely different data languages, and require the bridge to translate the node address supplied by one network into an address that is recognized by the other. The bridge uses special software that accepts data from the sending network, recognizes the address as one belonging to the other network, translates the address so that the receiving network can understand it, and sends it to the receiving network.

The bridge examines all the traffic on both networks, but it can distinguish between "foreign" data, which is sent between the two networks, and "domestic" data, which is sent between nodes on the same network. Data that does not require translation is allowed to pass through the bridge unchanged, and is not routed to the other network at all. This process, called *filtering*, increases efficiency by reducing unnecessary data traffic between the two "foreign" networks. The filtering mechanism sees to it that the two networks handle each others' data only when they have to.

Networking the World

The first complex networks were computer bulletin board services, which proliferated at the start of the desktop computer revolution because they were a convenient means for users to share information, often centered around some area of common interest, using modems and telephone lines. A single user, often an extremely dedicated enthusiast, would offer his machine as a central sending and receiving point for anyone with the necessary hardware, software, and knowledge required to call up and access the information stored there. Computer bulletin boards are still a good source of advice and support for specific hardware and software products, and you might look for one that has information and advice regarding local-area networks. Check retail computer stores in your area and local computer newspapers for more information.

Large commercial enterprises took the bulletin board idea to the next evolutionary step, the on-line service provider. These large, mainframe-based enterprises offer access to huge databases of information, plus on-line messaging between users, and charge a monthly subscription fee. For example, CompuServe and America Online are two popular commercial on-line services.

More and more desktop computer users are connecting to the Internet, a loosely organized, world-wide network of computers connected by telephone lines. To access the Internet, you must use your computer's modem to make a telephone call to another computer that is already connected to the Internet system. Once connected, you can establish contact with any other computer on the Internet using its complicated addressing scheme.

Right now, there are dozens of software packages and Internet service providers who will, for a fee, help you log onto the Internet and navigate your way around it. For starters, ask a local software vendor about Internet-in-a-Box, a software package that simplifies the process for beginners. Or consult a service provider, such as Netcom, that offers a simple software interface (called NetCruiser) along with the Internet connection. Additionally, there are a number of good books that explain Internet access in detail. Two excellent sources of Internet information are *Easy Guide to the Internet*, by Christian Crumlish, and *Mastering the Internet*, by Glee Harrah Cady and Pat McGregor, both published by Sybex; or browse the computer book section in your local bookseller for a title that suits you.

Routers

A *router* is similar to a bridge, but can handle more complex types of communications between dissimilar networks. Routers are usually employed by widearea networks, which often connect networks using different communication protocols and dissimilar addressing schemes. A router maintains a table of pathways between nodes and can select an optimal route of node addresses over which to send data. If the router detects an error condition after attempting to send data over one selected pathway, it can try again using an alternate.

A router is programmed to understand the communications protocols of its attached networks. However, some complex networks can be accessed by remote networks using any possible protocol. In these situations routers can function as bridges. The router simply translates the address and passes the data along the network data path to the receiving node.

Gateways

A *gateway* is used when simply transferring raw data between networks is not enough. Some network systems (in particular mainframe- or minicomputer-based systems) require specific instructions on how data is to be managed once it is received onto the network. A gateway is also required when connecting two or more networks that are running on top of different operating systems. A gateway incorporates the functions of routers and bridges, but in addition can translate the instruction set of the sending network into the corresponding instruction set of the receiving network. For example, a nationwide on-line database service, running on a large mainframe system, would employ a gateway system because it is open to telephone connections from dozens of different types of computers and networks. The gateway translates requests from the connected computers (for example, a request to download a file) into instructions the mainframe can understand. The gateway also translates messages from the mainframe (starting and ending the download, monitoring progress and possible error conditions, and the like) into instructions the receiving computer can understand. All of this is "transparent" to the human being sitting at the receiving computer. From this person's point of view, it appears as if the entire process is taking place in the user's native format.

Enterprise Computing

T IS COMMON for networks to grow in complexity as the needs of an organization evolve over time. What starts out as a small peer-to-peer LAN can, in a few years, grow into a far-flung network composed of other networks, dozens of different machines speaking their own electronic "language," and individuals with portable machines accessing central repositories of data from anyplace in the world with a cellular or pay phone. This type of "network of networks," usually organized around some large business model, is called an *enterprise*, a loosely-applied term referring to any complex network. In enterprise computing, shared data is usually stored in several different locations; in technical jargon, it is *distributed* throughout the enterprise, producing the frequently heard terms *distributed data*, *distributed processing*, and *enterprise computing*.

Enterprise computing represents a middle ground between the absolutely centralized world of mainframe computing and the completely decentralized world of stand-alone desktop PCs. Ideally, enterprise computing attempts to maximize individual productivity while keeping its foundation of raw data as tightly controlled, safe, and reliable as possible. Results are often mixed. These systems require much supervision and maintenance; when they run well, they live up to expectations and justify their cost. When they do not run well, they can be a nightmare.

Subsequent chapters in this book will take up a more detailed exploration of the basics of network hardware, software, and design. This knowledge will serve as a platform on which you can base good buying and configuration decisions and create—or remake—a reliable, cost-effective network for your business.

Communication Protocols and Standards

3

COMMUNICATION BETWEEN human beings depends upon our agreeing about the meanings of words and the rules for using them. Without such agreement, we cannot communicate. The closer and more consistent these agreements, the greater our chance for understanding. Nevertheless, one charm of human communication is its inexactitude. Most of the time, we don't need to spell out exactly what we mean, because we know the listener or reader can infer a great deal from context. We understand (and sometimes misunderstand) one another because of the assumptions we make about what our words and style of communication mean.

Computers, alas, are not so good at drawing inferences, and computer network communications cannot afford any degree of inexactitude. Consequently, network vendors establish a *protocol*, or set of rules that govern the electronic communications process. These rules must govern every aspect of network communications, down to the smallest detail. For example, separate protocols must apply to how data communication begins, continues, and ends. Protocols have been established for different types of hardware, software, and data. When all these different protocols work together to make data communication possible, the set of protocols is called a *protocol suite*.

It is the responsibility of the developers of hardware, network operating systems, and application software to develop their products so that they conform to the rules of communication. When a product conforms to a particular protocol suite (or set of different suites), the product is said to *support* those protocols.

In a simplistic world, there would be only one protocol suite, which would by necessity use a limited set of hardware and software, and networks would have to conform to it. Life would be easier: every network would then be able to communicate predictably with every other network; and, once the necessary hardware and software was installed, all the computers in the world would easily be able to talk to each other.

In the real world, there are multiple vendors competing with each other for your money. They are continuously developing and refining network systems that work better, faster, and sometimes even cheaper, and that customers can apply to all sorts of unique circumstances. Manufacturers, industry leaders, researchers, developers, and vendors all pay close attention to the way systems work, what customers respond to, and what aspect of computing and networking offer a competitive edge in the marketplace. Experts gather together to work out a balance between adopting standard rules of communication and maintaining the kind of competitiveness that leads to improved products. All this activity results in support for different protocols that apply to different types of networks.

Some of these evolving protocols have become *de facto standards*, meaning that they are in such widespread use that network vendors try to develop new products that are consistent with them. It is a difficult task, since protocols put constraints on how network products work. As the need grows for more powerful networks, the hardware, software, and standards evolve and become more complex. Old networks become obsolete, businesses feel the pressure to upgrade to newer systems, protocols evolve along with everything else, and the vendors make more money.

This chapter discusses some standard communications protocols in use today. These protocols are likely to be the reference rules for new communication standards that will evolve in the future. It is important to have an understanding of standard protocols because computers cannot communicate without them, and vendors will use these terms and concepts as a way of promoting the advantages of their products over their competitors'. If you understand the protocols your system uses, you can make better decisions regarding selection of hardware and software, avoid incompatibility problems, and manage your system's evolution with less anxiety and more productivity.

OSI/RM and the Seven-Layer Model

N AN EFFORT to develop a structured model for computer network communications, the International Standards Organization (an international body of experts who define a variety of different technical standards for governments) set up the *Open Systems Interconnection Reference Model*, or *OSI/RM*.

The purpose of OSI/RM is to demonstrate how the parts of a network communication system should work together. The model specifies only what needs to be done—it does not specify how those needs are to implemented. Actual implementation is left up to individual developers and programmers who work out the protocols that conform to the OSI model.

The OSI model organizes communication services into seven groups of specifications. These groups are called *layers*. Each layer specifies a greater degree of functionality in network services, building on the services of the previous layer. Together the OSI/RM forms a complete *Seven-Layer Model* (SLM) for network communicating. The layers are:

Physical Layer 1. This layer describes the electrical, mechanical, and functional specifications for handling network data. The physical layer describes processes that handle data as streams of binary bits flowing through hardware, but does not include standards for the hardware itself.

Data Link Layer 2. This layer describes processes for detecting and correcting low-level data errors during transfer of data between the physical layer and the layers above the physical layer.

Network Layer 3. This layer describes processes for routing data between network addresses, and verifying that messages are sent completely and accurately.

Transport Layer 4. This layer includes functions for establishing appropriate connections, initiating data transmission, and releasing the connection after the transmission is complete.

Session Layer 5. This layer includes processes for controlling the transfer of data, handling transmission and transport errors, and managing records of transmissions sent.

Presentation Layer 6. This layer controls rules for formatting data transmissions; for example, this layer includes specifications for encoding and decoding character sets.

Application Layer 7. This layer describes specifications for the environment in which network applications communicate with network services.

The OSI/RM provides a way of thinking about network communications. It is a general-purpose model. Its significance derives from its use by governments. Governments can select standards from the OSI model that meet their needs and issue a profile of OSI standards, called a *Government Open Systems Interconnection Profile*, or *GOSIP*. The GOSIP is made available to manufacturers who intend to sell products to these governments. Governments have heavy financial clout in the marketplace, so manufacturers who service government markets pay serious attention to OSI/RM specifications. These OSI-compliant products, often with some degree of modification, can be distributed in private-sector markets as well.

TCP/IP

CP/IP STANDS FOR *Transmission Control Protocol/Internet Protocol.*
Although TCP/IP has only recently become a standard protocol suite,
it is more than twenty years old; it was first used to link government
computers, and is now the basis for the Internet, the largest network of computer networks in the world. Its evolution as a standard was boosted when it was incorporated into the UNIX operating system in the early 1980s. Nowadays, TCP/IP has the advantage of being compatible with a large number of different hardware and software systems.

The primary responsibility of the Transmission Control Protocol is to receive an electronic message of any length and break it into 64K sections. (The last section can be smaller.) By breaking up the message into sections, the software controlling the network communication can transmit each section and subject it to verification procedures one section at a time. If a section is corrupted during transmission, the transmitting program need only repeat the transmission of that section—it does not have to repeat the transmission from the beginning. Since data corruption can and does occur from time to time, especially over long distances, this method is more efficient in the long run.

The Internet Protocol (IP) takes the sections, verifies each section's accuracy, addresses them to their intended destination, and makes sure they are sent in the proper order. The IP includes information on many different addressing schemes, and uses the correct addressing scheme based on the intended destination. This feature allows TCP/IP to be compatible with different types of networks.

As it prepares the message for IP, TCP can handle different types of messages in different ways. In effect, TCP is the host for a small set of protocols:

Simple Mail Transfer Protocol (SMTP) processes text messages that contain only a series of ASCII characters (A–Z, numbers, and standard keyboard punctuation marks) and a destination address.

File Transfer Protocol (FTP) is a larger set of message-processing rules used to process more complex messages; messages that require non-ASCII characters, or contain machine-readable binary characters. FTP also can be used to automate message sending; for example, sending a batch of different messages after hours.

Telnet is a set of rules that allow a person stationed at a computer on the network (called the *local terminal*) to access and run a different computer on the network (called the *remote terminal*). This process, called *remote access*, is more efficient than sending large amounts of data across the network. Telnet sends the local keyboard commands to the remote terminal, and sends the remote screen's display of the command results back to the local terminal.

TCP/IP is used by almost any UNIX-based system, Banyan VINES, Microsoft LAN Manager, and Novell Netware. Figure 3.1 charts the relationship between the protocols in the TCP/IP protocol suite.

NetBIOS

NETBIOS STANDS FOR *Network Basic Input/Output System*. The IBM Corporation developed it to provide a standard way of using the computer's underlying operating system to access network services. NetBIOS can be used by any IBM-compatible network system. Because different systems have unique ways of tapping the features of the underlying operating system, individual implementations of NetBIOS tend to differ just enough to make them incompatible with each other. In other words, if you are using NetBIOS and change your network operating system, there is some chance you'll have to use a new version of NetBIOS as well.

Still, NetBIOS has the advantage of hiding all those arcane and idiosyncratic aspects of network/operating system communication from the user. Instead, the user sees a more understandable set of network functions.

Network software can access NetBIOS functions by instructing the operating system to perform some network function. The software accomplishes this by sending a small chunk of data called a *network control block* (NCB). The NCB is passed to the operating system, which is programmed to understand it and respond with the correct network service; for example, to send a message to another computer.

FIGURE 3.1

TCP/IP protocol suite, showing relationships between protocols and their functions.

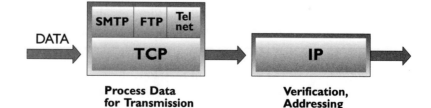

NetBIOS has several useful functions. Here are some examples of those most commonly accessed:

Configuring the NIC. This function allows you to make changes to the settings of your network interface card, or obtain information on its current configuration.

Message Broadcasting. This function allows you to send a single message simultaneously to every other computer that happens to be connected at the time.

Node Names. This function allows you to attach meaningful names to various nodes on the network. For example, you could name a shared printer "LaserPrint1" and forward printing documents to this name instead of some arcane node address.

Virtual Circuits. This function allows you to establish a direct connection between two computers over the network, in situations where the connection may involve complicated physical connections. This can speed up communications over complex networks.

NetBIOS Redirector

The Redirector is software that acts as a network "traffic cop." Its purpose is to control the flow of data between the various nodes on the network. It is responsible for seeing to it that the printers, servers, and clients all get data intended for them, and for handling the flow in such a way as to eliminate bottlenecks along the network's data path.

The Redirector accomplishes this by using a *Server Message Block* (SMB) protocol. This protocol intercepts requests by computers on the network and creates instructions that NetBIOS can understand. We might paraphrase such instructions like so: "Send this chunk of data to the screen on Roscoe's computer, send that chunk of data to the printer connected to Elaine's computer," and so on.

NetBIOS is a common standard for peer-to-peer networks; for example, LANtastic and Invisible NET/30. Microsoft's LAN Manager also uses a form of the SMB protocol. It is not generally used for very large or complex network systems. Figure 3.2 charts the NetBIOS protocol suite.

FIGURE 3.2

The NetBIOS protocol suite, showing relationships between protocols and their functions. Notice that data is passed to the NetBIOS operating system from software.

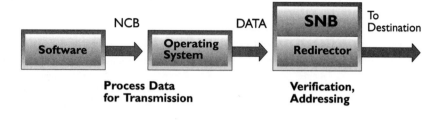

XNS

NS STANDS FOR *Xerox Network System*. The Xerox Corporation developed it for use by smaller local area networks as a simplified protocol suite. It does not support the more complex functions of other protocols that are generally not required in small, local systems.

The basic protocol in XNS is the *Internet Datagram Protocol* (IDP), which handles data verification and addressing responsibilities similar to those found in TCP/IP. This protocol is a suite of smaller, dedicated protocols:

Clearinghouse translates device and user names to internal network addresses.

Packet Exchange Protocol (PEP) processes messages for reliable transport along the network.

Remote Courier Protocol (RCP) allows instructions by software to access and run services available on other network nodes. To the local software program, these services appear as if they are running on the local terminal. This allows programs without network-specific functions to access network services.

Routing Information Protocol (RIP) establishes the best data path for messages from one node to another.

Sequenced Packet Protocol (SPP) verifies that data is transmitted accurately.

The XNS protocol suite is used by Banyan VINES. A subset of these protocols is implemented in Novell Netware versions 2.*x* and 3.*x*.

AppleTalk

PPLETALK IS A SUITE of protocols for Macintosh systems. The suite is complicated, and involves many integrated protocols that manage the various detailed aspects of the Mac's data communications system. Macintosh, in keeping with its ease-of-use philosophy, keeps these protocols well out of sight of the everyday user. Still, it is important to understand some Mac-specific jargon used to describe the Mac's networking services:

The heart of the AppleTalk suite is the *Datagram Delivery Protocol* (DDP). Each message sent to the DDP is accompanied by data indicating a specific computer on the network, and an address in the computer's operating system that stores a procedure for handling that message. The computer is called a *station*, and the procedure address is called a *socket*. DDP receives messages and routes them to stations and sockets, where the processing takes place. Several protocols are used to facilitate and monitor the process:

AppleTalk Data Stream Protocol (ADSP) monitors the flow of data between two computers, to verify that it is not interrupted or corrupted by internal errors.

AppleTalk File Protocol (AFP) handles requests for data files, and it manages file security—for example, not allowing overwrites of read-only files.

Appletalk Session Protocol (ASP) checks messages that are sent in sections. It tests to see that the sections are the correct size and are received in the correct order.

AppleTalk Transaction Protocol (ATP) verifies the accuracy of network messages.

Echo Protocol (EP) repeats each message back to the sending node to confirm that it has been sent completely, to gather information on delays, and to test the data path for maximum efficiency.

Name Binding Protocol (NBP) translates user-defined network node names into network node addresses.

Page Description Language (PDL) is a set of functions used by printers to control the formatting of text on paper. For example, Macintosh-compatible printers understand a PDL called Postscript.

Printer Access Protocol (PAP) monitors the flow of data that is sent in a continuous stream instead of sections.

Routing Table Maintenance Protocol (RTMP) monitors the location of nodes on the network, and maintains a database of reliable connections between them. If one node fails, RTMP can establish an alternate route.

Zone Information Protocol (ZAP) analyzes the network configuration and collects device addresses into groups, or *zones*, to establish efficient access.

Appletalk is specific to Macintosh networks. It is noteworthy in that it is integrated into the Macintosh operating system and is, largely, transparent to the user. Figure 3.3 charts the functions of the protocols in the AppleTalk suite.

EtherTalk and TokenTalk

APPLETALK SUPPORTS two variations of its proprietary implementation, which allow it to coexist with other LANS: EtherTalk, also known as the EtherTalk Link Access Protocol, or ELAP; and TokenTalk, also known as the TokenTalk Link Access Protocol, or TLAP. Simply put, EtherTalk is AppleTalk over an Ethernet foundation at the physical and datalink layers. TokenTalk is AppleTalk over a Token Ring foundation at the physical and datalink layers. These variants require a special adapter card, which can be found in the more powerful Macintosh machines (such as the Mac Quadra).

FIGURE 3.3

The AppleTalk protocol suite, showing relationships between protocols and their functions.

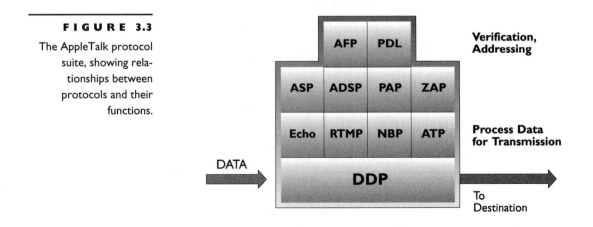

NetWare Protocols

BESIDES ITS SUPPORT for the standard protocols listed above (except AppleTalk), NetWare has introduced some additional protocols that are specific to itself. These protocols often duplicate functions found in standard protocols, but they are integrated more fully into NetWare's own system. NetWare protocols are for use on NetWare networks only, are additional to standard protocols, and are designed to give NetWare a competing edge over other systems that confine their implementations to standard protocols only.

Internetwork Packet Exchange (IPX) handles data verification and addressing responsibilities similar to those found in TCP/IP. This protocol can handle *internetwork messages* (messages sent between NetWare and other networks).

NetWare Core Protocol (NCP) manages the flow of data between NetWare clients and file servers for maximum efficiency.

Sequenced Packet Exchange (SPX) uses NetWare NOS functions to verify the accuracy of data.

Server Advertising Protocol (SAP) monitors the process of logging on and off the network, and it manages the transfer of messages between nodes throughout the entire internetwork.

Windows NT Protocols

WINDOWS NT SERVER supports four protocols. TCP/IP has already been discussed. The other three are:

Microsoft NWlink: A version of Novell's IPX/SPX protocols, discussed in the previous section of this chapter, included for compatibility between Windows NT and NetWare.

NetBEUI: An extension of the NetBIOS protocol. It uses NetBIOS as an interface to the network, but adds functions that enable it to work with a wider range of hardware and software.

Data Link Control: A limited protocol, designed for connections to IBM Mainframe computers or for hardware devices that connect directly to the network cable, instead of a workstation or server.

Sorting Out Standards

THE IMPORTANT THING to remember about protocols is that they are the means by which networked computers understand each other. Remember that computer networks have a tendency to evolve into larger and more complex systems, containing more nodes and devices, and increasingly sophisticated software.

The protocols discussed in this chapter are standard and in widespread use. It can be helpful to know about protocols, to know what vendors are referring to when they advertise support for various protocols in their networking products. Also, if you know the rules your current system lives by, you have a basis for knowing whether proposed upgrades and changes to your system will be compatible.

Network Hardware

PART

2

Workstations

URING THE STAND-ALONE era of desktop computing, the term *workstation* was used to describe extremely powerful desktop computers, whose applications were usually complex graphic and engineering tasks. As all desktop computers steadily became more powerful, the term now applies to just about any computer on a desktop.

Network Workstations

N A NETWORKING context, a workstation is any node on a network that is accessed and used by a human being (at a keyboard, for example). At a minimum, the workstation includes the standard items we normally associate with a desktop computer: a keyboard for entering commands, a monitor for displaying output, and a central unit for processing data. The central processing unit (CPU) includes random-access memory (RAM) for making changes to data and managing data communication instructions. Most network workstations also include a hard disk for data storage, although in certain circumstances they may not need one—for example, if a high-security application requires that all data reside on a remote file server. The workstation includes an internal transport system, called the *bus*, which moves data between keyboard, RAM, monitor, and hard disk.

Other optional equipment may be connected to the workstation—for example, a *mouse*, a pointing device used with graphic user interfaces like Windows, OS/2, and the Macintosh, or a *digitizer*, a drawing device often usedwith computer-aided drafting applications.

The key issues that affect a workstation's performance on a network are processing speed, memory, and bus performance. These issues are interrelated, and their relationship is discussed in detail in the following sections.

Choosing Your Workstation

Keep in mind that every user's needs are special to one extent or another. If your network is going to run only word processing and spreadsheet software, your workstation needs are going to be easier and cheaper to fulfill than if your network is going to run space engineering design software. When in doubt about what workstation design is best, extend your implementation deadline and go over available options in detail with your vendor. Give yourself time to test a variety of workstation configurations to decide which is best for your own situation. The extra time you invest now will save much more time and money in the future.

Processing Speed

ACH NEW MICROPROCESSOR design released by its manufacturer does its work faster than the previous one. There is no theoretical limit to the speed of a processor (other than the speed of electricity), so processors will continue to get faster and faster for some time to come, until we have reached the ideal of nearly instantaneous processing.

Speed is a burning issue for all computer users, more so now than ever, since recent software has become inordinately complex and graphics-driven. This software includes billions of separate computer instructions that must be processed inhumanly fast. Computer vendors have exploited this need for speed by heavily promoting microprocessor speed ratings in their advertising.

Microprocessor speeds are measured in *megahertz* (MHz). One MHz equals one million cycles of a vibrating crystal in the microprocessor, which controls its internal flow of instructions and is thus known as the *clock*. At the time this book is being written, microprocessor speeds of up to 150 MHz, or 150 million cycles per second, are becoming quite common.

Microprocessor vendors have been able to increase their products' performance by developing a special chip called the Reduced Instruction Set Computer (RISC) chip. Some commonly-used RISC chips include: IBM's PowerPC Processor, Sun Microsystem's SPARC, the DEC Alpha chip, and the R4000 series by MIPS. RISC chips work faster because their internal architecture is simpler and is optimized for the most common types of internal operations. This makes them faster in most common end-user applications, and allows the

Is Processor Speed the Whole Story?

In the most simplistic terms, the higher the MHz, the faster the processor, and the better the software performs. However, the actual speed of a workstation depends not just on the speed of its central microprocessor but on its slowest individual component. In other words, if the microprocessor is fast but the hard disk is slow, or the microprocessor and hard disk are fast but the video display system is slow, then the speed of the fast components is wasted while they wait for the slower components to catch up. (Later in this chapter we'll look at other components that can affect performance.)

The lesson to be learned here is to pay attention to the ratings of all the system components before you buy any computer. If you spot a "bargain" computer with the latest and greatest microprocessor and a temptingly low price, be certain the low price does not mean that some inferior component is lurking inside.

manufacturer to boast a higher speed rating than would otherwise be possible. RISC chips are fine for most network and stand-alone workstations, but may not be a good choice for sophisticated high-end applications—for example, complex engineering and construction projects—where the full processing power of a Complete Instruction Set Chip (CISC), such as the Pentium, K5 or P6 chip, is required.

Memory

MEMORY SPEED AND SIZE are also crucial to workstation performance. It is a common misconception to believe that you can save money and install a relatively small amount of memory on a workstation, then run applications remotely across the network. This is possible, but will usually cost you more—in terms of lost productivity because of slow performance—than was saved skimping on workstation RAM.

RAM size is measured in *megabytes*, a megabyte being space sufficient to hold one million bytes of data. At the time this book is being written, a size of eight megabytes (8MB) is usually considered the practical minimum for networking, with 12–16 megabytes a likely standard for machines running sophisticated graphic user interfaces, such as Windows 95.

Is This Application Right for My Network?

Applications specify their RAM requirements on their packaging, usually in very small print so you won't be deterred from purchase by reading them carefully. Squint, and read them carefully anyway. While you're at it, check to see if the application is programmed to be network-aware, and if it requires a specific network operating system to run, and it has any esoteric hardware requirements as well.

The amount of RAM each workstation requires depends on the size and complexity of the operating system and applications that you intend to run on it. Each workstation will devote a certain portion of its local RAM to those parts of the network operating system that it must access locally. The remaining RAM will be used to store software applications while they are running, plus the data beinpg processed by those applications.

Most recently developed software will make use of *virtual memory*; in other words, if the software detects that there is not enough RAM available (above a certain required minimum needed to run at all), it will store excess operating instructions in temporary files on your hard disk. Then, if it needs instructions stored on the hard disk, it will swap the needed instructions into RAM, and swap out some unneeded instructions to make room for the needed ones. This process allows the software to function in less-than-sufficient RAM, but it is grindingly slow. Such a situation is at best a stopgap measure, and you would be well advised to consider adding more RAM to your workstation.

Ideally, each workstation on your network would have sufficient RAM to access and run every application *locally* (that is, in its own random-access memory). However, it is not absolutely necessary. In situations where it may be deemed practical, a single copy of an application can be stored remotely, accessed once by the workstation and run out of its own local RAM. This is not usually the best alternative, as it tends to increase network traffic.

The speed at which RAM chips function can have a noticeable effect on your workstation's performance. Memory speed is measured in *nanoseconds*, a nanosecond being one-billionth of a second. The smaller the number, the faster the chip. For example, 70-nanosecond chips are faster than 120-nanosecond chips. The faster the chip (as you might have expected), the more expensive it is. Still, if you are buying a workstation with an ultra-fast processor, buy the fastest RAM you can afford. Check with your dealer to decide the best RAM for your chosen microprocessor.

RAM, Storage, and Licensing

Be aware that most network software is sold based on user licensing. This means that the software vendor requires that a separate software license be purchased for each user of an application on the network. The license is not sold for the actual physical copy of the application. If you have ten people using a software program and they all access a single copy on a central server, you will in all likelihood be expected to purchase ten licenses. Some vendors offer site licensing, which permits an unspecified number of users to run an application at a single physical location. Site licensing can be limited. Read your licensing agreement carefully before agreeing to purchase any network application.

Memory speed is an often-overlooked feature, and knowing this, some vendors may attempt to lower their prices by shipping workstations with slower-than-required memory. The speed of a fast microprocessor is wasted by slow memory chips; be wary of these too-cheap machines.

File Server Memory

F YOU ARE RUNNING a client/server system, you will be running the network operating system from the file server, while simultaneously sending and receiving both applications and data between the server and its various clients. These operations require vast amounts of RAM, and the requirement will only increase as your network operating system software becomes more robust and complex, more users are added, more applications are added, and existing applications are upgraded.

At the time this book is being written, server systems on the average require between 32 and 64 megabytes of RAM. With regard to file server RAM, be sure that any file server you consider for purchase be expandable—that is, that it can accommodate additional RAM in the future. Ask your vendor to explain expandability issues fully before approving the purchase of any machine.

Bus Performance

THE *bus* IS AN electrical pathway inside a workstation's CPU. Data travels along this pathway between the CPU's components— keyboard or mouse to video card to hard disk to network interface card to other optional add-on controller cards and back again if required. Data flows along this path continuously while the computer is in operation.

There are two features of the data bus that determine its performance effectiveness: data transfer speed and the width of the data path. The rate at which data can move along the bus is set by the manufacturer. It is important that fast microprocessors use a correspondingly fast bus; otherwise the processor speed is wasted. In addition, bus speed is also important when selecting add-on cards for the machine; a card designed for a slower bus will not work with a fast bus.

In the earliest desktop computers, the width of the data path was eight bits. This meant that the data moved between components along eight parallel tracks of copper that were printed onto the computer's main circuit board (or *motherboard*). The 8-bit bus width allowed data to move one byte at a time. This system was soon replaced by a 16-bit data bus, using 16 parallel copper tracks so that data bytes could move between components in pairs, called *blocks*, making the data flow that much faster. The latest systems, such as those built around 80486 and Pentium microprocessors, use a 32-bit data path, which increases the speed of data transfer by an order of magnitude, using 4-byte blocks.

The data bus is constructed according to a standard physical architecture. The most obvious aspect of the bus architecture is the shape of the slots into which the peripheral cards must be inserted. The network interface card in your workstation must be manufactured to fit with the type of bus architecture your workstation is using. There are five major types of bus architecture currently in use in networked systems:

Industry Standard Architecture (ISA). This is the oldest standard bus still in widespread use. It is a 16-bit design, but can handle peripheral cards designed for earlier 8-bit systems. It has the advantage of being less expensive, but it is slow. This architecture can be found in IBM-compatible machines using 80286 processors, or better.

Extended Industry Standard Architecture (EISA). This is a 32-bit design that is an enhanced version of the ISA architecture, developed by Compaq Corporation in cooperation with other industry leaders, for use in IBM-compatible machines. Besides cards specifically designed for EISA, this bus can handle most cards designed for ISA machines. Its chief drawback is the expense—EISA-specific network cards cost too much to make them popular for anything but file servers.

Macintosh NuBus. This is a proprietary bus used by the Macintosh, and is not available on any other type of computer. It is a fast 32-bit system. Recently, Macintosh abandoned this bus in their new PowerMac machines, in favor of the PCI bus specification, as described below.

Micro Channel Architecture. This was a proprietary 32-bit design developed by IBM for its PS/2 line of desktop computers. It does not support any cards developed for any other bus. IBM developed Micro Channel Architecture in hopes that it would become a new standard bus architecture and drive competing machines off the market. The system is very fast, but has not caught on as well as it might have because of the compatibility issues. The PS/2 computer has faded in the marketplace, and IBM has indicated that it is phasing out the technology.

Peripheral Component Interconnect (PCI). This is the most recent bus design. The Intel Corporation developed it to take advantage of the advanced processing power in systems that use 80486 or later microprocessors. It also borrows some concepts that were introduced in the Micro Channel Architecture bus; for example, PCI cards have a direct connection to both the system's main memory and CPU. This allows the card to function as a *bus-master*, transferring information directly to the memory, bypassing the CPU. This bypass technique can speed up network performance dramatically; however, a single machine can handle only one or two bus-mastering peripheral cards at a time. PCI cards also have the advantage of a lower price than comparable EISA cards. They use fewer hardware jumpers and configuration switches, making them easier to install and maintain. At this writing, PCI is still a maturing technology. If it proves itself in the marketplace, living up to its potential for reliability, cost savings, and speed, it can become a long-lasting standard.

Data Storage

DATA STORAGE ON A network usually involves a compromise of one sort or another. Networks have to weigh several concerns against one another when designing network data storage systems. These concerns include access speed, convenience, application performance, and security.

Data on the network (including application programs as well as the text, numbers, graphic images, and other information they work with) is stored on workstation hard disks, on the file server hard disk, or split between workstations and one or more servers. It is the responsibility of the network administrator to guide users on where to store data, as well as to keep track of what data is stored where, how to keep it secure, and how to be sure that its integrity and accuracy are upheld as it moves throughout the system. See Chapter 12 for more details on network administration.

In a client/server system, the ideal data storage solution is to centralize all stored data on the file server, and keep nothing of consequence on workstation hard disks. Some client/server workstations may have no hard or floppy disks of their own, requiring that all requests for data be handled by the central server, and preventing the workstation operator from copying any data off the network. For example, in a high-security environment (such as military defense or commercial research), such diskless terminals would be a simple and practical means of preventing individuals from removing sensitive information on disks.

In most everyday circumstances, it is necessary to store some data on workstation hard disks, when security and data sharing is not an issue and such local storage will reduce network traffic and speedup system performance. Usually, client hard disks tend to be small (around 500MB) and file server hard disk are by necessity many times larger.

Peer-to-peer systems distribute data across a series of workstation hard disks, and it is up to the network users, in cooperation with a network administrator and sometimes with the help of internally-programmed access rights, to agree on systems to protect the data's integrity and accuracy.

The size of the hard disk on the server and workstations will be determined by the amount of data your system must handle weighed against the amount of money you can afford. However, there is a general law of computing that says all stored data will eventually grow to fill any hard disk storing it. (Application programs, in particular, have a way of growing as they are upgraded—a phenomenon known as "software bloat." One current accounting package, for example, now requires 300MB minimum, with 500MB recommended.) Unless you know there is a fixed upper limit on the amount of data you will handle, buy the largest hard disk you can afford.

Like RAM, a workstation's hard disk size is measured in *megabytes*. A megabyte equals space to store one million bytes of data. These days, a 540MB hard disk is considered small. On a network file server, such a size would be hopelessly inadequate. Thus, large network storage devices today are measured in *Gigabytes* (GB), each gigabyte being space for a billion bytes of data. Nowadays, up to ten gigabytes is common for file servers.

Hard disks access data at varying speeds, measured in *milliseconds*, indicating the amount of time it takes the hard disk to find data. A millisecond is one-thousandth of a second; the lower the hard disk's millisecond rating, the faster it is. Thus, a 17ms hard disk is faster than a 28ms hard disk. Because networks must access and store far greater amounts of data than stand-alone systems, buy the fastest hard disk you can afford. Fortunately, hard disk prices are falling and those made by the major manufacturers tend to be reliable. As long as you stick to the popular brand names, price can be your overriding concern when selecting hard disks for your system. For file server storage devices, choose one with a good warranty.

Network Interface Cards

THE NETWORK INTERFACE CARD was described generally in Chapter 2. This peripheral card is the key component of the network workstation. Its chief purpose is to send data out onto the network and receive data sent to the workstation in which it resides.

Although several manufacturers produce network interface cards, they can all be used to talk to each other in any of the popular network systems (LAN Manager, NetWare, Windows NT, and others). A more important compatibility issue is the type of workstation bus in which they are being installed. For example, you cannot use a 32-bit card in a 16-bit bus. However, most 16-bit cards can work accurately, although more slowly, in a 32-bit bus. Cards are designed for specific bus architectures as well; many ISA cards will fit in EISA slots, but all other types of cards will only fit into the specific bus slot for which they were built—PCI in PCI slots only, EISA in EISA slots only, and so on.

Each network card is manufactured with a unique, permanent electronic address. Manufacturers license blocks of addresses to encode onto their cards, and barring some egregious mistake on the manufacturer's part, this licensing system ensures that no address is ever duplicated. This address is a 16-bit binary code, which limits the total number of available addresses to about seventy trillion. Manufacturers probably will not run out of network card addresses anytime soon.

Network cards allow for a set of configuration options that ensure the card's ability to coexist with other peripheral devices in the workstation and respond correctly to your network operating system. If you are using a Macintosh network, the hardware and software are already fully integrated and you need not

Why Not Just Use the Defaults?

Almost all NIC vendors ship their cards with widely used standard configurations already set. Network software vendors, wishing to avoid customer support problems as much as possible, try to respect these default settings in their software. Still, take the time to check each board's configuration settings before you install it, even if you have decided to go with an "all default" configuration. Mistakes in setting default configurations do creep in when a card is being manufactured, and once an incorrectly configured card is in place and cabled up, the smallest incorrect setting can cause all kinds of mysterious and maddening behavior to occur. What's worse, these errors often seem to be software-related. Since you have assumed that all the NICs have only default settings, the NIC is the last place you'd expect to find the problem, and sure enough, that's where it eventually is found.

concern yourself with configuration options. If you are using a PC-based network, you should consult your network operating system manual for information about the required settings for the NIC you are using, and check the settings in use by other add-on equipment for each workstation, to prevent conflicts.

The two most important variables governing the behavior of a NIC are its *port address* and *interrupt*. The port address is different from the card's permanent address. Whereas the permanent address identifies the card throughout the network, the port address is a hexadecimal number used by the workstation to select a local electronic circuit through which it directs the NIC's incoming and outgoing data. A common default port address is 300h. The workstation must be configured to send network data to the correct port address; the NIC must be configured to recognize when data is sent to that address. If the hardware configurations do not agree, the data will get sent elsewhere (to the printer, to the mouse, or nowhere at all), the network will fail to respond, and the workstation may simply shut down.

The interrupt is also a local electronic switch used by the operating system to control the flow of data. The interrupt, as its name implies, is used by the workstation to stop the flow of data temporarily and allow other data to pass through the system. Interrupts prevent different data flows from using the same physical circuitry simultaneously. PCs have a limited number of interrupts, and a workstation loaded down with many peripheral devices (such as modems, mice, page scanners, bar code readers, extra printers, dual monitors, joysticks, and more) must be carefully configured to allow all those devices to share interrupts without bringing the whole affair to a crashing halt.

Interrupt conflicts are a common cause of network problems. If you suspect that your workstation is locking up because of conflicts between network cards and other peripheral devices, the only solution may be to take out one or more of the extra devices (bye-bye, beloved joystick), or spend hours experimenting with various optional configurations until the whole mess finally works harmoniously together. In these circumstances, you may need the services of a network engineer, a person with the detailed technical knowledge necessary to straighten things out. Have the coffee ready.

Configuring a NIC usually involves setting *switches* or *jumper block connectors* (both are shown in Figure 4.1). It is always a good idea to set these devices before pushing the NIC down into its slot on the workstation's motherboard. If they need to be changed later, turn off all power, lift the card gently out of its slot, reset them, and gently replace the card.

Switches are usually found clustered together in a switchblock, a tiny plastic box. Switches are extremely small levers that must be set in combination to achieve particular configurations.

Switches are often too small for fingers to handle. Electronic supply stores carry miniature toolkits that contain tiny screwdrivers you can use to move switches.

FIGURE 4.1

A switchblock and pin jumper block. A switchblock sets configuration options by adjusting the positions of small switches. A jumper block sets configurations by shorting, or establishing a connection between, exposed connector pins.

Switchblock

Short Pins 2-3

Short Pins 1-2

Jumper Pins

Jumper Block

Jumper-block connectors are set by pushing a separate small connector down on a pair of exposed pins. A good set of tweezers can help make this job easier. Move the connectors carefully— they have a tendency to fall away and hide in the recesses of your workstation's internal hardware, and if you handle them too roughly, they may bend or even break the pins.

The switches and jumpers do more than set interrupts and port addresses. They can also configure the NIC to handle other optional features:

Cable. Some NICs can be configured for different types of cabling—thin Ethernet, thick Ethernet, 10baseT, and others. Refer to Chapter 5 for more information on cables.

Remote Booting. Some NICs are designed to be used in diskless workstations and have a special chip that allows the workstation to boot from a file server or other node on the network. A jumper or switch must be set to enable this chip.

Direct Memory Access (DMA). Some NICs have special circuits that allow them to bypass the microprocessor for certain data-transfer operations. These circuits can be enabled or disabled with switches or jumpers.

ARCnet addressing. Older ARCnet cards have configurable base addresses. These cards are not recommended, because the potential for address conflicts looms large in these systems. If you are using a system like this, keep a log of workstation addresses, and use exceptional care when installing new nodes or making changes and upgrades.

If you are using more modern NICs (for example, 3Com's EtherLink III 3C509-Combo or Cogent's eMaster+ EM964 Quartet, to name but two among the many currently competing in the NIC market), you can configure them entirely with software. This feature is a tremendous advantage over hardware-based configuration, and can save hours of tedious problem-solving. It also allows a network administrator to change workstation configurations from a single node on the network.

Good workstation design can reduce the number of headaches you may encounter running your network. Keep copies of the NIC instructions handy, along with manufacturer's manuals for the workstation and the network operating system. Read the manuals carefully, take your time during installation, and test the results as you work. You will find that a little hands-on experience goes a long way, and the process will quickly become less daunting than it first appears.

The next chapter explores in detail the fundamental means by which all these workstations are able to communicate with each other: the network cabling that connects them.

Cabling

CHAPTER

5

HE CABLE is the most vulnerable of your network's physical components. Cables must be installed and connected carefully, and in many installations you will need to take extra care to safeguard them from hazards such as excessive heat and moisture, electrical interference, and physical damage. Cable installation isn't pretty—it's often a matter of crawling around in cramped spaces feeding long segments of cable between rooms and machines.

Cables are not exciting—they tend to be perceived as simple wires, and once installed they are easily forgotten. However, when an established, reliable network develops sudden problems, seemingly out of nowhere, you should check your cabling first as a possible source of the problem. If you know what kinds of cables your system is using and understand their characteristics, you are better prepared to identify and solve problems that might arise.

This chapter will acquaint you with the language of cables and the basics of how they are installed and used. If you are installing a very small system—for example, a system with less than ten nodes in a single room or small building—this chapter will give you enough information to select the proper cables and connect the network reliably. Bear in mind, though, that cabling issues become more complicated and elaborate as the size of your installation increases. If you are installing a very large system, covering several floors in a building or running between different buildings, you should leave the installation to a reputable professional cabling service. They have more experience designing intricate wiring schemes and avoiding potential hazards. You will save money in the long run.

You may want to hire a cable installer even for the smallest networks. Learning to install cables neatly requires considerable practice.

Whatever the size and scope of your network, this chapter will give you the basic information you need for choosing the type of cable that best meets your requirements.

Cable Transmission Rates

THE CAPABILITIES of different types of cable are described using a standard terminology that anyone involved in planning a network needs to understand.

A cable that transmits only one signal is called a *baseband* cable. This term is often abbreviated to *BASE*. Some cables can handle simultaneous transmission of different signals, by sending them at different frequencies. These cables are called *broadband* cables. Broadband cables are more expensive and require additional frequency-modulating equipment; baseband is the cable used for networking.

Cables are also described by the maximum speed of data transmission they are built to handle. Data transmission speed is expressed in numbers of megabits (one million data bits) transmitted per second. Thus, *10BASE*, a very common type, indicates that the cable is of the baseband type and is capable of transmitting data at a rate of 10 megabits per second (abbreviated as 10 Mbits/s). 100-BASE cable is becoming more common, and can handle 100 Mbits/s.

Cable is further described by a numeral indicating the maximum length, in hundreds of meters, of any single segment you can use without degrading the electronic signal. For example, the term *10BASE2* indicates that the cable is baseband, handles ten megabits per second, and can be used to a maximum length of two hundred meters.

Finally, if the cable is a twisted-pair type (discussed later on in this chapter), the letter *T* is added to the end of this descriptive shorthand. Thus, 10BASET (pronounced *Ten-Base-T*) describes baseband, twisted-pair cable that handles 10 Mbits/s.

Bandwidth

The point to remember is that the BASE in cable terminology comes from the standard networking cable, which is baseband cable. The terms broadband and baseband are related to a frequently used piece of network jargon: bandwidth. Bandwidth is a general term describing the amount of data that can be carried on a network; the more data, the greater the bandwidth. Broadband cable can carry a network with a large bandwidth because a single cable carries simultaneous data transmissions along multiple frequencies. It is used, for example, in cable TV systems to carry multiple channels. But baseband, or BASE cable, is what you will use for local area networking.

Cable Types

B ESIDES THE DIFFERENCES in their transmission capabilities, cables are classified according to their type of physical construction. There are several different types of cable, each suitable for specific network configurations and rates of data transport. The most common types of cable currently in use are coaxial, twisted-pair, and fiber-optic.

Coaxial

Coaxial (or *coax*, pronounced *co-ax*) cable is the most common type of network cable. This cable consists of an inner wire surrounded by a layer of insulating material, a conducting layer of woven wire, another layer of insulation and a plastic covering. Figure 5.1 shows the structure of coaxial cable.

Type RG-58 cable (10BASE2) is a thin coaxial cable in widespread use. It can connect many local area networks that are limited to a single office or small building. It is relatively inexpensive and easy to handle.

Older, larger and more complex networks might use RG-11 (10BASE5) cable. This is a coaxial cable that is much thicker and sturdier, can withstand more rugged surroundings, and as its descriptive type indicates, can be used with much longer segment lengths.

Twisted-Pair Cable

Twisted-pair cable looks something like telephone cable. It consists of two pairs of wires twisted together. Figure 5.2 shows the structure of twisted-pair cable.

FIGURE 5.1

Coaxial cable.

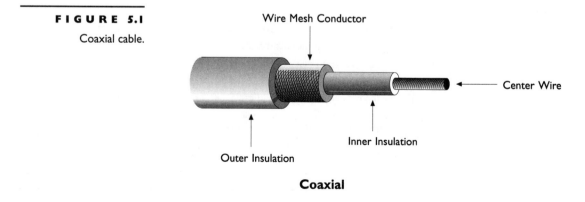

Wire Mesh Conductor

Center Wire

Inner Insulation

Outer Insulation

Coaxial

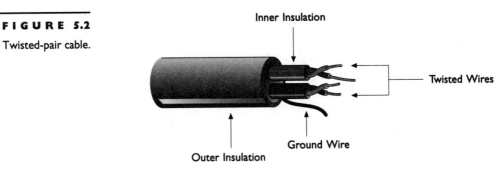

FIGURE 5.2

Twisted-pair cable.

Twisted-Pair

Twisted-pair cable is less expensive than coaxial. However, coaxial has the reputation for more durability because, compared to early twisted-pair cable, coaxial's central wire was more durable and better-protected by the surrounding insulation and outer casing. To see the difference for yourself, compare a cable TV wire (coax) to the wire between a desk telephone and the wall (twisted-pair). Twisted-pair wires were thinner, more subject to breaks and line problems when the cable got twisted or creased. The outer casing was thinner, too. But more modern construction has produced very durable T-P cable. These improvements in cable manufacture have made twisted-pair cable as reliable and durable as coaxial at speeds up to 100 Mbits/s. Another important advantage of twisted-pair cabling is its effect on the network as a whole: if a portion of a twisted-pair cable is damaged, the entire network is not shut down, as well may be the case with coaxial.

Fiber-Optic

Fiber-optic cable (shown in Figure 5.3) is becoming more common as demands for transmission speed increase. This type of cable consists of a thin glass or plastic filament, about as wide as a human hair, protected by a thick plastic padding and an external plastic sheath. Fiber-optic cable uses a pulsing laser light instead of an electronic frequency to transmit a signal.

Using light offers important advantages over using electricity; the light signal can travel further, faster, and more reliably. This is because the light signal is not subject to electrical impedance from copper wires, and can pulsate at faster rates than electric frequencies. In addition, the light signal is immune to external electrical interference. Fiber-optic cable can send reliable signals as far as 10 kilometers, at speeds approaching 100,000 Mbit/s.

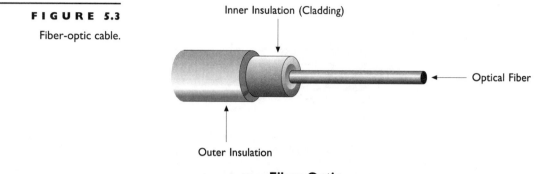

FIGURE 5.3

Fiber-optic cable.

Inner Insulation (Cladding)

Optical Fiber

Outer Insulation

Fiber-Optic

You may wonder why, if there is no electrical impedance to get in the way, fiber-optic has any distance limit at all. The answer is that after about 10 kilometers, the fiber has absorbed enough of the light to weaken the signal.

This type of cable can also be more expensive to buy, install, and maintain. It also requires special equipment (called *fiber line drivers*) to translate the electronic signals that are sent to and from workstations into pulsing light signals sent along the cable. Its use is limited to very large and extensive networks where distance, speed, and security issues are important enough to justify the extra expense.

Hubs and Repeaters

Star networks and complex bus networks (see Chapter 2 if you need a refresher on network topologies) may require special devices to connect various nodes. For example, a shared printer may need multiple connections from a variety of sources. A *hub* is a device that accepts such multiple connections. There are many different types of hubs. Some are simple hardware devices that only accept connections (called *passive* hubs); others are complicated electrical components that monitor and control the flow of information to various network locations (called *active* hubs).

A *repeater* is a special device, similar to a hub, whose function is to amplify and reduce electrical interference with a cable signal, and relay that signal from one cable to another. It is usually used to enlarge a network, in effect joining two networks together by passing a cable signal between them.

Backbones

A BACKBONE IS A TYPE of linear-bus cabling configuration, often found on multiserver, widely dispersed networks. Its purpose is to group nodes closest to the server that holds the data they access most often, or to connect multiple servers close to each other, or to group nodes close to bridges, repeaters, or routers.

Backbone cabling is effective on networks with nodes that are physically far apart from each other but still connected via cable—occupying several floors in an office building, for example. In such broadly dispersed networks, the distances between nodes and servers can have a noticeable effect on performance. Backbone cabling configurations try to put no more than one or two nodes between any node and its most frequently accessed server. Fiber-optic cable is often used for backbone cables to further improve transfer speeds. Figure 5.4 shows a typical backbone-style layout.

Backbones, using fiber-optic phone lines, are used to speed up connections between networks that must frequently communicate with each other. Although the connected LANs may be some distance apart, the use of a fiber-optic line as a backbone-style configuration over the wide area can mean a significant improvement in network performance.

FIGURE 5.4

A backbone-style cable layout. Notice that each node is no more than two nodes away from the server it will presumably access most often. Also, the servers are connected for fast data transfers between them.

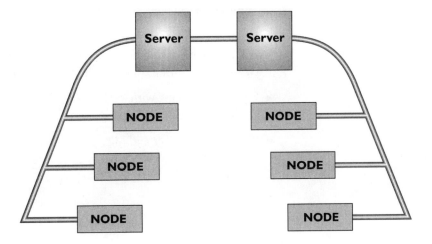

Selecting Cable

A T ONE TIME, cable choices were determined by the chosen topology; for example, Ethernet (and ARCnet) used coaxial, and token ring used shielded twisted-pair. Nowadays, networks are more accepting of a variety of cable types, and thus your cable choices are a balancing act between budgets and performance needs. The selection is normally worked out on an installation-by-installation basis when you are initially designing and budgeting your proposed network. Here is an admittedly broad generalization of how cable choices tend to be worked out:

- Ethernet supports all cable types. Coaxial cables have the reputation of supporting higher data rates, longer distances, greater durability, better protection from electromagnetic interference, and better protection from electronic eavesdropping (compared to unshielded twisted-pair cabling).

- Modern shielded twisted-pair cables, however, have performances specifications virtually equal to coaxial, with the addition of greater flexibility, and less impact on the network as a whole if they should suffer damage. For this reason, twisted-pair cabling is becoming more and more popular as the chosen cable for Ethernet networks.

- Fiber-optic cable provides the highest data transfer rates, less susceptibility to transfer errors, and protection from electromagnetic interference, but is expensive and more difficult to install than the alternatives.

- If you are working with one of the older ARCnet systems, chances are you will be using coaxial; however, some later variations of ARCnet support twisted-pair or fiber optic, with the same considerations as listed above.

- If you are working with a token ring system, you will most likely be using shielded twisted-pair cabling.

- If price is no object and high performance is the goal, and you have chosen an FDDI (Fiber Distributed Data Interface) topology, you will use fiber-optic cable.

Tables 5.1 and 5.2 summarize these considerations.

TABLE 5.1	CABLE TYPE	COMPATIBILITY			
Choosing a Cable Type: Network Compatibility		ETHER- NET	TOKEN- RING	ARCNET	FDDI
	COAXIAL	Yes	No	Yes; on later systems	No
	TWISTED-PAIR (SHIELDED)	Yes	Yes	Yes	No
	TWISTED-PAIR (UNSHIELDED)	No	Yes	Yes	No
	FIBER-OPTIC	No	Yes	Yes; on recent systems	Yes

TABLE 5.2	CABLE TYPE	SPEED	RELIABILITY	PRICE	COMMENTS
Choosing a Cable Type: Performance and Other Considerations	**COAXIAL**	Fast	Better	MidRange	Used less often than twisted-pair in modern systems
	TWISTED-PAIR (SHIELDED)	Faster	Good	Lower	Recent improvements in speed and durability
	TWISTED-PAIR (UNSHIELDED)	Acceptable	Subject to EMI	Lowest	Not often used in modern systems
	FIBER-OPTIC	Fastest	Immune to EMI	Highest	Technology still evolving and improving

Installing Cable

CABLE IS CONNECTED to workstations and other nodes along the network by means of special connectors, which are specific to the type of cable being used. Even if you leave the installation to someone else, being familiar with the physical connections will help you make informed cabling decisions.

Coaxial Connections

Coaxial cable requires a connection called a *BNC plug*, a metal cylinder with a slot cut in the side. As shown in Figure 5.5, the plug fits over a smaller cylindrical receptacle with a small knob. The slot in the plug slides around the knob as the plug is fitted into place. You secure the plug by turning it, tightening it against the knob.

A special BNC connector, called a *T-connector* (also shown in Figure 5.5), is used to join workstations in a ring or daisy-chain topology. A T-connector is attached to each network interface card and protrudes from the back of each

FIGURE 5.5

Coaxial cable uses either a BNC plug or, for ring and daisy-chain topologies, a BNC T-connector.

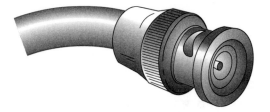

BNC (Bayonet Connector) Plug

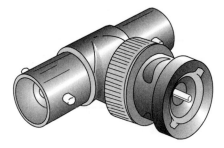

BNC T-Connector

workstation. The network is linked by cables that are attached to the open ends of the T-connectors. In a daisy-chain topology, two workstations (one on each end of the chain) will have only one cable attached. On these end workstations, the open end of the T-connector must be capped using a *resistor plug*, a small cap that absorbs the signal and prevents distortion along the line. This type of connection is fairly easy to set up and maintain.

Ethernet bus-topology networks, which share a single cable, are connected in a different way. In this topology, a cable is connected directly to each network interface card, and extended to the shared cable. The shared cable is marked every 1.5 meters to indicate where a *tap connector* (sometimes called a *vampire tap*) can be installed. A tap is a small device that stabs a hole into the shared cable and makes a connection to the core (hence the "vampire" nickname). The tap is used to attach a device called a *transceiver* (or *media attachment unit*, or *MAU*) to the shared cable. This device includes an attachment for a special nine-wire cable that connects the shared cable with the network workstation. This type of connection requires more precise and careful handling, to ensure that solid connections are made at exact locations along the shared central cable. Imprecise connections lead to signal distortions and bad network communications, and therefore this job is best left to a responsible professional.

Twisted-Pair Connections

Twisted-pair cables use connectors that look like the plugs commonly found on telephone wires inside homes. These connectors are called *RJ connectors*. They are built to different specifications for different types of twisted-pair cable. The most familiar type, called RJ-11 (shown in Figure 5.6), is the type used for telephones. A larger version of this connector is the RJ-45, which can handle cables with as many as eight wires. The RJ connector is simply inserted into a corresponding socket on the network interface card until it locks in place. This type of cabling technology is improving, and can equal coaxial-cable performance at reduced cost.

FIGURE 5.6

An RJ-11 connector, used with twisted-pair cabling.

RJ-11 Connector

Fiber-Optic Connections

Fiber-optic cable is made to order and comes equipped with its own connectors (shown in Figure 5.7). These connectors fit into special receptacles and lock in place. If you are connecting a workstation with equipment that is not compatible with fiber-optic cable, you must attach the workstation to a conversion device called a *fiber-line driver* (Figure 5.8). This device takes the light signal and converts it to an electronic signal, and vice-versa. It can become expensive to install a lot of extra equipment in order to provide compatibility between the nodes on your network and the cable, and the extra equipment requires additional maintenance as well. But if you have a very large system and need the enhanced performance, this option may be worth it.

Handling Cable

Unlike other kinds of electrical wiring, network cable is subject to performance problems because of bending and pinching. For aesthetic reasons, people like to install cable out of sight—behind walls, above ceilings, and in crawl spaces. This is fine, provided that you protect the cable from hidden damage. Water leaks (from old plumbing, worn roofs, or whatever) and heat (from nearby heater vents, sunlight through windows and skylights, and so on) can ruin cable and shut down a network. In addition, cable signals are subject to distortions from nearby electrical appliances. Neon lights have been known to cause

FIGURE 5.7

A fiber-optic connector.

Fiber-Optic Connector

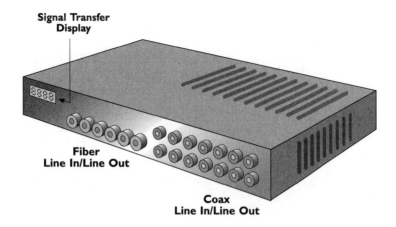

FIGURE 5.8

A fiber-line driver.

problems; other potential problem spots are elevator shafts and nearby industrial machinery. When necessary, you may have to protect your cable from environmental interference by installing special insulating pipes and running the cable through them.

Sniffing Down a Cable

Because cabling problems are frequently the source of network problems, it makes sense to inspect the cables when troubleshooting almost anything—from intermittent slow-downs to the terrifying, out-of-nowhere system crash.

Check the cable connectors first. Loose or disconnected cables cause big problems and are often easily reconnected.

Check for signs of physical damage. Cables can get cut or broken (when heavy ojects move across them, for example) and the damage is usually easy to spot.

If the cables are not easy to inspect (they are threaded through air ducts or behind building walls, perhaps), you can use a device called a time-domain reflectometer (informally, a cable sniffer) that transports a signal down a cable and measures the time it takes the signal to reflect back from blocked points. The elapsed time is translated into cable distance, and you then have a pretty good idea where the trouble is.

Common Cable Problems

Many network problems can be traced to cable problems. If you are experiencing bizarre network behavior, check the cable first. Some problems are easy to solve: The cable connection has simply shaken loose, or come disconnected. If all the connections are still solid, check the cable for signs of damage. If you find such evidence (for example, torn or sliced insulation), replace the entire cable.

Some network systems have built-in diagnostic procedures that can send signals down a cable and report on the status of the transmission.

Cabling ARCnet

ARCNET IS AN OLDER technology. Despite its venerable status, some users have an affection for it—like those people you occasionally see on the highway, driving restored classic cars. (ARCnet was first developed by the Datapoint Corporation in 1977, which could qualify it for "antique" status in the computer industry). Even so, ARCnet had a number of interesting features, worth a brief mention in a discussion of networking principles. ARCnet was fairly easy and inexpensive to set up and maintain. It had the capability of establishing alternate routes along the network as users logged on or off, by making extensive use of *hubs* to connect all the nodes. Hubs could be either *active* (meaning that they established connections and amplified the signal) or *passive* (meaning that they simply established connections).

ARCnet had a reputation for performance limitations such as slow speed and a low limit on the number of available nodes. Some modified derivatives of ARCnet can still be found, with modifications that increase its speed and data-handling capabilities.

Here are some of the basic cabling specifications that you would find in a standard ARCnet network:

- Cable type is RG-62 A/U coaxial. This is an easy-to-handle, lightweight cable grade).

- The longest cable segment carrying an unamplified signal is 100 feet.

- The longest cable segment carrying an amplified signal is 2000 feet.

- The total cable length along the entire network cannot be greater than 20,000 feet.

- You cannot directly connect two passive hubs. In other words, if you want to connect two hubs that do not amplify a signal, you must install a signal-amplifying hub between them.

- You must install a resistor cap on all unused connectors.

Cabling Ethernet

E THERNET IS A FLEXIBLE topology supporting a wide variety of hardware and configurations. It can use both coaxial and twisted-pair cabling. Coaxial cable can be RG-11 (also called *thick Ethernet*), using transceivers to connect to workstations, or RG-58 (also called *thin Ethernet*), using T-connectors to link workstations directly. Thin Ethernet is good for relatively small local networks, especially using peer-to-peer topologies (discussed in Chapter 2). Thick Ethernet is good for larger, more demanding systems, such as client/server systems with a lot of nodes and data traffic. Twisted-pair cables are used to make direct links between workstations and a central hub. Regardless of the physical topology that you choose, Ethernet functions as a logical bus topology.

If you are using thin coaxial cable with T-connectors, the following rules apply:

- The longest allowable cable segment between nodes is 300 feet.

- The shortest distance between T-connectors is 1.5 feet.

- The maximum number of nodes on a network (without repeaters) is 30.

- The total cable length along a network (without repeaters) cannot exceed 607 feet.

- Up to four repeaters can be used, joining a maximum of five cables and 138 nodes.

- The total cable length along the entire network (with repeaters) cannot exceed 3035 feet.

If you are using thick coaxial cable, the following rules apply:

- The longest allowable cable segment between nodes is 300 feet.

- Special 9-wire cable is used to connect the workstations to the shared cable.

- The shortest distance between transceivers is 1.5 meters (8 feet).

- The maximum number of nodes on a network (without repeaters) is 100.

- The total cable length along a network (without repeaters) cannot exceed 1640 feet.

- Up to 4 repeaters can be used, joining a maximum of 488 nodes.

- When using repeaters to join cables, up to five cables can be joined, but only three can have computers attached to them. The other cables are empty, and serve only to extend the overall length of the network.

- The total cable length along the entire network (with repeaters) cannot exceed 8200 feet.

If you are using twisted-pair cable, the cabling rules are determined by the type of hub used to make the connections to the workstations. In general, you can expect to be allowed up to 300 feet or so of cable between the hub and each workstation.

Some Ethernet hubs can be connected to other hubs using coaxial cables. In such cases, the rules for coaxial cabling apply.

Cabling Token-Ring Systems

TOKEN-RING NETWORKS use a ring topology to support large, complex systems. These systems use shielded, twisted-pair cables in most cases. Workstations are connected using a special token-ring hub called a *multi-station access unit* (MSAU). Each MSAU contains up to 24 ports for network nodes. In addition, each MSAU has two special ports, called Ring-In (RI), and Ring-Out (RO). If you choose, you can use these ports to connect several MSAUs together. Figure 5.9 shows a simple token-ring cabling topology.

If you are using shielded twisted-pair cables, the following rules apply:

- If you choose to connect more than one MSAU to your network, you must connect each MSAU's RO port to another MSAU's RI port, thus chaining them all together in a physical ring. If you are using only a single MSAU, the RI and RO ports are ignored.

- The longest allowable cable segment between an MSAU and a workstation is 150 feet.

FIGURE 5.9

Cables and connections in a token-ring topology.

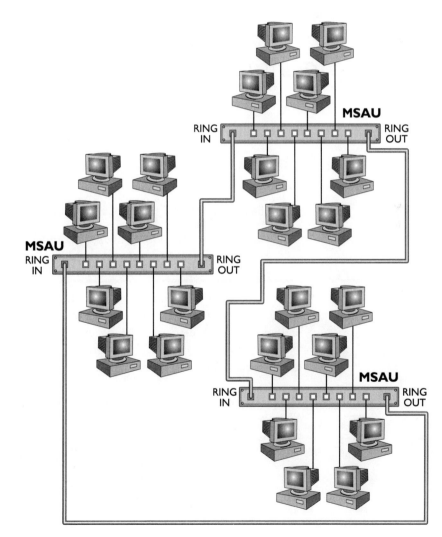

- The maximum distance between two MSAUs is 150 feet.

- The maximum number of nodes on the network is 260.

- The maximum number of MSAUs is 33.

Token-ring networks can become quite complicated, more so if you use bridges, routers, and gateways. Connecting these types of devices to a token ring network can force changes and exceptions to the above rules, and such an installation should be undertaken by an experienced professional.

Cabling Macintosh Networks

MACINTOSH (APPLETALK) networks use shielded, twisted-pair cables. Each workstation uses a *drop cable* to connect to a small connector called a *LocalTalk connector.* Other cables connect the LocalTalk connectors to each other. The system is simple and easy to set up. Cabling rules are simple as well:

- The maximum total length of cable along the network is 1000 feet.

- The recommended maximum number of nodes is 32. (LocalTalk hardware supports up to 254 nodes, but with this many nodes, performance would be seriously degraded; therefore it's not recommended.)

Other types of cable can increase the recommended specifications. For example, you can use Farallon's PhoneNet cabling system to increase the size of your Macintosh network. This system uses unshielded twisted-pair cabling and standard phone connectors. It allows a maximum of 48 nodes and 1800 feet of cable total along the network.

These cabling rules apply to AppleTalk networks. As discussed in Chapter 3, Apple also offers the EtherTalk and TokenTalk protocols, which allow links to Ethernet and Token Ring networks.

Cable Development—What's Next?

SPEED, SPEED, and more speed is the holy grail of networking. Network hardware design is centered around making things faster than ever, and cabling specifications are likely to change dramatically as newer and faster networking systems are developed. As the process continues, expect to see lower prices for fiber-optic cable and different standards and specifications emerge. This chapter has given you a foundation for understanding the unpredictable, emerging standards of the future.

In the next chapter, we will discuss the most important node on a network, the hardware through which all client/server traffic flows: the file server.

Servers

ILE SERVERS HAVE BEEN discussed in previous chapters (especially Chapters 2 and 4) in relation to other network technologies. This chapter explains in detail what file servers do, how they do it, and how they came to be. Understanding something about file server technology and its purposes will help you decide whether a client/server network is the right kind of network for your business.

This chapter focuses on the need to share centralized data as the driving force behind the use of file servers. In some client/server network installations, however, the need for communication may be independent of data storage issues. In Chapter 10 you'll learn about messaging systems and other network applications.

How Servers Came to Be

BEFORE FILE SERVERS there were print servers. Their development, in response to a need for sharing resources, provided a model for that of file servers; so a brief look at their history will be instructive.

The computer revolution has yet to fulfill its ideal of a paperless office. As computers have become more powerful, they produce increasingly sophisticated information. However, most of this information, sooner or later, is put back on paper. With today's word processing programs (or even spreadsheet and database software), any computer user with sufficient understanding of page design can produce professional-looking documents incorporating various fonts and page layouts, tables, charts, graphic images, equations, and the like—all intended to be printed on paper.

Sophisticated printed information requires sophisticated printing hardware. Printers have evolved in response to this need, but the most powerful (for example, high-resolution, full color) printers are also the most expensive.

This problem has existed since the first days of desktop computing. Because a printer connected to a single computer often sits idle for hours at a time, it was a natural response on the part of information experts to look for a way to make expensive printers more cost-effective by allowing a number of users to share the same printer.

Sharing a printer presented scheduling and resource problems: it wouldn't be cost-effective to tie up computer time waiting in line to print. Printer sharing required an intelligent management scheme to store and line up ("spool") print jobs separately, allowing computers to continue other processing while the printer churned out information on paper. The solution was a *print server*, a separate computer that received printing instructions from several computers, stored them and fed them to the shared printer in turn.

Management eventually caught on to the idea that the print server could save resources (read: money) and increase productivity (read: profits). They increased demand for more sophisticated print services. In large organizations, print servers could manage several printers. Print servers could run in unattended batch mode, at night, leaving more time for human workers to focus on company business. Print servers could analyze the printing process and offer information that could be used to streamline printing. In this way the print server became the genesis of client/server networking.

Enter the File Server...

If it worked for printing, why not for data? Storage media were also expensive. Why not share a single storage location, both saving money and eliminating the kinds of inconsistencies that arise when copies of the same document are scattered on hard disks throughout the organization? The goal of achieving consistency and reliability of information throughout the organization became the business ideal of desktop computing's infancy.

File sharing, unfortunately, was a much more complicated and expensive process than print sharing. Whereas print services involved mostly one-way transfer of data (computer-to-printer), file sharing would involve transfer back and forth throughout the organization. Bottlenecks and collisions would have to be avoided, and centrally-located, shared information would have to coexist with local, individually-owned information. There were immense technological problems to solve.

The current solution is the *file server*, a computer dedicated to storing shared information and managing, by means of software and transmission hardware, the distribution of that information throughout the enterprise.

How Many Servers Is Enough?

File servers must be doing something right. The demand for these powerful computers increases each year. In the United States now, according to the Bureau of the Census, there are over 11 million business establishments (defined as locations with at least one worker). By the turn of the century, every business establishment in this country and most in the world will have at least one computer, and many will have more than one.

These computers are linking together. As a conservative estimate, there are easily 30 million business locations worldwide, now in the process of linking up and transmitting data. In ten years or less, some experts estimate, the business world will make use of more than 50 million file servers.

File Server Functions on the Network

F THE LOCAL AREA NETWORK is the nervous system of a business, the file server is the system's brain, as illustrated in Figure 6.1. Servers process orders, manage inventory, schedule shipments, balance accounts, issue paychecks, manage schedules, update personnel records, and analyze the organization's use of its resources, including the network itself. Overall, file servers provide the following general solutions for businesses:

- They function as a central repository for shared business data.
- They enforce enterprise-wide rules that (ideally) make this data into consistent, meaningful information.
- They facilitate communication between work team members.
- They facilitate sharing of technical resources (for example, expensive printers).

Storing Shared Data

Servers to a large extent follow a hierarchical model of information storage and retrieval as it evolved in the precomputer world. Before the rise of computers, the fundamental building block of business information (the first level) was a

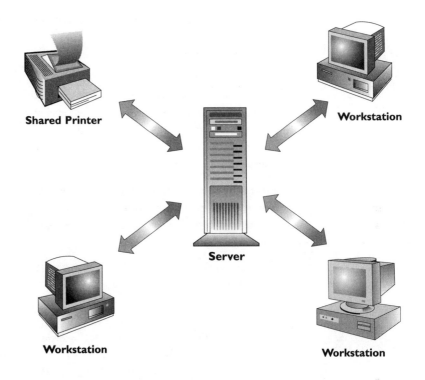

FIGURE 6.1

In a network with a single file server, the server stores data and distributes it throughout the enterprise. This model provides a balance between convenient access, consistency, and security. Notice that this model is a logical model, and is independent of the physical topology of the network.

Shared Printer

Workstation

Server

Workstation

Workstation

sheet of paper on which information was printed. At the next level, sheets of paper could be gathered together and secured with a staple or clip of some kind. Related documents could be gathered into file folders, file folders gathered together into larger hanging folders, and so on up through the system: hanging folders in file drawers, drawers in cabinets, cabinets in rooms, rooms in buildings. If a document was relevant in more than one context, physical copies of it needed to appear in each appropriate file folder.

Servers translate the ink/paper storage model into an electron/magnetic media storage model, but the fundamental arrangement is the same. The basic building block (the computer equivalent of information-on-paper) is called *data*. Data is information in its simplest form, meaningless until related together in some fashion so as to become meaningful. Related data is stored on a server's disk under a unique name, called a *file*. Related files are gathered together into directories, and related directories are gathered together into larger and larger directories, until all the required information is stored in a hierarchy of directories on the server's hard disk.

The server's "filing cabinet" is a database; it offers a number of advantages over the paper model. You can search electronically for a particular file, even if you can only remember a tiny portion of what the file contains.

The Database

A database, generally defined, is a flexible, hierarchical structure for storing raw data, which facilitates its organization into useful information. Under this definition, just about all data on computers is stored in one kind of database or another. A spreadsheet is a database, arranging data in a grid of rows and columns; a word processing document is a database, storing data in an arrangement of characters and formatting instructions.

What a database does, then, is break information down into its most fundamental components, and then it creates meaningful relationships between those components. We depend on databases of varying configurations and complexity for all our computerized information needs.

A specialized form of the database is the relational database, which follows the hierarchical component model to its logical conclusion. The relational database breaks a series of related forms of data down into fundamental units, which are arranged according to common attributes, called fields. Then it arranges the fields into sets called records, and the records into sets called tables. It also forms relationships between tables based on links between different fields. All of this data crunching is handled by a piece of software called a Database Management System (DBMS), more details of which you will encounter in Chapters 10 and 13.

Many people, when they hear the term database, think of a DBMS. But in the client/server context, the term database is extended, to include any hierarchically-arranged data. And, as you'll see in Chapter 10's discussion of network applications, the concept of data sharing—that is, information sharing—embraces tools such as e-mail and discussion media as well as databases.

Using a database, you can *tag* data, relating it to other data in several different ways, without having to replicate the data in different physical locations. This ability to access and organize data in a flexible manner without making physical copies of it (and thus preserving the integrity of the information at its most basic level) is what has led to the increasing use of client/server technologies as a widespread business information model.

The Server and the Database

With regard to information processing, storage, and retrieval, servers exist to manage data. Without a central store of information to be shared, servers would be impractical as business tools. True, you could still use them to share resources and facilitate communication, but a peer-to-peer network would be a more cost-effective tool for handling these jobs in the absence of business databases. (Another solution, particularly for larger enterprises, is to maintain the centralized data on a mainframe and use the client/server network for communications.) So the question of client/server becomes a question of whether or not your business needs centralized databases. Sharing and communications are built on top of that.

Data Distribution

Distributed data and *distributed processing* (also called *distributed computing*) are terms used widely in the world of client/server networking, and you will come across them often. Figure 6.2 illustrates the difference between these two terms. Following is an explanation of what they mean.

Distributed data and distributed processing are two sides of the same conceptual coin. Distributed data refers to the basic data stored in the server, which is accessed by (or in client/server jargon, "distributed to") different members of the work team. Or in other words, if two or more workers access the same data in order to get their jobs done, the data is distributed.

Distributed processing refers to the way different tasks are organized among members of the work team. If a set of information-handling tasks is thought of as a single step-by-step process and is split among members of the work team so that they can handle the steps more efficiently, that process is distributed.

Here's an example: a customer's ordering and payment information is stored in a central customer record on the server. This record is accessed by many departments in various locations throughout the company (say, accounting and shipping/receiving, to name two). Thus this data is an example of distributed data. In addition, because accounting and shipping/receiving work with the data in unique but related ways in order to accomplish a specific goal (updating the customer record), their activities are an example of distributed processing.

FIGURE 6.2

Distributed data (shared
access) and distributed
processing or computing
(shared tasking).

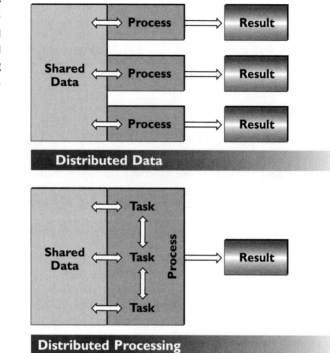

Enforcing Enterprise-Wide Rules

In addition to centralized storage, the file server performs a less-understood, but equally important function: preserving the integrity of the data by enforcing rules on how it may be processed and communicated.

For example, practically every business derives its income from invoicing customers. A well-run business follows generally accepted rules for handling invoices in order to determine how best to record charges and payments. Charges must be related to both customers and products ordered, records must stored consistently and accumulated accurately, and payments must be applied against the correct customer and correct invoice. Back orders, late charges, and other anomalies must be accounted for, and all this must be done in a consistent manner to avoid the kind of confusion and mistakes that will alienate the customer and undermine the business. If everyone in the business could access the data and make whatever changes to it they deemed appropriate, it would be impossible to maintain consistent, reliable information for the enterprise.

Throughout any business, rules are set up for handling all sorts of different information. These rules can be formally designed, like those for bookkeeping and accounting, or they can evolve out of the day to day handling of the business, but they are there and their consistency is vital.

Centralized data storage provides a narrow access point through which data is made available to the enterprise, and through which the enterprise transmits data for storage. It is at this point that the server can be programmed to accept or reject the transmission if the information does not conform to vital rules. For example, the server can assure that charges are not billed to customers without an accompanying order for products. Also, the server can perform necessary security operations, such as preventing data from being unintentionally lost, or making sure that sensitive business information is not available to competitors.

What's a Business Rule?

The concept of business rules is so important in the world of networked computing (and for that matter, in business overall), it's worth defining in some detail.

In general terms, a business rule is a process that specifies some action (or set of actions) that occurs as the result of another; to put it in computer-specific terms, a business rule is an if-then process. An example: If the minimum shipping order is 25 items, then orders of less than 25 items must be combined to meet the minimum. If the minimum is met, then we ship the order.

Businesses are full of these rules. Together, they form a series of steps that define the nature of business and keep it running. And of course, business rules are organic—they tend to evolve and become more complex over time.

If you are running a one-person business (or at least a very small one), the rules may be informal, kept in your head ("If it's Tuesday, then I stay open an extra hour"), and subject to momentary exceptions. A medium-size or large business cannot afford to keep informal or constantly-shifting rules, because time would be wasted determining the course of action instead of taking it. ("What were we supposed to do with government purchase orders again?" or "How do we account for customer defaults again?")

The short-term, if-then decisions of a business work together to become the real policy and business plan of an enterprise, more so than idealized mission statements or advertising copy. To whatever extent you have formalized the business rules you work by, and communicated those rules clearly throughout your enterprise, you can expect to have pretty much that same extent of success using computers to model your business procedures.

This last point is worth bearing on. All businesses compete, and an advantage in competition is often based on specialized knowledge (access to information). Centralized data storage and retrieval often involves a delicate balancing act between ready access to information by those who need it and securing proprietary information against those who might use it against the enterprise. The balance is seldom perfect. Most companies will tend to make data more secure than accessible, and thus day-to-day accessibility issues can take up a significant amount of a network administrator's time. We will discuss data security in greater detail in Chapter 11.

Facilitating Communication

The file server, because of its centralized nature, is a natural repository of ad-hoc information between work team members. The server can send a single copy of a business memo from one team member to selected other members, or to the entire enterprise, nearly instantly. The server can inform team members that a message exists for them, provide access, and keep track of who has received the message and who hasn't.

Network communications systems (also called e-mail) have evolved into complex messaging systems that provide sending, storing, and receiving services for a virtually unlimited number of potential users, as well as managing complicated security and access issues. E-mail is discussed more fully in Chapter 10.

Resource Sharing

Finally, the original purpose of the server, allowing shared access to expensive peripherals, remains as important a function as ever. These days, however, more than just printers are involved. A server can manage access to such devices as high-speed, multiline modems that permit simultaneous access to the network from remote sites; data scanners for more efficient data input; sophisticated graphic output devices, such as pen plotters; high-speed data backup devices. In effect, just about any information-processing device can be attached to the server and shared, provided that it is cost-effective to provide the necessary supporting technology to make the connection. We have come a long way from the lowly print server, but the principle remains the same.

Print Servers Then and Now

From its beginning as a dedicated workstation (with perhaps a switchbox attached), the modern network print server has evolved into as much a logical process as a hardware device. For example, in NetWare, a dedicated workstation can run software named PSERVER.EXE to manage the flow of data to printers on the network. If you choose not to use a dedicated workstation, you can install software on the file server, a NetWare Loadable Module named PSERVER.NLM, which does the same job (at the cost, however, of using up some of the file server's RAM and disk space).

The Server's Technical Requirements

F THE BENEFITS to businesses just discussed sound interesting to you, and you believe that you are in the market for client/server networking, be ready to open your wallet. File servers must be capable of handling thousands upon thousands of requests from users. This means that servers need:

Massive Storage: You need plenty of storage capacity not only to hold the data that is to be shared by many individuals, but also to hold network application/management/communication/interface data. Furthermore, the need for storage space is increasing, because all software becomes more feature-laden and complex as vendors compete to provide upgrade incentives. We are already at the point where immense storage capacity is required for software applications alone. It isn't unusual for some server disks to use more space for application software files than the data files they manipulate.

One strategy is to put applications on individual hard drives and use the server only to back them up. You'll learn more about this in Chapter 11.

Massive Random-Access Memory: From the user's point of view, graphic interfaces and advanced application features make data processing easier and more intuitive. From the computer's point of view, they are diabolically complex, involving billions of individual data processing instructions. An ocean of RAM is now required to keep vast amounts of data processing instructions, plus the data being processed, in a place where it can all be handled efficiently.

Blazing Speed: What good are billions of instructions if the machine executes them slowly? At the positively glacial pace of one second per instruction, a computer would take more than 31 years to process a billion instructions, and a billion instructions aren't nearly enough to do any serious processing on your network. Computers must therefore execute billions of instructions in scant seconds. They must also be able to transfer data between storage and RAM fast enough to keep up with their processing speeds. This means hard disks that are not only big, but can access stored data as close to instantaneously as possible.

Bigger and faster servers are more expensive. The larger your network, the more speed and storage you need, and you (or your trusted network engineer) must determine your exact requirements. For purposes of comparison and as a thumbnail estimate, consider that a 20-node client/server network running an average database for a company of that size, with room for individual applications and standard communication features, might want to start with a single-processor, 120-MHz Pentium server, with 1GB hard disk storage and 32MB RAM, costing roughly $6,000. But these figures are not hard and fast. Every business is different. Your server will be custom-designed.

Of course, you can wait, and today's power machine will be cheaper next year. That's the good news. The bad news is that it may well be obsolete as well. To keep today's servers from falling by the wayside, more and more hardware designers are building upgradable servers, meaning servers that will accept more powerful or additional processors, additional RAM, and larger or additional hard disks, as they are needed and become available. This type of server promises to have a longer life-span, and for the additional money may well be worth it.

Servers, like workstations, tend to feel obsolete after about three years. It is wise to know before purchase that the server you are considering includes a clear upgrade path, in order to maintain the usefulness of your investment.

Servers and Mainframes

THERE IS SOME controversy as to whether servers will someday replace mainframes. They may, but not someday soon. Mainframes still serve a purpose in managing the complex business rules of very large organizations, and enterprises that are spread out over a very large area. But the increasing processing power of servers combined with their lower cost make them the logical replacement to mainframe-based systems in the future.

The question of whether client/server networks have already replaced mainframes is an on-going debate in the enterprise computing world. You'll find that arguing about it at any length is like arguing Macs vs. PCs—devotees on both sides have their arguments mastered. In any case, we'll all know more someday, just by sticking around. "Film at 11..."

In the interim, client/server networks will often find it necessary to connect to mainframe-based systems. This is because some data can only be found in the mainframe environment, usually because the business rules for handling it are sufficiently complex, or the data itself is massive or sensitive enough that as a practical matter it remains stored there.

Connecting to a mainframe requires some form of network-like access. Even if you are using a telephone and modem as your access hardware, you still require special software to make your workstation appear to the mainframe to be just another network terminal. Many vendors can provide the necessary software to handle this type of network extension.

Reading Server Ads

B ECAUSE SERVERS ARE COMPUTERS, much of their sales promotional lierature deals with the same specifications touted for workstation computers: processing speed measured in megahertz (MHz); hard disk capacity measured in gigabytes (GB) instead of megabytes; data transfer rates measured in milliseconds (MS). There is some server-specific jargon that is useful to know, however. Following are some common terms you're likely to run across.

RAID

RAID stands for Redundant Arrays of Inexpensive Disks. Borrowed from mainframe technology to provide security for data. RAID systems utilize a set of hard disks to write data onto more than one disk simultaneously. If one disk fails, the operating system can retrieve the data from a backup disk. The more disks (and thus the more redundancy), the safer the system.

RAID can also speed up disk access. If a file server uses only a single disk, any request from a user for data must wait until all previous requests from other users have been accommodated. Using RAID, because redundant copies of data are stored on multiple disks, requests for data can be accommodated simultaneously, speeding up access. Figure 6.3 illustrates this process.

Symmetrical Multiprocessing

Symmetrical multiprocessing (SMP) was discussed in Chapter 4. Briefly summarized, SMP is a feature that adds power by integrating more than one central processor into a single file server, along with the necessary additional hardware and software to divide processing chores between them. Other terms for this same feature indicate the number of processors involved: *bi-processor* (two processors); *tri-processor* (three processors); *quad-processor* (four processors); and so on.

Using multiple processors can have a dramatic effect on server speed and efficiency, and an equally dramatic effect on price. It is a feature suited for very large-scale networks.

FIGURE 6.3

RAID technology, in addition to providing data security by simultaneously creating multiple copies of data, allows faster data throughput by providing the means for different subsets of data to be distributed simultaneously along the network.

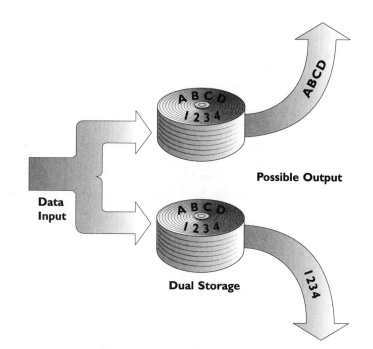

EDC Memory

EDC stands for Error Detection and Correction. EDC memory is configured at the hardware level with special circuitry that verifies RAM output, and resends output when memory errors occur. This type of memory is becoming standard equipment on modern servers, and boosts overall reliability. Vendors include this type of memory to remain competitive in the marketplace, so its impact on the price of the server depends on what value the vendor believes it can market to the customer.

Memory Cache

Memory cache sets aside a portion of the server RAM to store the most frequently-used network instructions, so that they can be accessed as quickly as possible. Cache storage is dynamic, meaning that it is constantly updated while the server is in operation. During network processing, instructions that are accessed less frequently are pushed out of cache, replaced by instructions that are accessed more frequently. The larger size of the memory cache, the more instructions the server can keep "on hand" for fast access.

You can find cache sizes of up to 2 megabytes per processor. In general, if you have a great many nodes on your network, or rely on your server for application processing, you will probably benefit from a large memory cache. If your network is relatively small (20 nodes or less), you can achieve satisfactory results with about 512KB memory cache.

Rack Mounting

A rack-mount server is actually multiple servers stacked on top of one another in a single cabinet to save space. It is used in very large and powerful client/server systems that require more than a single file server. This type of configuration is for highly centralized and complex systems, and further blurs the distinctions between network and mainframe technology. As such, it is beyond the scope of this book. If you have the kind of budget for this kind of networking muscle, you should allocate a significant portion of that budget to experienced, professional consultants and support personnel. You will need them.

Power Protection

A redundant power supply (RDS) is a good idea for businesses that can afford insurance against downtime. The power supply is the unit that distributes electricity within the server. As the name implies, a redundant power supply is a backup power supply that takes over in the event that the main power supply fails. This feature is different from an uninterruptible power supply (UPS), an external device that provides continuous electrical power to the server, usually for a short time, in the event of an electrical power failure. The RDS keeps the network running indefinitely, as long as electricity is being fed to it; the UPS keeps the network running just long enough after a power failure to store and protect your data before shutting down.

Do I Need a File Server?

SERVERS ARE ABOUT finding a balance between empowering users to access needed information immediately, and at the same time protecting the integrity and consistency of that information. Servers do this by allowing work teams to access information directly, instead of applying for access to information through centralized, mainframe-based information management services.

Because the data on a file server is still centralized, it can be protected from arbitrary access and changes. If access to data remains unlimited, then anybody—by error or design—can make false or misleading changes to your data. In the client/server environment, the network administrator is responsible for designing automated systems that enforce the business rules that secure your data's integrity and assure that it has meaning.

However, effective business information management does not start with networks—or even with desktop computers. Computing technology can only facilitate and hasten the flow of information. You must begin to computerize your information services by understanding how information is used and communicated throughout your enterprise, and implementing a sensible set of business rules for organizing and communicating that information. Only then will computing technology make your information services more productive.

The next chapter will discuss remote access to your network, technology that increases its power and allows you to connect your network to larger networks around the world.

Remote Connections to Your Network

A S NETWORKS PROLIFERATE and become more powerful, an interesting irony develops: Data becomes more and more centralized, but the work teams accessing that data become more and more decentralized. In other words, once you have a local area network installed and running smoothly, don't be surprised if more and more members of your work team want to access that network from remote outposts in your business territory (for example, their homes instead of the office). This development is a logical step in the evolution of your information-management system. If you manage it properly, it can be another means to greater efficiency and productivity.

This chapter looks at the resources currently available to make remote connections to your network, and some of the problems and pitfalls you will want to avoid.

Decentralizing the Team

W HEN DATA IS CENTRALIZED, all access to it across network lines can be viewed as remote—some access is simply more remote than others: "Across town" is conceptually more remote than "across the hall." However, the time required to access the centralized data does not necessarily reflect the actual physical distance between user and storage.

The Rise of the Portable PC

The evolution of the portable PC has done a lot to widen the market for remote access products. Portable PCs have expanded the concept of remote access beyond the process of connecting from fixed remote sites (for example, telecommuting from a home office) to highly flexible systems of access from mobile remote sites.

At first, the portable PC was not practical because of the bulk and weight of early hard disks. Early portable PCs, weighing eight pounds or more, with 40 MB hard disks, could not store the large amounts of data capable of being stored on desktop systems. Nowadays, the best of these portable machines are every bit as powerful as desktop systems—as well as small, reliable, and lightweight enough to carry nearly anywhere. In addition, networking technology has evolved to the point where it can be adapted to make direct connections over existing communication lines. In fact, you have several methods of remote access from which to choose. Once you've decided, modern software and graphical user interfaces make the connection easier to establish.

Who Needs to Connect?

There are four types of users who make use of remote access to centralized data:

1. **Home users, also called** *telecommuters*: More and more individuals no longer travel from home to office every day of the week. Instead they access the office via a workstation at home.

2. **Mobile users:** These individuals have jobs that demand their presence at work sites away from the office. They "bring the office with them" via remote access using portable PCs.

3. **Remote offices:** The remote office is a permanent or long-term site, either with a single workstation or another network, located at a distance too great to make direct network connections practical.

4. **Remote clients:** These individuals (for example, purchasers of products direct from the manufacturer through on-line catalogs) access centralized data directly because business considerations like speedy customer service, high volume, or customer convenience make offering such access profitable.

Establishing a Remote Connection

WHEN IT WORKS RIGHT, remote access can produce enormous gains in business productivity, reliability, and efficiency. But this is true only when reliable remote connections can be made. Reliable, cost-effective connections require your understanding of which of several variations of remote access are best for your type of business and (as usual) your budget.

Currently, people looking to access their LAN from a remote location have a choice of two basic types of connection service: *direct access* and *dial-up connection*. There is also the *wireless* connection, but this is—for the time being, at least—simply another form of dial-up connection, using radio and cellular technology to replace wire lines. Right now, the advantages and limitations of wireless technology are, from the end-user's standpoint, the same as wire-based dial-up technology.

For dial-up connections, there are for the present time two communication methods: analog (the most widely available) and ISDN (increasing in popularity and gradually becoming as available as analog). These connection technologies and communication methods are described in detail in this chapter.

Direct Access

DIRECT-ACCESS CONNECTIONS are the most reliable. They also tend to be the fastest, and they connect the remote PC directly as another node on the network. Direct access connections are expensive, and are best suited for connections being made to remote sites that are long-term or permanently established, and need near-constant availability of LAN services.

Direct access is established by leasing a dedicated telephone line (called a T1 or T3 line). You acquire these lines by contracting with a long-distance telephone carrier for their installation and lease. The line is hung between telephone poles or buried underground, usually alongside existing telephone installations. The cost for the dedicated line depends on the length, difficulty, and complexity of the installation, but you can expect that it will be expensive. A relatively simple installation between two networks in the same town might cost a few thousand dollars; installing a more complex system (say, for example, a nationwide van rental service for do-it-yourself home movers) could run into the millions.

Once the dedicated line is installed, you make the final connection between the cable, your host network, and the remote PC using dedicated hardware devices or high-speed modems. With a dedicated line, the choice of appropriate connecting devices will depend on the type of network you are using and the communication protocols it supports. Your direct-access provider will inform you of what options are available and you will work out appropriate choices together.

The obvious disadvantage of direct access is its high cost. However, it can be cost-effective if you have sufficiently large needs for fast and reliable transfer of high volumes of data. Most users will prefer to make the connection using the less-expensive dial-up options.

Dial-Up Access

D IAL-UP ACCESS is based on the idea of tapping into existing communications technology to establish remote connections. Using this method, establishing a remote network connection is like making a telephone call to your network. In general terms, there are two dial-up options, and both use standard modems to make remote connections using telephone lines: you can make the link using *remote-control software*, or using a specialized hardware device called a *remote node server* to accept the incoming telephone connection and establish the remote user as a node on the network.

Remote-Control Connections

Remote-control access is the easiest and least expensive means of remote access to your LAN. This solution uses specialized software to establish a connection, via modems and standard analog telephone lines, to a host workstation connected to the LAN. Once the telephone connection is established and the remote-control software takes over the host workstation, the remote user can access LAN services as if he or she were sitting locally at the host. There are several relatively inexpensive software products that will do the trick. You might look at Close-Up (Norton Lambert Corp.) or PCAnywhere (Symantec Corp.), among others that are available.

The process has some limitations, however:

1. The connection is strictly one-to-one. Each remote connection requires a separate, dedicated host PC.

2. Only those services available to the host PC are available to the network. While this can provide some measure of security, it also can be inconvenient for some remote users who might need fuller access to the network.

3. The host workstation must be remote-aware, using the same software as the remote PC.

4. Performance is likely to be slower than other types of connection, especially when using graphical interfaces.

The issue of performance is critical. A remote-control connection normally does not send network data over the telephone line. Instead, traffic over the remote link consists of remote commands to the LAN and host screen changes sent back to the remote PC. In most cases, the remote user only monitors processing on the network. The remote user who wants to use a local application to process data on the host network must resort to entire-file transfers to and from the network, or put up with slow data communications across the remote link. The former puts data at risk and limits local access; the latter is likely to be frustratingly slow, especially if there is a lot of other traffic on the host network.

Setting up a remote-control connection requires that the software be installed, properly configured for the modem being used, and running on both ends of the connection. When the remote PC dials the host workstation, the software sets up the necessary digital "handshaking" and transfers control to the remote PC. When the connection is ended, the software senses this and returns the host PC to normal operations along the LAN. This process is illustrated in Figure 7.1.

FIGURE 7.1

A remote-control connection. The remote PC takes over a host PC and directs its behavior at a distance. Any process available to the host PC is available to the remote.

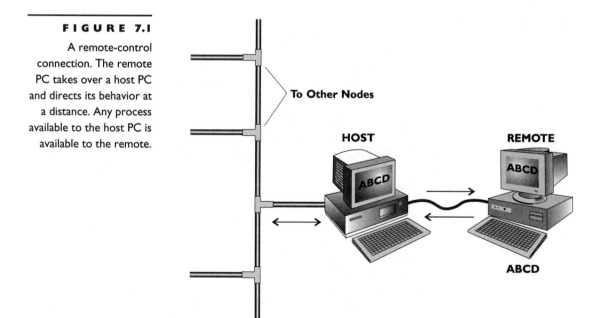

Computers, Talking on the Phone

Computer modems are well-established devices with a language all their own. Here's a quick run-down on common modem jargon:

Baud Rate: The speed of the data transfer, expressed in bits-per-second (bps). These days, 14.4 bps is a practical minimum; for Internet access, 28.8 bps is recommended. Expect modems to get faster as the telephone system updates its technology to fill the increasing demand for faster data transmission.

Data Bits: The number of bits used to send one character (for example, a single letter or number) over the line. Characters are sent using either seven or eight bits.

Duplex: A display control setting for the display of transmitted characters. In Full Duplex mode, characters you type at the keyboard are not displayed on your screen. In Half Duplex, they are displayed.

Handshaking: The process by which two connected modems analyze each other's transmissions and exchange data without conflict. A sending modem interrupts its transmission when the receiving modem indicates that it has received a maximum allowable number of characters. Then the receiving modem becomes the sending modem and the transmission goes the other direction. This back-and-forth process occurs at very high speed so that the communication appears smooth and steady to the user.

Parity: A form of error checking that interacts with the number of data bits. When you use 7 data bits, you can set Even or Odd parity, to coincide with the parity setting at the other end of the communication. If you use 8 data bits, parity is set to "None."

Port: The connection point between the computer and a modem or other peripheral device. Most modems communicate through a serial port. A PC can have up to four serial ports, named COM1, COM2, COM3, and COM4. Modems are configured to use one of these ports to transmit data.

Stop Bit: A delay after a character is sent, to indicate to the receiving modem that the single-character transmission is complete. The modem's stop bit setting is almost always set to 1, unless you have been instructed to set it to some other value.

Remote-Node Access

A remote node server is a hardware device that allows a remote PC to function as a full-fledged member of the LAN, operating network applications and accessing network data directly across the remote link. Figure 7.2 shows how a remote-node server is set up. Remote-node servers have distinct advantages over simple remote-control access:

1. The host LAN can support a single access point to multiple remote sites, without tying up the services of a dedicated LAN workstation.

2. The same access point can be used to provide an array of network services to the remote PC.

3. Easier-to-manage network security. For example, the remote node server can identify callers and allow different levels of access.

4. Better performance through the use of local interfaces on the remote PC.

5. Access across different networking environments and protocols (in effect, the remote node server acts as a bridge to other networks).

In theory, remote-node server connections should be fairly easy to set up. After you acquire the server box from your vendor, you connect it to your LAN using the included connection hardware, install however many modems you are using (the number will depend on how many remote users must have access at the same time), configure the server (using the LAN remote-node

FIGURE 7.2

A remote-node server. The remote-node server can establish a direct connection to the LAN and allow different users different levels of access to the network.

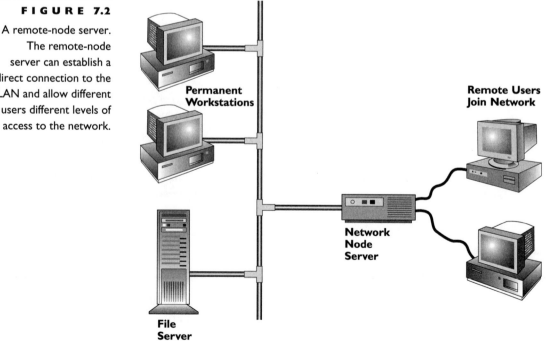

Permanent Workstations

Remote Users Join Network

Network Node Server

File Server

administration software supplied by the vendor), and distribute disks containing access software to your remote users. Sounds simple, but in practice, you can expect that some fine-tuning will be required before things run smoothly. This is another case where an experienced network administrator, one who thoroughly understands the design of your network and its supported communication protocols, will ease the installation and configuration process.

Data Signals—Something Old, Something New

There are two types of electrical signals that carry data: analog and digital. Analog signals are represented as regular waves of varying voltage (the signal's amplitude), that cycle between a maximum and minimum voltage level a given number of times per second (the signal's frequency). Analog signals are sent over a transmission medium—for example, over a telephone line—or as a wireless signal, like cellular microwaves. Multiple analog signals can coexist on the same sending medium if each one starts and completes its wave cycle at a different voltage level. Computers can send and receive binary data (that is, data coded into ones and zeros) using analog signals. To do this, specific levels of frequency or amplitude are assigned one binary value or the other.

For example, amplitude above a certain level may mean one; below that level, zero. Alternatively, a given frequency can mean one; otherwise, the signal means zero.

The technology for sending and receiving analog signals has been around for a long time and is well established. Analog signals can travel great distances (an international telephone call, for example). However, analog signals are susceptible to static and other electrical "noise," called electromagnetic interference (EMI). This is the cause of some distortion you may hear on a long-distance telephone call, and can create errors when sending computer data.

Digital signals work differently, by alternating between the presence of a given electrical state (one) or a contrasting state (zero). For example, a digital signal can consist of a positive electrical polarity changing to no polarity (meaning one), or a negative electrical polarity changing to no polarity (meaning zero). Digital signals are better suited for sending binary data because the binary encoding is locked directly into the signal. They are less susceptible to EMI, so they tend to be clearer. They are sent over digitally aware transmission media, which can be either wires or digital wireless transmission signals. However, (and here's the meat of the matter) analog circuitry does not handle digital signals very well. If you have an analog signal and digital equipment (like an analog telephone signal coming in to a PC), or a digital signal and analog equipment (like a

(continued on next page)

CD-ROM sending musical signals to a set of non-digital speakers), some conversion of the signal is needed. Analog-to-digital conversion equipment analyzes the amplitude and frequency of the analog signal, in a process called sampling. The equipment tests the signal many thousands of times per second, and creates a digital representation of the analog signal; it then sends the digital signal along to the digital equipment. In the reverse conversion, the digital signal can be used to generate waveforms directly.

The most efficient and least expensive means of working with binary data is to use digital equipment to send and receive digital signals. In this scenario, the equipment does not have to perform complex signal processing. For this reason, digital wireless communications have become desirable for remote access. But because a tremendous amount of analog equipment is installed throughout the world, analog-based communications (and analog-to-digital conversion) will remain part of our remote-access world for the time being.

Telephone Line Communications

THERE ARE TWO TYPES of communication methods available for dial-up data connections over telephone lines: standard analog and ISDN. Following are brief explanations of each.

Analog Connections

Analog communication is the most widespread communications method available. When you use the telephone to make a local call, you are using analog technology to carry the voice signal. Analog telephone technology (which can be carried over wire and cellular telephone lines) may seem old-fashioned in this high-tech age, but it offers some advantages for remote LAN users:

1. Remote access links can be established from any spot in the world that has telephone service.

2. Long-distance charges are relatively inexpensive compared to ISDN.

3. Analog-compatible modems are low-priced and easy to configure, use, and maintain.

4. The technology is traditional, and supported by vendors and application developers.

Analog has some disadvantages as well:

1. The transmission rates are slow. Currently, the fastest analog modems handle 28.8 kilobytes per second (KBs).

2. Connections can be noisy, with line static and echoes that cause communication failures.

ISDN Connections

ISDN, or Integrated Services Digital Network, is a set of technologies (circuits and upgraded telephone lines) that allow specialized data pathways to coexist

Remote-Connection Security

Providing secure access to valid remote sites involves special configurations to your host LAN. For remote-control connections, you should secure the host PC as if it were available to any walk-up user. Remember that any access available to the host machine is automatically available to the remote machine as well. The remote-control software will provide a certain amount of basic password protection at connect time, but do not rely on this level of security alone.

It is easier to provide security for remote-node servers or remote connections to other networks. Products for these types of connections normally include protocols that limit the initial connection to authorized users. You should verify that any remote connection products include compatible security protocols. Some readily-available standard security protocols include:

PAP (Password Authentication Protocol). A no-frills, Internet-standard protocol for verifying passwords from remote callers.

CHAP (Challenge Handshake Authentication Protocol). This is an Internet-standard protocol for verifying encrypted passwords.

CLI (Call Line Identification). This protocol identifies the calling number and checks against a stored list of authorized callers before making the link.

You'll learn more about security in Chapter 11.

with voice pathways. It is, in effect, an upgrade to the existing analog system. To use ISDN lines, you must use ISDN-compatible modems and connecting devices to establish the remote link to your LAN. ISDN offers some significant advantages over analog communications:

1. Processing speed is nearly as fast as direct connection to the host LAN.

2. Low cost for the performance, compared to direct-access.

Telephone systems are gradually upgrading to ISDN. All vendors of remote-connection systems support ISDN. However, no firm standards yet exist for optimizing ISDN's communication features at the local connection sites. This means that, if you intend to make use of ISDN (especially to connect networks to one another), you are likely to find that vendors' current product offerings are proprietary. Proprietary technology will limit, at least for the time being, the ISDN links you can establish to those remote LANs that support your vendor's products, or have licensed the vendor's proprietary standards.

Connecting via the Internet

F YOUR REMOTE LINK is primarily for the purposes of message communication (E-mail) and transfer of data files, the Internet presents a practical method of establishing remote links to your LAN. In this case, the LAN and its remote access sites all connect, via modems, to one or more local Internet access providers, and establish permanent Internet addresses for storing transmitted data.

Instead of making direct links to the LAN, all parties to the communication send data at the desired receiver's Internet address, which is accessed at will by the receiver.

The main advantage of this arrangement is that there is minimum technical overhead for the LAN administrator or remote user, other than a modem and access to a telephone, and communication is sent and received at the convenience of all participants. The disadvantage is that access to host LAN services, if it exists at all, is limited and slow.

Right now, Internet access technology and service providers enjoy a booming market. The promise of easy, global access between LANs and PCs is a powerful lure that may lead to the development of revolutionary products for remote LAN access. It is worth your time to pay close attention to developments in this field, but be cautious. Brand-new digital technologies often have problems, and it is often a good idea to wait for a new technology to prove itself in the real world before rushing in with your scarce purchasing dollars. In addition, by the time a new technology is established, the price tends to fall.

Bandwidth

B ANDWIDTH IS A TERM you will hear frequently when discussing network data traffic, especially when discussing remote and LAN-to-LAN communications. It is jargon that is used to describe the maximum amount of data that can be transmitted simultaneously on your network or between LANs and remote sites.

Data moving between all the connections to a network is called, colorfully enough, *data traffic*. The more data traffic that can be transmitted along your network data pathways, the wider your network's bandwidth.

Much network technology (and remote connection technology in particular), is devoted to reducing unnecessary data traffic and conserving your network's precious bandwidth. There are several ways of accomplishing this.

Local Processing

Local processing can occur at the level of the workstation, the remote site, or the network server. At the workstation level, the workstation accesses data from the network server, performs all processes locally, and returns modified data to the server. Network resources are used only to access and return data. At the remote-site level, the remote connection is used only to transmit data to and from the remote PC, where all processing takes place.

At the server level, the LAN workstation (or remote PC controlling the LAN workstation, or PC directly connected via a remote-node server) transmits instructions to the network server to perform processes, and the server transmits the result of those processes back to the workstation. Because a remote link has a much narrower bandwidth than the LAN, the LAN handles all remote requests for processing as locally as possible.

Dial on Demand

This bandwidth-conserving method takes the concept of remote local processing one step further. Dial-on-demand software senses when a remote PC is engaged in extended processing, and ends the telephone connection, which can speed up processing on both ends. When the remote PC needs to access the LAN once again, the dial-on-demand software senses this as well, and reestablishes the connection automatically. While some time is lost in continually redialing the host LAN, the elimination of the need to maintain a telephone connection during periods of extended local processing can speed up overall processing times on both ends.

Dynamic Bandwidth

Dynamic bandwidth is an optimization technology for ISDN remote-node connections. In this method, the remote node server monitors the rate of transfer for various types of data along the connection. When data is dense (for example, when transmitting graphics information) and the designated speed of transfer falls below a predetermined level, a second communication channel is opened to accommodate more data and speed up the transfer rate. When data density levels return to normal (for example, E-mail messages) the two-channel data transfer is no longer required, and the second channel shuts down to conserve transmission overhead.

Making the Connection

The decentralization of the work force surrounding centralized data offers competitive advantages to businesses. Some of these advantages include: direct client services on site; order processing direct to vendor by client; short production and development cycles; faster responses to marketplace changes; and direct access to distant markets.

In addition, employers can be more flexible when hiring, and employees can benefit by a decreased emphasis on physical location as a condition of employment. Reducing the number of commuters would help lower—somewhat—our dependence on oil for gasoline, and help reduce smog. It remains to be seen what other social advantages (and problems) may crop up as a result of these new ways of working.

The possibility of significant economic advantages for businesses make remote access worth looking into, even at the current costs for implementing remote-access systems. You may find that remote access is a good investment in your business's competitiveness and market penetration.

In the next chapter, we will look at the software that ties your entire network together: the network operating system, or NOS.

Network
Software

PART

3

Network
Operating
Systems

ALL DESKTOP COMPUTER SYSTEMS require an operating system in order to work. The operating system is software that provides a platform of low-level services shared by various applications. An application (for example, a database management program) calls upon the operating system continuously for the common tasks (sending data to the monitor, updating files on disk, receiving input from the keyboard and mouse, and so on) that support its processing.

A network operating system (NOS) does everything a stand-alone operating system does, and more, in a much more complex environment. Some network operating systems work on top of a foundation operating system; for example, LANtastic works on top of DOS. Others, such as NetWare, are independent operating systems in their own right. In addition to the usual lower-level computing tasks, a network operating system is responsible for all of the following:

- Directing data traffic throughout the network

- Allowing and preventing access to data based on security requirements

- Preventing access to data files while they are being processed

- Managing the flow of data between a variety of different (and sometimes otherwise incompatible) workstations

- Managing requests for printer services

- Managing communication and messages between network users

- Managing connections between the network and remote sites

In addition, the network operating system must make its services as transparent as possible to each user; when a user must access NOS services, the network should present as intuitive an interface as possible, translating complex digital tasks into simple instructions using words and pictures that are readily understandable to nontechnical human beings. Depending on what it is doing at any given moment, a NOS can function as a digital traffic cop, international ambassador, interpreter, teacher, pupil, file clerk, secretary, janitor, repairman, or watchdog.

Networks in a Box

If you are new to networks and installing one for the first time, look into the possibility of obtaining complete starter kits from the operating system manufacturer. All major operating system vendors offer some type of start-up kit; these kits include two or more NICs, standard lengths of cable, and all necessary software. In addition to the convenience, you can be assured of compatibility between your software and hardware.

There are several different network operating systems available, and the ones discussed here support the hardware configurations we have discussed in previous chapters. Some are more complex and have more features than others. Your choice of an operating system for your network will be based on the best combination of features you can afford. This chapter looks at the most common NOSes currently available and offers you an overview of what they can accomplish.

LANtastic

LANTASTIC IS A CLASSIC operating system for peer-to-peer networks. It is manufactured by the Artisoft Corporation, which also manufactures network hardware. LANtastic's advantages are ease of setup, relatively low memory requirements, good security for a peer-to-peer system, and fairly low cost.

LANtastic can run with minimal hardware. You can make a LANtastic workstation out of any IBM PC or compatible with at least 640KB RAM (and using either DOS 3.1 or later, or Microsoft Windows). LANtastic can run using most standard Ethernet NICs, or you can choose Artisoft's own proprietary cards that boost the network's performance.

The LANtastic operating system is NetBIOS-compatible, meaning that it sits on top of DOS (or any other NetBIOS-compatible operating system) and makes use of certain file and data-flow services belonging to the underlying system, in order to manage its network operations. (Think of LANtastic as a network running on top of a more basic operating system.) For more information on NetBIOS, see Chapter 3.

Once you have the adapter cards installed and connected, you can install the network system software at each machine on the network using LANtastic's automated installation program. During the installation procedure, you can designate each workstation as one of two types:

Server: This type of workstation can send and receive data across the network. Server workstations have data that must be accessed by other workstations on the network. A server can also receive data from other workstations.

Client: This type of workstation can only receive data from server workstations. An example would be a computer whose sole function is to drive a shared printer.

Once LANtastic is installed, other workstations are identified on each local workstation using DOS-like drive letters. This procedure is very easy to understand if the user is familiar with basic DOS commands, and since drive letters are used, most DOS-based software can access the data directly. LANtastic also supports a basic e-mail system for sending messages between workstations.

LANtastic offers a number of optional security features for controlling access to data throughout its peer-to-peer system. LANtastic controls access rights to files using *access control lists* on each workstation. You can adjust access rights to files, directories, disks, printer ports, and other workstations, any of which can be designated as having a specific right of access:

Search only: The user can look up files in directories but cannot access the files' contents.

Read only: The user can read but make no other changes to the files (or the directory).

Create only: The user can create new files or directories, but cannot overwrite or delete existing ones.

Delete only: The user may be allowed to delete only designated data files and data directories.

Change attributes only: The user can modify file attributes (for example, designating a file as a hidden or system file).

Execute program files: The user may launch specific application software.

Full access: The user can access designated files and directories without restrictions.

Who Gets Access?

Access rights to nodes on a network are based on two underlying security issues: keeping unauthorized people away from data, and preventing errors that can occur when several people access the same data.

For example, users in an order-entry department would need full access rights to order-entry files, so that they could create and modify records of customer orders. On the other hand, the shipping department might be given read-only access to the same files, because their business need would be only to review them if there is a question regarding order fulfillment. Other workstations in the business with connections to the outside world (for example, workstations connected to a modem for access from the field) might be denied even read-only access, to prevent competitors from slipping in and acquiring sensitive information about customers.

Why Choose LANtastic?

LANtastic is an inexpensive solution for workgroups that need to share data in a free-flowing environment that nevertheless requires some basic security. In addition, you can purchase additional utilities that make it possible to connect a LANtastic workgroup to a larger NetWare network. A LANtastic network can handle more users than most other peer-to-peer systems. It is a good choice when cost and simplicity issues outweigh power and foolproof security.

Windows for Workgroups

N WINDOWS FOR WORKGROUPS, Microsoft Corporation has integrated a set of peer-to-peer network services and network-aware applications within what amounts to an expanded version of Windows version 3.1. The advantages of Windows for Workgroups are the ease and efficiency it offers to first-time networkers already familiar with the Windows operating system.

Windows for Workgroups requires the same hardware that Windows 3.1 requires to run in Enhanced Mode: a PC with at least an 80386 (or compatible)

CPU, running DOS version 3.1 or later. In addition, each workstation should be equipped with the following:

1. 4MB RAM (3MB is possible, but not recommended). A larger amount of RAM is a good idea, as it will increase performance. 8MB to 16MB is common; even more in very demanding situations.

2. A minimum of 13.5MB of hard disk space (or 8.5MB if you are installing over stand-alone Windows). This is just for the operating system; other software will require additional space.

3. One floppy disk drive.

4. Windows-compatible display and printer drivers.

Using Windows for Workgroups

After installing your network cards and cables, you install the operating system on each workstation, using an automated Install program. If you are installing over an existing copy of Windows Version 3.1, Windows for Workgroups will attempt to use your current Windows configuration settings. Windows will allow you to do either a fully automated (express) setup, or an interactive (custom) installation that allows you to fine-tune your system at installation time.

During the installation procedure, you must assign a name (up to 15 characters long) to each workgroup, and a unique name to each workstation. You must tell Windows what types of network communications hardware you have installed on each workstation and how it is configured. You must also identify your shared printers and the local ports to which they are connected. When the installation process is complete, Windows 3.1 restarts as Windows for Workgroups.

Once fully installed, Windows for Workgroups offers a useful set of new Windows utilities:

New File Manager: The WFW File Manager includes a customizable toolbar and a dialog box for connecting logical drive letters to network workstations and file directories. You can also assign *alias* names to nested subdirectories. For example, if you wanted to access files on directory \ACCOUNTS\ INVOICES\BACKORD\PAYABLE, you could shorten the name to PAYABLES, or whatever name you like. Directory aliasing makes it much easier to access files in complicated file directory schemes.

New Print Manager: This Windows utility includes a toolbar in Windows for Workgroups. It also has a larger, easier-to-read display.

New Control Panel: The Control Panel contains a network icon, which you can use to manage names of workgroups and PCs and adjust the amount of time spent on local applications before allowing data to flow across the network. You can also make configuration changes to cards and drivers that allow such changes at the software level.

Windows for Workgroups also offers some useful network-aware applications:

Microsoft Mail: This application allows workgroup members to send and receive messages through a central database that resides on one member's machine.

Schedule+: This application is a calendar and time scheduler for workgroups; it facilitates appointments and meetings, and allows team members to find each other's whereabouts.

ClipBook: This application is like the Windows Notepad, but its contents are accessible to everyone in the workgroup.

Chat: This application allows real-time messaging between workgroup members. Outgoing messages are displayed in an upper window, and responses are displayed in a lower window.

WinMeter: This program charts the balance of time spent between local and network services. You can use this information to make adjustments at the Control Panel and optimize your workstation's performance.

NetWatcher: This utility displays an overview of network activity. For example, you could use NetWatcher to discover that one shared printer is being used far more often than another, and make the necessary changes to equalize the time spent printing.

Windows for Workgroups, following a peer-to-peer standard, also identifies network drives using drive letters, permitting you and your Windows applications to access them as local drives. You can access shared printers and other hardware with familiar Windows interface commands and use them as locally connected devices. Windows for Workgroups allows read-only and read-write access to files and directories, with optional password protection.

It is possible to connect Windows for Workgroups to a NetWare server, but doing so requires patience and the right set of communications drivers. This is a job best left to an experienced technician. It should come as no surprise that connections to Windows NT and NT Server are much more straightforward than NetWare connections.

Why Choose Windows for Workgroups?

Windows for Workgroups is a good solution for users who are committed to the Windows environment, who want the convenience of a familiar interface with good connections to other Windows-based systems and software, and who don't require a lot of file security. Some stand-alone users have switched to this operating system, just to use the improved versions of File Manager and Print Manager.

Windows 95

MICROSOFT CORPORATION has also integrated peer-to-peer network services within its latest version of the Windows operating system. The advantage of Windows 95 is its integration of basic peer-to-peer capabilities into an independent operating system, without the purchase of additional software.

Windows 95 does have significantly large hardware requirements:

1. PC with at least an 80386 (or compatible) CPU, with an 80486 or better recommended.

2. 8MB RAM (not a realistic minimum; 12–16MB RAM is the more practical minimum; even more in very demanding situations).

3. Approximately 100MB of hard disk space for a fully-featured implementation; other software will require additional space.

4. One floppy disk or CD-ROM drive.

5. Windows-compatible displays and printer drivers.

Using Windows 95

After installing your network cards and cables, if your network cards are plug-and-play compatible (check this out with your vendor before you buy), you install the operating system on each workstation using Windows 95's automated Install program. Windows 95 will see your adapters and install the appropriate drivers. Otherwise, you can open up a DOS window and run whatever DOS-based configuration software is required by the card you have purchased.

Then, click on the Add New Hardware icon in the Control Panel and specify what network cards and drivers you have.

Double-click on the Network icon in the control panel and bind any necessary protocols to your network adapter card. (Most peer-to-peer network cards will use either NetBEUI or IPX/SPX.)

While you are using the Network Control Panel, be sure to add File and Print sharing services for each workstation on the network, if they aren't implemented already. Be sure to give each machine a unique network name, but the same workgroup name.

Windows 95's simple peer-to-peer networking allows you to share resources, such as other machines' disk drives and printers, right away. However, to take advantage of more sophisticated networking features, consider using Windows 95-based machines as clients in larger networking systems. For more information on Windows 95 as a client workstation, see Chapter 9.

Why Choose Windows 95?

Windows 95 is a good solution for users who need only file- and resource-sharing capabilities in a peer-to-peer context, want a low-cost, low-maintenance solution, and don't require much in the way of network security.

OS/2, Warp, and Warp Connect

BM'S ANSWER to Windows, OS/2, enjoys a reputation as a very robust and reliable operating system, which has inspired enthusiastic devotion from its users. Nevertheless, it somewhat surprisingly lacks built-in networking features, beyond a rich and elegant set of Internet-access features called the *Internet Access Kit*. (IBM adds local-area networking features to the latest release, called OS/2 Warp Connect.)

Previous versions of OS/2 obtain networking capabilities using add-on software. For example, Artisoft has released a 32-bit version of LANtastic for OS/2, which gives OS/2 peer-to-peer networking features similar to DOS-based LANtastic, while allowing users to take advantage of OS/2's smoother graphical interface and more powerful internal architecture.

Another networking add-on is IBM's *OS/2 LAN Server*. In performance tests, this product appears similar to Windows NT—this is not surprising, since IBM and Microsoft worked together in the early development of Windows NT.

Like its Windows competitors, OS/2 Warp Connect supports peer-to-peer networking, sharing applications, data files, and printers using standard NICs and network cables. In addition, Warp Connect supports peer-to-peer connections using the PC's parallel ports, for faster transfer of data between workstations.

Macintosh NOS

APPLE COMPUTER INTEGRATES networking services with its Macintosh operating system. Once your Macintoshes are up and running and the cables are connected, your network operating system is ready to go. The system requires Macintosh machines; more powerful models, as you would expect, offer more efficient network service.

The integration of network services with the operating system is smooth and reliable. You access the Control Panel to designate local printers and directories as shared and specify what access levels are permitted. Access levels are similar to those offered by LANtastic.

To access shared services, use the Finder. The Finder will display all shared resources, including any found on AppleShare servers. You select services from what is displayed, and access them like locally connected devices.

Macintosh networks offer a convenient process called *interapplication communication* (IAC), which means that applications can access data from other applications dynamically. For example, a word processor can search an IAC-compatible database for a name and address and bring it directly into the document. This kind of dynamic linking can take place across the network.

Another nice feature is the *Publish/Subscribe* system. Using this utility a user can "publish" a message (make it available to other users on the network), and it will be instantly available to all "subscribers" (those users who have opted for immediate display of "published" messages). This makes for convenient sharing of up-to-the-minute information.

Why Choose Macintosh?

Macintosh is the obvious solution for users who have all-Mac systems and want to take advantage of Mac's legendary ease-of-use. Also, the security system is more fully featured than most other peer-to-peer systems, making Mac more attractive as a peer-to-peer system for sensitive data.

Why Combine?

It may seem like overkill to connect a peer-to-peer system to a larger, client/server type network. Why not just plug all the workstations into the large network? The answer is based on the workgroup concept. Within a workgroup, users want fast access to locally-shared resources and quick communications, group scheduling, and the like. At the same time, the workgroup needs access to the corporate-wide information on the file server. It makes sense to connect the members of the workgroup together for direct communications and not tie up the server with what is essentially local data traffic. Then, to get at the corporate-level information, one or more workgroup member workstations can connect to the enterprise. Provided, of course, that you have room for all this convenience in your budget.

Banyan VINES and UNIX

VINES (VIrtual NEtwork System) is a file-server based network operating system designed as an extension of UNIX System V or SCO UNIX. It was developed by Banyan Incorporated in 1984. Banyan's intent was to use the acceptance of UNIX in the large corporate computing marketplace as a platform to launch VINES as a networking standard. They succeeded not only in distributing their product widely, but in influencing the development of file server systems in general.

VINES can be used to operate very large UNIX-based networks spread out over large geographic areas, and at the same time present remote services as if they were local to the workstation. The concept of localizing remote services, introduced with VINES's *StreetTalk* technology, has now been incorporated into all major network operating systems.

StreetTalk is the commercial name for a feature called *global directory services*, which helps integrate the complex UNIX networking system running on more than one server. From the user's point of view, the VINES multiserver network appears as a single, unified system. Individual users do not need to know which server provides which services, nor do they need to log onto multiple servers to access those services. Instead, the user logs onto the network and requests services by accessing the global directory, and the operating system keeps track of which server provides the requested services. In very large networks, this greatly simplifies the day-to-day work of both the users and the network administrator.

VINES requires at least 80386 or better workstations and servers, but is extremely adaptable and flexible. It requires either UNIX System V or SCO UNIX as a base operating system. When installed, VINES takes over the base operating system and controls its functions.

You can connect workstations from many different vendors into a VINES network. It supports clients running DOS, Windows, OS/2, and Macintosh as well as UNIX workstations. However, Banyan recommends that you use only workstations certified as VINES-compatible. Some individual manufacturers may have introduced components into their machines that will cause problems on the VINES network. (For more information on whether a particular machine is compatible, contact the vendor or Banyan Systems Incorporated, 800/828-2404.)

Using VINES

VINES consists of dozens of utility programs that control its various network operations. The utilities that control connections to the network are installed on each client workstation, while those that control shared services are installed on the network server. When you start a VINES client workstation, you must run the BAN command to load the NIC controller software and system connection software (for example, VINES Redirector and VINES NetBIOS).

After the connection has been made, you run the LOGIN program, which prompts you for your user name and password. After VINES verifies your LOGIN name, it searches for your *user profile*. The user profile is a set of information that has been previously set up by the system administrator. It determines which shared network services (directories of data files and remote services, like printing and e-mail) are available to you.

At this point, you can access the network services you need by calling upon them by name. Using its StreetTalk system, VINES gives each node on the network a three-part name that identifies the location of the node within the network's directory structure. Each node is named according to its type (workstation, printer, server, and so on), the workgroup to which it belongs, and the location of the workgroup in the network's directory. The three parts of the name are separated by @-characters. The StreetTalk name looks like this:

```
node@workgroup@location
```

A remote printer can be named *LaserPrinter@Accounting@ LosAngeles*, for example. The first part of the name, LaserPrinter, is the identifier of the node (in this case, a printer). The second part of the name, *Accounting*, indicates the workgroup to which the object belongs (the Accounting Department). The third part of the name, *LosAngeles*, indicates the location of the workgroup (the Los Angeles business office).

Another example, for a more localized network, would be *Bob Thomas@ Programming@First Floor*. In this case the node is a workstation, logged on-to the network under the name *BobThomas*. The workstation is part of the programming workgroup, located on the first floor (of an office building, presumably).

You can also omit parts of a name, and VINES assumes you intend to access your own workgroup or location. In other words, if you are accessing a node in the same location as yours, you can omit the location in the node name. Like-wise, if you are accessing a node in the same workgroup as your own, you need not include it in the node name.

VINES networks can have dozens of node names, and complicated names like these can be difficult to remember. StreetTalk includes a feature called *Directory Assistance* (STDA), which you can access to see lists of node names on the network. The system administrator controls the names that can be included in the directory assistance list.

VINES Security

Security on a VINES network is thorough and sophisticated. Virtually every connection can be controlled by the system administrator (SA).

The first level of security is the user password. The SA can configure the op-erating system to accept only certain types of passwords (for example, only pass-words of a specific minimum length). The SA can also prevent users from chang-ing their own passwords, or force them to change their passwords periodically.

Login procedures are subject to security controls as well. Logins can be re-stricted to specific times of the day, and connections can be sustained for preset lengths of time. The system can limit some log-ins to specific geographical loca-tions; for example, a user named Bob Thomas could log in from Programming on the first floor, but not from Accounting on the fourth floor.

The user is also subject to security limitations after logging in. Files and directories are controlled by access rights, settings that allow only certain per-missible operations. For example, PC workstations can be granted one or more of the following access rights:

Search: The user can view the names of files and directories. This is the most restricted access right. Other rights are not granted without this one.

Read-Only: The user is allowed to view the contents of files but cannot make changes to them.

Execute: The user is allowed to run executable files (in other words, run applications).

Write Directories: The user is allowed to create and change the attributes of files and directories, and change the contents of files. The user with this access right may also create new files and directories.

Write Files: The user is allowed to change the contents of files only.

Delete: The user is allowed to delete subdirectories and files.

Control: The user is allowed full access to the system. This right is usually reserved to the system administrator. The user with control rights can make changes to the access rights of other users on the system.

As mentioned earlier, access rights are put in place to reduce the chance of errors across the network. Many users in your business may need to view data, but only a few may actually need to make changes to it. For more information on security, see Chapter 12.

Files and directories are also subject to security features called *attributes*. File attributes control how a file can be handled by anyone on the system. On DOS-compatible workstations, these attributes are in addition to the normal DOS file attributes:

No delete: This attribute prevents a file from being erased.

No Rename: This attribute prevents all users from renaming the file.

Shared: Allows different users to access the data file simultaneously. This is a risky attribute for files that are not read-only, since when two or more users can write to a file, its contents can become corrupted.

Executable: Allows executable files to be run, but not copied or written to. They can be renamed or deleted.

Finally, it is possible for the SA to grant users one of three levels of printer access rights:

User: This is the lowest level; it allows the users to control only their own printing jobs.

Operator: This level allows the user to change the order of print jobs that are pending, stop jobs that are printing, change the print format parameters, and start new print jobs. In effect, a user with operator status functions as a print queue manager.

Administrator: This level allows the user complete access to the print queues. An administrator can assign hardware to a particular queue, set up printing filters to automate control of the printer, and delete print jobs from the printing queue.

Why Choose VINES?

VINES is a good solution for experienced users who need a powerful client/server network and are comfortable with the intricacies of its UNIX base. It is useful when you need to set up a very large network, need extensive security, and want all users to have a consistent view of the whole system.

NetWare

NetWare is a large client/server system developed by the Novell Corporation. Currently, more than half of the PC-based file server systems run using NetWare.

There are three different versions of NetWare in use at this time, numbered Versions 2, 3, and 4. (NetWare Version 2 is no longer sold, although many networks are still running this version.) Each new version of NetWare introduces a number of advancements, new features, and improvements over the previous version.

Although Novell would probably prefer that everyone upgrade to the latest Version 4, NetWare 3 remains in the marketplace because it is well established and widely supported by hardware and software vendors; it is also less expensive than Version 4.

Version 4 is much larger, more feature-laden, and more complicated than NetWare's previous versions. It includes significant changes in its file system and introduces global directory services.

NetWare Versions 3 and 4 are loaded on top of the DOS operating system, but once up and running, NetWare takes over the entire network. DOS can continue to exist below NetWare (shoved into the basement, so to speak), and if you close the NetWare operating system, you can return to the DOS prompt. However, NetWare includes a command, REMOVE DOS, which you can invoke once it is up and running, which deletes the DOS operating system from RAM, freeing up additional memory for NetWare.

NetWare's file system is proprietary, and optimized for the networking environment. It has many unique features that can improve a network's overall performance, speed, and reliability.

PC-based NetWare Versions 3 and 4 require the following minimum hardware for workstation and server nodes:

1. Intel 80386-compatible processor, or better.

2. 4MB RAM for Version 3, 8MB RAM for Version 4.

3. A minimum of 80MB of hard disk space.

These requirements are minimums, and they don't account for performance or the overall usefulness of your NetWare network. Workstations may get by if they aren't running any really demanding applications, but for servers, 32–64MB RAM and 1–4 gigabytes (trillions of bytes) of hard disk space are more practical requirements. NetWare can support up to 4 gigabytes of RAM, and 32 gigabytes of hard disk space.

NetWare also supports a wide range of network adapter cards and cabling systems. Your choice of specific network interface hardware for NetWare will be based on the kinds of performance and budget considerations that were discussed in previous chapters of this book.

Using NetWare

NetWare uses many different utility programs to control its various operations. When you start a client workstation, you must first load the software driver for the network interface card that you are using, followed by an important piece of software called the NetWare Shell. All workstation requests for network services are handled by the NetWare Shell. If you want to run NetWare using Windows, you must also load additional driver software for Windows.

When the NetWare Shell loads, it polls the network for the first server it can find, which becomes the default server for that session. Once you are connected to a server, you can run NetWare's LOGIN program. This program prompts you for your user name and password, and (assuming that you enter them correctly) executes a *login script*, which (if it exists) is a series of commands that set up network environment parameters for all workstations logging in. Among other configuration commands, this script can establish a link to a specific server other than the default.

The login script is followed by the *user login script*, another series of commands that set up custom parameters applying only to the individual workstation. If the user login script for a workstation is not present, NetWare looks for a *default user script* to run. This script exists on the file server and can contain generic workstation configuration commands that apply to everyone, or to any workstation that logs in to that particular server.

Finally, in Version 4, a third script can be run, behind the login script but before the user login script. This is the *profile script*, which sets up network parameters for a predefined group of users. This script is set up by the NetWare Administrator.

NetWare Versions 3 and 4 rely on a modular architecture. The network designer can choose specific network services to include in the operating system, from a set of small programs called *Virtual Loadable Modules*, or *VLMs*. A VLM is essentially a utility program that specializes in performing a narrowly-defined network service (for example, a network management and resource tracking system, a database driver, an e-mail system, and so on). VLMs conserve memory by allowing the NOS to load only those services NetWare actually needs to run on your system. VLMs have another significant advantage: They can be written by third-party developers, making it possible to customize your NetWare network along lines not necessarily envisioned by Novell.

NetWare Directory Services

In its latest version of NetWare, Novell has introduced a special feature called NetWare Directory Services (NDS), a system for organizing network locations into a hierarchy. This hierarchical structure is often referred to as a *tree* structure because of its branch-like nature. Figure 8.1 shows a simple NDS tree.

Network Directory Services begin with a *root directory*, which contains any number of *objects*. There are two types of objects: a *container* or a *leaf* object. A container object holds other objects; for example, a country, an organization, or a workgroup within an organization. A leaf object identifies a single node on the network: for example, a workstation, file server, workgroup, or user name.

To locate an object on the network, you can identify it using its complete directory name. An object's complete name includes the various branches in the directory that are connected to it, starting with the object name and moving up to the root, the branch names are separated by periods (also called *dots*):

```
COMMON NAME.ORG UNIT.ORGANIZATION.COUNTRY
```

For example, using the directory tree in Figure 8.1, the complete name of user Bob Thomas would be:

```
THOMAS.PROGRAMMING.PRODUCT DEV.TEL CORP
```

The purpose of NDS is to identify network locations based on function and physical location rather than network addresses. Although the Directory can get quite complicated on very large networks, it is still much easier to look for information about other users and shared hardware using recognizable names,

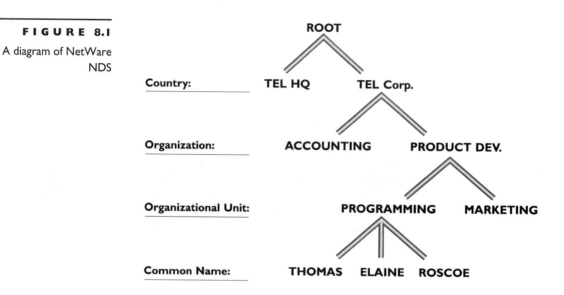

workgroups, and organizational units. To assist users in navigating NDS, Net-Ware includes utilities for searching NDS and looking up lists of names based on NDS object specifications.

NetWare Security

NetWare security is implemented at every level throughout the system. You can set levels of security that are customizable, that form-fit every user on your network.

The System Administrator

The system administrator can configure the operating system to require a password from selected users at log-in time. The SA can also configure NetWare to do any of the following:

- Accept only passwords of a defined length

- Prevent users from sharing the same password

- Force password changes at defined intervals

- Put limits on the times of day when a user can log in, the calendar period during which log-ins are valid, or the amount of time the user is allowed to remain on the network.

The User

The user, once past the log-in level, still cannot roam the network scot-free. The user may be made subject to one or more of the following *file access rights*:

Supervisory: Grants complete access to the network data files, and the right to assign other file access rights to other users.

Access Control: Allows the user to grant other rights, except Supervisor.

Scan: Allows the user to display the contents of files and directories.

Read-Only: Allows the user to view the contents of files but not to make changes to them.

Create: Allows the user to make new files and directories.

Modify: Allows the user to change the name of a file or directory, but not have access to its contents.

Write: Allows the user to change the contents of files and directories.

Erase: Allows the user to delete files.

Files and Directories

NetWare also establishes attributes for files (in addition to the usual DOS file attributes—read/write, system, hidden, and archive). The following file attributes apply to both directories and files, and limit what any user can do with them:

Delete Inhibit: This absolutely prevents file/directory deletion, even by users with the right to erase files.

Rename Inhibit: This prevents name changes to files and directories, even by users with the right to modify files.

Purge: Completely removes a file or directory from disk when deleted. Without this attribute, a deleted file remains on disk but is subject to being overwritten by new data. (Until the deleted file without this attribute is overwritten, it can be restored using NetWare's FILE RESTORE command).

The following attributes apply to files only:

Execute Only: Prevents copying and erasure of executable files.

Indexed: Places file name in NetWare's directory index for faster access.

Shared: File can be accessed by more than one user. (Dangerous unless the file is read-only. As mentioned earlier, two users attempting to write to the same file at the same time can corrupt the file.)

The following additional attributes are available in NetWare 4 and apply to files:

Compressed: The file is stored in compressed format.

Can't Compress: The file was subject to compression, but could not be compressed (usually because it's too small to begin with).

An infrequently-accessed file has been moved to a backup storage area.

The following NetWare 4 attributes apply to both files or directories:

Normal: No NetWare 4 attributes set.

Immediate Compress: Compress files (or the entire directory) when saving to disk, to conserve disk space.

Don't Compress: Save files in uncompressed format.

Don't Migrate: Keep a seldom-accessed file or directory on the hard disk— do not automatically move it to a backup storage system.

File Transaction Tracking

NetWare can protect data from system crashes during write operations using its *Transaction Tracking System* (TSS). This system is handled at the file server level. Certain files stored on the file server can be flagged as *transactional* files. When NetWare senses that such a file is about to be overwritten, it marks the current file as a backup and writes the entire updated file to the disk in a new location. When the copy process is completed, NetWare deletes the backup file.

TSS can be used to recover files that would otherwise have been lost if a power interruption occurred during the write operation. In that event, the untouched backup file would remain on the hard disk, flagged as a backup. Upon restoration of normal operations, NetWare can sense the existence of this backup file, understand that the write operation was aborted, and restore the backup automatically.

System Fault Tolerance

As a further security mechanism, NetWare uses special disk-storage techniques to prevent data damage because of hard disk failure. These mechanisms are collectively called *System Fault Tolerance*, or *SFT*.

NetWare provides two levels of system fault tolerance (plus a third in NetWare 4). SFT Level One performs an operation called *read-after-write verification*, to account for the possibility of bad sectors that may appear on the hard disk over time as the result of normal wear and tear.

STF Level One is a complicated read/write/compare mechanism. In simple terms, NetWare does the following:

1. Before NetWare begins a write operation, it stores the data in a special comparison buffer in memory.

2. NetWare then writes the data to disk.

3. After writing, it reads the data back into a second memory buffer.

4. It then compares the two buffers.

If the comparison matches, the buffers are flushed and only the verified disk copy remains. If the comparison does not match, the sectors are marked as bad, and NetWare tries writing the data again at another location on the hard disk. It repeats the process until the data has been saved successfully.

STF Level Two provides support for *disk mirroring* or *disk duplexing*. Disk mirroring is a process by which duplicate hard disks are run off the same controller, and data is copied to both disks simultaneously. If one disk fails completely, the other disk can serve as a backup. In addition, because the same data is stored in two places, NetWare can take advantage of this to speed up access. (For more information about this process, see Chapter 6.) Disk duplexing works the same way, but the duplicate hard disks are attached to separate controllers. This system guards against data loss resulting from controller failure in addition to disk failure.

SFT Level Three provides support for *mirrored file servers*. In this system, the data is stored on a primary file server and immediately transferred at high speed to a secondary file server. NetWare can also use the secondary file server to access data and boost performance. This system guards against disk, controller, and file server damage—short of some massive disaster such as a flood or earthquake that destroys all your file servers at once.

Why Choose NetWare?

NetWare can handle extremely demanding client/server networks, and because it is in widespread use, virtually all vendors support its features. Because of its complexity, however, you must use a well-trained, experienced network administrator to maintain it.

Windows NT Server

WINDOWS NT SERVER is a Windows-based client/server operating system developed by Microsoft Corporation. It is positioned in the marketplace as a direct competitor to Novell's NetWare. As such, Windows NT Server looks to provide the same levels of security, features, and robust performance as NetWare, with the added convenience of a fully integrated Windows interface.

Windows NT Server can be run on file servers using advanced Intel processors (at least an 80486 is recommended) or DEC Alpha RISC processors. It is designed to interact with its companion client product, Windows NT Workstation, but it can interact with other platforms as well: MS-DOS (using Microsoft LAN Manager), OS/2, Windows 3.1, Windows for Workgroups, and Windows 95. Client software is discussed in greater detail in the next chapter.

Windows NT Server supports virtually all network adapter cards and cabling systems. You can choose your own based on personal evaluation, performance and budget considerations, or purchase Windows NT Server in kits with network interface cards and cables included.

NT Server Protocols

NT supports four protocols. Of these, TCP/IP has been discussed in detail in Chapter 2. The other three protocols are:

NWLink: This protocol is compatible with NetWare's IPX/SPX protocol, and provides compatibility with Novell's NetWare.

NetBEUI (NetBIOS Extended User Interface): This is a small but very fast protocol that is suitable for self-contained networks (where all nodes establish direct links with the server).

Data Control: This protocol is provided to establish communications with mainframe computers (which also must support Data Control), and peripheral hardware (for example, a network-aware shared printer with an internal NIC) that is connected directly to the network cable.

Using Windows NT Server

Windows NT Server is a fully integrated system. Installation on the file server is automated; you run it by inserting an installation disk and booting the server. During installation, NT creates a special database called the *Registry*, containing information that you enter about the server system and clients who have logged on. The registry controls the overall configuration of the network and its clients.

If you are installing Windows NT Workstation clients, you can install the client software over the network from the server or from other workstations, a convenience when installing many workstations spread out over a wide area.

Client data is centralized in the NT system. Each client is given a *user account*, which gives the user access to network services. The network administrator has centralized control over client accounts and can restrict access to specific services for security purposes. User accounts include the following information:

User name: The unique log-in name for each user.

Password: The user's access password.

Full Name: The user's true, full name.

Logon Hours: Times during which the user is permitted access.

Logon Workstations: Workstation names from which the user is permitted access.

Expiration Date: The date on which the account is deactivated (user no longer permitted access).

User Directory: Private directory on the server for the user.

Logon Script: A batch file of operating system commands that executes when the user logs on.

Account Type: Either global or local. A global account gives the user normal access to the network. A local account gives the user access to the single local domain. (See the later section on Windows NT domains.)

In addition to the user account, each client has a *user profile* that is stored on the server. This profile contains configuration settings and preferences for the user's workstation. Because the user profile is stored on the server, the user can log in from different workstations and still see a familiar working environment.

Windows NT Server Organization

Windows NT Server is organized into *domains* and *trust relationships*. A domain is simply a server, or group of servers, that process a set of client accounts. When a group of servers share client account information, one server is designated as a *primary domain server*, and all changes to client account information are handled by this server. The other servers function as *backup servers* that store copies of the primary server's account database.

A trust relationship is a communication link between two domains. When a trust relationship is established, the first domain (called the *trusting* domain) allows access by users in the second domain (called the *trusted* domain). This type of communication allows users to access different domains without requiring that they set up separate accounts in each one. At the same time, because these communication links are controlled by the network administrator, security can be maintained.

Trust relationships can be established between domains so that only one has access to the other, or so that both have access to each other (in effect, two trust relationships between a pair of domains). You can also establish trust relationships between several domains in a series. However, trust relationships are not passed through domains. In other words, each relationship must be established separately between two domains. Trust relationships are diagrammed in Figure 8.2.

In a small network, there is only one server to which all clients are linked. There is no need for trust relationships because only one domain exists. In larger and more complicated networks, however, the concept of domain and trust relationship can be used to develop highly organized models of data sharing and secure access. For example, in networks with several domains, you can establish different types of relationships:

Many-to-One: Multiple domains have access to a single master domain, but not to each other.

Many-to-Some: Multiple domains have access to a number of master domains.

Many-to-Many: Multiple domains have two-way access to each other (no master domain).

Windows NT Server Security

Windows NT Server maintains security by means of password access to the network, and user access rights to network services. On the network-access level, the network administrator has all the usual controls over password usage: for

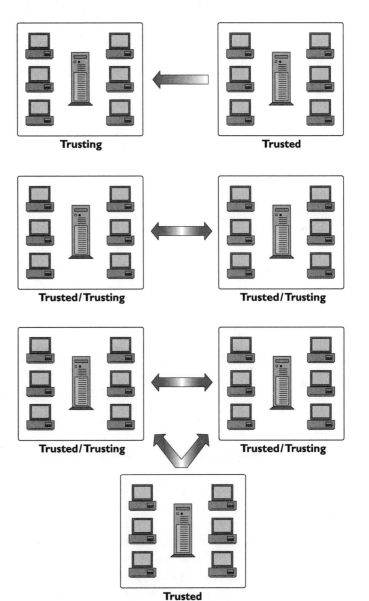

FIGURE 8.2

Trust relationships among
Windows NT Server
domains. The arrows
indicate which domain
(trusted) has access to the
other (trusting).

example, minimum and maximum length of passwords, and frequency with
which passwords must be changed.

User-level security is implemented by classifying users in categories based on
the network services they are permitted to access, and the degree to which they
are allowed to manipulate data files. The network administrator (or administrators—there can be as many as you deem necessary) has the power to control

file and directory access, and the power to modify files, for each category of user. Following are examples of common NT user categories:

Administrators have control over network organization. For example: managing all client accounts; client access to files; backup procedures; security assignments; and so on.

Server Operators control server functions. For example, back up files, control file sharing, control print services.

Account Operators create and modify client accounts (but not server operator or administrator accounts) and user profiles.

Print Operators manage print services only.

Backup Operators manage backup procedures only.

Power Users log on as clients, but have reading, writing, or modifying access rights to files on the server as granted by the system administrator.

Users log onto the system to access network services and applications, and have more limited server access rights than power users.

Network access rights are granted on the domain level. A right granted on one server in a domain is extended to all servers in that domain; but not to servers in other domains. Access rights must be set separately for each domain to which a user has access.

Why Choose NT Server?

Windows NT Server is a good choice if you need an operating system with power and features comparable to NetWare, but with a smoother integration with the familiar Windows interface. Windows NT Server also offers a well-integrated, centralized management package that can be used to ease the management problems associated with large, multiserver networks, as well as networks that must support different communication protocols. It is also competitively priced for its array of features.

Making NOS Comparisons

YOUR CHOICE of operating system is largely a function of how information is normally communicated in your business. Assuming that your business is well organized and the lines of communication are clear, the operating system should model the way information flows in your existing real-world system. For example, if your business depends on access to centralized data, a client/server system such as NetWare or Windows NT might be most appropriate. If, on the other hand, you have a greater need to move files back and forth between users, a peer-to-peer system might be preferable.

On the other hand, perhaps your real-world information and communication system may need revising. If it is subject to systemic bottlenecks because your business communication rules aren't clear, you may need to take a step back and establish clearer information rules before deciding on which computer network to install. It is axiomatic that a computer does not replace an organizational model, it merely amplifies it. Be sure that you are amplifying an understandable and efficient real-world system.

Now that we've looked at some operating system software, the next chapter will describe the other aspect of the client/server model: client software.

Client
Software

LOCAL AREA NETWORK isn't always put into place as an integrated, turnkey solution. Many businesses turn to networking technology as a means to connect and integrate a variety of different client workstations (DOS, Windows, OS/2, for example) that have landed on different users' desks over time. For this reason, modern file server systems support a variety of client platforms. This chapter describes common client software and compares how they go about making a connection to server-based networks. The technical information you'll find here should also provide a basis for deciding which operating system best meets your needs if you're upgrading from stand-alone computers to a network.

DOS Clients

NDUSTRY EXPERTS were surprised that DOS has lasted as long as it has, hanging on for dear life as the operating system of choice for IBM-compatible stand-alone computers. The users who have stuck with it have done so because it has been a cheap, reliable, familiar, and fast operating system. These features outweighed its nearly nonexistent native user interface and cryptic command structure. It's worth noting that Windows has played a role in extending the life of DOS, by adding a graphical interface and shielding the user from its idiosyncratic line commands, a response to market demand inspired, in no small part, by Apple's Macintosh interface. Windows, up through version 3.1, put a graphical layer and specialized application platform on top of DOS, which ran, more or less quietly, underneath. This dual operating system configuration is thorough enough to give users a friendlier gateway to applications.

Although DOS's desktop domination is now beginning to fade, machines using it will be around for several years to come. Some users of these machines will want to connect to networks.

DOS Clients on NetWare

Connecting a DOS client to a NetWare server requires installation of protocol drivers and NetWare shells that handle communication between the local client DOS and NetWare. In older versions of NetWare, the connection was made using two executable files, IPX.COM and NETx.EXE. IPX.COM was custom-configured for the particular workstation's NIC by the system administrator. NETx.EXE was the NetWare redirector; it received user commands and determined whether to direct them to the local operating system or the network.

NetWare Versions 3 and 4 have a more flexible and powerful connection scheme, based on a standard called the Open Datalink Interface. Under this specification, the network interface card must be equipped with a special software driver, called a Multiple Link Interface Driver (MLID). MLID drivers accept different kinds of data protocols; for example, AppleTalk, TCP/IP, and NetWare's IPX. When the driver receives data, it passes it on to a link support utility, which identifies the protocol type and passes the packet to a protocol stack, which translates the data so that the NetWare redirector can understand it and react appropriately.

When you initiate the NetWare connection, these processes are loaded into the client workstation's memory by means of executable files, in the following order:

1. LSL.COM—This is the link support utility

2. The MLID-compliant NIC software driver (supplied with the NIC)

3. Protocol Stack utilities (for example, IPXODI.COM to support NetWare IPX, TCPIP.EXE to support TCP/IP protocol)

After the ODI connection is set up, you can load the NetWare redirector, VLM.EXE. This program, like NETx.EXE, directs data flow between the workstation and the network. However, this version of the redirector is more modular and flexible than NETx.EXE. Specific network services can be loaded into the redirector on an as-needed basis, thus conserving memory. These services are stored in files called *virtual loadable modules*, or VLMs. VLMs perform services such as verifying data accuracy, providing compatibility with older versions of NetWare, handling file and print services.

NetWare DOS client configuration is a richly detailed topic, well beyond the scope of this book. For more information, refer to *Novell's CNA Study Guide*, by David James Clarke IV (SYBEX, 1994), which covers configuration issues in depth.

DOS Clients on Windows NT

Windows NT supports DOS clients running Microsoft's LAN Manager (or fully-compatible) software. To make the connection to a Windows NT network, use LAN Manager's NET USE command. For example, a DOS client could use the following command to access Windows NT's \ACCOUNT\INVOICES directory and see it on the client workstation as drive letter I:

```
net use I: \\account\invoices
```

There are restrictions on how a DOS client will view Windows NT file names. Windows NT supports long file names, up to 255 characters. As DOS users know all too well, DOS can only read file names that are up to eight characters long with an optional three-character extension. Windows NT automatically translates long names into shorter names that comply with DOS's restrictions. When you create an NT long name, NT shortens the name using specific rules, in the following order:

1. All spaces are removed from the long name.

2. Illegal DOS characters (for example, ? : = \ |, among others) are changed to underscores in the long name.

3. If the resulting name is less than six characters long, skip to step 6.

4. If a period exists within the first six characters of the name, the name is truncated to include just the characters before the period.

5. If the name is longer than six characters, it is shortened to six characters.

6. NT then adds a tilde (~) and a single-digit number to the truncated name, to create a unique eight-character name. (For example, SAMPLE~1, SAMPLE~2, and so on.)

7. If NT requires a two-digit number to create a unique name, only the first five characters of the truncated name are used, followed by a tilde and two-digit number.

8. If any periods exist in the original long name, the last period and the first three characters following the period are appended to the DOS-compatible name. (These characters are also subject to the translation rules in steps 1 and 2.)

Windows NT network users should also use caution when assigning alias names to shared NT files and directories. DOS clients can see only those NT alias names that conform to its own 8/3 character-naming conventions. This means that, even though NT supports alias names up to 12 characters in length, you should use only DOS-compatible alias names for shared NT directories that are to be accessible to DOS clients.

Windows Clients

ALL CURRENTLY-AVAILABLE versions of Windows (version 3.1, Windows for Workgroups, Windows NT, and Windows 95) support connections to the most popular file-server networks. They differ in the number of features they offer once the network connection is made.

Windows 3.1

Windows 3.1 is supplied with drivers that support a number of popular networks: for example, NetWare, LAN Manager, LANtastic, and VINES, among others. However, your network vendor may have supplied a Windows network driver that is more fully-featured and reliable than the default Windows driver. It is prudent to check for such an updated driver before setting up the network driver that comes with Windows 3.1. For example, all versions of NetWare include Windows drivers that should be installed before making the network connection.

To make a client connection using Windows 3.1, you must first make Windows network-aware using Windows Setup. From Setup's Options menu, pick Change System Settings and open the Network drop-down list to choose the correct network driver from those supported. If you're using a vendor-supplied driver, its diskette should be in your A: or B: drive. Pick "Other Network" from the list and, when prompted, enter the appropriate drive letter. After you pick the driver, Windows copies the driver file to its System directory, and restarts itself with its new configuration.

Once Windows 3.1 is set up to recognize your network, you can establish a network connection using the File Manager. First, pick Network Connections from File Manager's Disk menu. In most cases you will see a dialog box with prompts to enter the network drive and your user password. Pick the connect button to establish the connection.

Once the connection is made, you can access network drives and directories using the File Manager. You can also define Windows program items using network drives; however, this process is a little smoother if you connect to the network before you set up a new program item.

Windows for Workgroups

Windows for Workgroups (WWG) works similarly to Windows 3.1, but in addition has network connections built in for peer-to-peer access (as discussed in Chapter 8), and support for connections to other server-based networks such as NetWare and Windows NT. If the controlling software driver furnished with your network adapter card supports the changing of network configuration settings from within Windows for Workgroups, you can use a feature called Smart Setup to configure network settings such as an exact percentage of computer time for shared and local programs.

Setting up the connection works as described under Windows 3.1: You use commands and dialog boxes in the File Manager to point to server drives and directories, subject to security-based access limitations, if any.

Windows for Workgroups includes two useful network applications that are not found in Windows 3.1:

Microsoft Mail: This application allows messages of any type to be sent between connected workstations, provided they have Microsoft Mail installed. (You will need a separately sold upgrade to this product if you want to send messages to other e-mail systems.) This message system works in the background, so that you can send and receive messages while working on some other application. It can alert you to messages you have received and file messages you wish to save. Microsoft Mail also allows you to "chat" electronically with other users.

Microsoft Schedule+: This application enables you to define your schedule, make appointments, and set meetings among users. You can view the appointments of other users and they can view yours, except for those defined as "private." If you want to set up a meeting, you can list users who will attend, and search for available time slots from among their schedules. When an available time is found, you can set up a "Request Meeting" form to be sent to the proposed attendees, who can respond using either Schedule+ or Microsoft Mail.

The advantage of Windows for Workgroups over Windows 3.1 is its integrated ability to access server networks and remain a member of a peer-to-peer workgroup, plus the mail, messaging, and scheduling applications that are included.

Windows NT Workstation

Windows NT Workstation is optimized for connection to Windows NT Server. Each NT client can participate either in an NT Server domain or in a separate workgroup. (Refer to Chapter 8 for more information on NT domains.) Connection to the network can be handled in typical Windows fashion, by accessing File Manager at the workstation, or the connection can be established remotely from another installed Windows NT Workstation over the network.

When a user logs on to the Windows NT Server, a logon screen prompts for the user's name, password, and domain. If the user has an account on an NT Server domain, the user enters the name of that domain. Windows NT Server checks the logon information against the user database on the domain server and if the data matches, the login is completed.

The user can also log onto the network independently of a domain, entering the name of the local client workstation. Windows NT Workstation then checks the log-in information against a local database of access rights, and if a match is found, allows the log-in for local client resources only.

Whenever a user logs in, Windows NT Workstation looks for a *logon script*, which is a batch file containing operating system commands. If NT Workstation finds the logon script, its contents are executed automatically.

The Windows NT Workstation environment is controlled by means of a *user profile*, a file containing client configuration data; for example, program items and groups, window sizes and locations, screen colors, and printer connections.

Windows NT Workstation accesses files and directories according to rights established by the network administrator. Directories available to different users are called *shared directories*. A shared directory is given an alias name, by which different users can access it. The directory alias can be the same name as the directory, but it is not required. In this way, a complicated directory name like C:\ACCOUNTING\PAYABLES\INVOICING can be aliased as simply INVOICES.

Windows NT Workstation permits integrated access to NT Server's powerful networking utilities:

Windows NT Backup is an application that provides centralized management of one or more tape backup drives across the network. You can use Windows NT Backup to back up data on servers or other workstations, but it will not recognize Windows 3.1 or MS-DOS workstations remotely, and to maintain security, it will not back up Registry or event log files except at the domain server.

Event Viewer is used to read NT Server's *event logs*, special files that record logons, file and application access, and errors. There are three types of event logs: the system log, which record logons, file accesses and hardware/software errors; application logs, which record application usage; and security logs, which record errors and events that may be related to breaches of internal security settings.

Server Manager monitors current system activity (who is logged on and what network resources have been opened for access).

Performance Monitor displays performance statistics for various technical aspects of the system; for example, number of data packets transmitted per second, wait time for processes, percentage of processor being utilized. These statistics are useful when diagnosing network performance problems.

Windows 95

Windows 95, the latest version of Windows, includes several useful networking client features, and supports connections to NetWare Versions 3 and 4, OS/2 LAN Server, and Windows NT Server. If you like, you can also link a group of Windows 95 users as a small peer-to-peer network using most manufacturers' NICs and cables.

Configuring and Connecting

To configure the Windows 95 client, you access the Network Connections dialog box from the Control Panel. You then define the network type, supported protocols, user name and password, network-specific security information (if any). Also, you can define your local workstation as a client or a server (including a dial-up server, with password protection, for remote access).

Windows 95 stores configuration information in a special database called the Registry. The Registry replaces the initialization files used in previous versions of Windows, and allows for an easier means of updating configuration information using the operating system interface.

If you connect as a NetWare client, the Windows 95 NetWare client software can execute your NetWare login script—but it will not load memory-resident NetWare applications except from a separate batch file. Windows 95 clients can share local disk drives and printers with NetWare clients, using utilities that reside on the Windows client only. However, you can choose only one or the other (files or printers), not both at once.

Networking Features

Although functionally similar to Windows for Workgroups and Windows NT, Windows 95 has some unique networking features that make it an interesting alternative to those other Windows versions. For example, Windows 95 supports 32-bit, protected-mode versions of TCP/IP, NetBEUI, and IPX/SPX protocols, which are faster and use less system memory than the 16-bit versions in Windows for Workgroups. Although Windows NT and Windows for Workgroups both have Microsoft Mail and Schedule+, Windows 95 lumps a variety of messaging programs together as the Microsoft Exchange. The Exchange permits you to have a single mailbox for e-mail, fax, data files, and connections to commercial on-line mail services, such as CompuServe, or an Internet mail provider.

In addition to Control Panel, there are three other networking utilities in Windows 95:

Network Explorer is an expanded version of the old File Manager, which allows you to access and modify files on the network server, assuming that the network's security features allow you the appropriate access rights.

Network Neighborhood is a display of available servers, domains, workgroups, and files. You access it through the Network Explorer. Using Network Neighborhood, you can map a local drive letter to a server directory, or attach directly to the server drive. Neighborhood also allows you to browse server resources—for example, file names and print queues—but in read-only mode.

Briefcase is a file transfer and compression utility for copying files between the workstation and floppy disks or portable PCs. File transfers between the desktop and portable PCs require a parallel or serial cable connection.

Security

File security in Windows 95 is limited. You can assign passwords to client directories or printers. If you want to assign more flexible access rights, or restricted rights to individual files, you can set them up using the security design of your attached file server (Windows NT or NetWare).

Windows 95 offers four useful network management utilities for system administrators:

Netwatch allows you to connect to a server and monitor connections to that server: who is connected, and what files they have open. System administrators can disconnect users remotely.

System Monitor allows you to track a client's performance and use of resources, either at the workstation or across the network. You can choose different display formats for the analysis: bar or line graph, or numeric chart.

Registry Editor allows you to access and make changes to users' system setting in the Windows 95 Registry.

System Policy Editor allows you to set each user's interface and network resource rights. For example, you can prevent certain users from accessing certain printers, or from setting up their workstation as a server.

OS/2 Clients

O S/2 IS ONLY SLOWLY attracting support from developers of broad-based desktop applications. Its earlier versions, up through OS/2 Warp Version 3, lacked significant local-area networking functions.

The latest version, called *OS/2 Warp Connect*, includes drivers and utilities for the most popular server-based and peer-to-peer networks. Warp Connect includes file requesters and redirectors that will allow direct connections to NetWare Versions 3 and 4, and support for IPX, NetBIOS, plus enhanced TCP/IP protocols that will permit concurrent access to both network services and the Internet.

Warp Connect also includes *LAN Distance* software to support dial-in remote access. Messaging services are provided by including Lotus Development Corporation's *Notes Express*, a messaging system with functions similar to Microsoft Mail.

Additional Warp Connect networking utilities, designed for larger corporate customers, can be purchased separately as a suite of applications called the *OS/2 Extend Pack*. These utilities include connections to mainframes, system performance monitors, remote software installation, and remote node configuration.

Warp Connect can run Windows applications as native programs (in other words, without requiring a copy of Windows itself). However, to do this, you must make a separate purchase of add-on Windows applications drivers called the Win-OS/2 libraries.

Macintosh Clients

I F YOU ARE USING Macintosh computers as clients in Macintosh environments, the AppleTalk network is built right in; you simply make the hardware connections and go. Refer to Chapter 8 for more information about networking the Mac, and Chapter 3 for more information about AppleTalk.

However, if you want to connect Macintosh machines as clients in networks that are not Macintosh-based, be aware that the necessary software drivers and connectivity tools will be the responsibility of your host NOS. For example, if you want to connect a Mac machine to a NetWare system, you will need an add-on product, NetWare for Macintosh (a set of NetWare loadable modules and a client desktop accessory that together support the connection between NetWare's protocols and AppleTalk).

In addition, you should make certain that there are available Macintosh versions of your network's applications. For example, Lotus Notes, WordPerfect and AutoCAD offer versions for the Macintosh. These applications (and presumably most others, otherwise why bother?) can share data files with other workstations on the mixed network while running under the local operating system.

My point is not to dismiss the idea of connecting Mac clients to non-Mac networks; it's a fine idea. However, if you know in advance that you intend to put Macintosh machines on a non-Macintosh network, take the time to be certain that the necessary software and drivers are available for your host NOS.

Making Client Software Comparisons

I N MANY CASES, your choice of client software will be a function of the network you are using; for example, you'll run copies of Windows NT Workstation on a Windows NT Server system. However, if you are just starting out, it is useful to pay close attention to client software options, because the client interface is what your network users will be working with every day. It makes sense to choose a network partly on the basis of how appealing the users find the features of the recommended client interface.

It is fairly common that as networks grow, different client platforms will join the network. This aspect of networking is always a challenge for system administrators. However, network operating system software continues to evolve and become more powerful, integrating support for a wider variety of client platforms, making this a bit less of a headache than it used to be.

At this point, you have become acquainted with some of the standard hardware and software that makes up a networked system. Many network operating system software includes some applications, like integrated messaging. The next chapter will take a more detailed look at network applications, the actual business-task software you use from day to day.

Network Applications

OST OF THE SOFTWARE discussed in this book so far has been *system* software, the software that controls computers. *Application* software is the software you use to get things done; writing letters and memos, reporting income and expenses, drawing pictures, printing paychecks, designing skyscrapers, balancing the bank account.

It is outside the scope of this book to evaluate individual software applications. There are simply too many. Software companies upgrade their products with such frequency that information on individual products (in book form, at least) quickly becomes out of date. Finally, it is not this book's intention to imply any recommendations for any specific product.

This chapter discusses three types of applications that have come into existence because of networks. For each of these, this chapter describes features that make these applications useful and what you should be looking for when making comparisons between various product offerings. This chapter also makes some observations about application software in general.

Stand-Alone Applications on the Network

N THEORY, AN APPLICATION that runs on a stand-alone desktop computer should run on the same computer connected to a network. In practice, stand-alone applications present some risks when running on a network, because they are not programmed to comply with the network's rules for shared access to data. It is up to you and your network operating system to enforce those rules and prevent the stand-alone application from inadvertently corrupting shared files.

You are better off running applications that are *network-aware*, meaning that they are programmed to recognize shared-access file systems and respect your network's rules for keeping shared data safe and sound.

Types of Desktop Applications

ALTHOUGH THERE ARE a great many competing applications being marketed out there, business software falls into five broad categories of purpose: Database, Spreadsheet, Word Processing, Communications, and Graphics:

Database: Includes applications for accounting, inventory, personnel, statistics, order entry, shipping and receiving records; in general terms, the kind of data that used to be stored in file cabinets.

Spreadsheet: Includes applications for making analysis, comparisons, and projections. Modern spreadsheets offer document-formatting capabilities to enhance their final output. Many small businesses use spreadsheets to maintain simple databases (inefficient, and not recommended, but possible).

Word Processing: Includes applications for both writing and document formatting, from simple in-house memos to glossy advertising brochures.

Communications: Includes applications for sending and receiving digital messages of all types; for example: e-mail systems, Internet access.

Graphics: Includes applications for communicating ideas using pictures: Computer-Aided Drafting and Design (CADD), charts and graphs, presentation slides, scanning, photo editing, sketch drawing.

Some applications combine these categories: A project-management application may combine a database of tasks with a graphic output showing how task schedules overlap. In another example, a spreadsheet is actually a specialized form of a database, using a row-and-column format for its user interface.

Many network-aware applications are stand-alone applications that are enhanced with additional features that provide secure multi-user access to their data files. As such, they do not differ, in a functional sense, from their stand-alone cousins. The three types of applications discussed here are those that rely on network services for their native functionality: the distributed database manager, electronic messaging, and groupware.

Databases

HERE ARE A LARGE number of networked database products on the market, but they all have the same fundamental purpose: to provide a centralized repository of data, then allow multiple users to access it, update it, and produce meaningful information based on it, all the while protecting it from accidental corruption and enforcing your business rules for keeping it accurate and reliable. That's a large job for a software program, and many programs will requires the ongoing support of a skilled database manager.

The integrity of the database is vital to the survival of many large and small businesses today. A Database Management System (DBMS) is an application that organizes data into a structured framework, and uses that framework to provide access to the data and a vehicle for processing (modifying) it.

The Structure of a Data Table

A database framework organizes raw data into a hierarchy of relationships. At the lowest level of this hierarchy, the data is broken down into fundamental building blocks, called *fields*. A field defines an aspect of the data that is common to all instances of it; for example, a Last Name field would contain persons' last names, and a First Name field would contain their first names.

Fields are combined into *records*. A very simple record might consist of first and last name fields, and each record would then contain the full name of a person.

A set of such records is called a *table* (or in some systems, a *datafile* or *file*). A phone book is a real-world example of a table. For each listing in the phone book, there are three fields: one for names, another for addresses, and another for phone numbers. One set of fields—a person's name, address, and phone number—form a record. The records are alphabetized into a list and bound together to make up the table/phone book.

By breaking up data into fields and records, a DBMS can access and sort the data very quickly. For example, a DBMS can sort a mailing list alphabetically using the Last Name and First Name field, and sort it in ZIP code order by using a ZIP code field.

Relational and Flat-File Databases

So far we've discussed the simple "flat-file" database, in which all the information is contained in a single table. But a DBMS can go one step further. Several tables can be related to each other and the DBMS can access them in a synchronized way to create highly detailed analyses and meaningful relationships between their various fields (or subsets of fields). In other words, the DBMS takes raw data and forms relationships that turn it into useful information. This ability to synchronize relationships between tables is far easier for a computer than a human being.

To visualize how a computer works with related tables in a database, imagine a company that ships a variety of products to customers. The company maintains a table of customers, including a customer ID number, name, and shipping addresses. If the company had to add a field to the customer table each time a customer ordered a product, the table would quickly become bloated, full of fields that all customer records wouldn't necessarily need.

Instead, product numbers, names, and prices are stored in a separate inventory table. When a customer orders products, just the product numbers, along with the customer's ID number, are copied into a third table: a shipping/invoicing table. This third table is very small, since only the relevant ID numbers are duplicated. The shipping/invoicing table can be sorted on the customer's ID number and invoice number, to keep all the ordered items together. The details about the customer and the products remain in their respective customer and inventory tables.

The DBMS can print shipping orders and invoices based on the small table, using the ID numbers to look up the details about customers and products. While this process would be tedious for human beings, it is easy for a computer. The relational database saves disk space and is more efficient, especially as shipping and invoicing records accumulate. The shipping/invoicing table, with its three fields, is much easier for a computer to sort and maintain than a single table with many fields. Figure 10.1 shows a relational database model.

The multiple-file, relational database model can be applied to many different types of business record-keeping. For example, you can relate a mailing list to a set of demographic categories; a single student to multiple records of classes taken and grades received; a single accounting code to multiple instances of expenses and income; and so on.

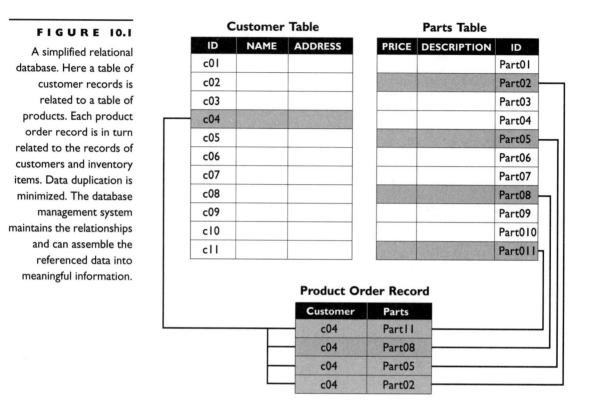

FIGURE 10.1

A simplified relational database. Here a table of customer records is related to a table of products. Each product order record is in turn related to the records of customers and inventory items. Data duplication is minimized. The database management system maintains the relationships and can assemble the referenced data into meaningful information.

Databases on a Network

A Networked Database Management System (NDBMS) is an application that synchronizes multiple users' access to centralized databases. There are two basic forms of networked databases:

Peer Level NDBMS: In a peer-to-peer network, each user accesses the database records directly, using the NDBMS software to read and assemble the information, and to make changes to the data as required. The system is simpler than client/server, but it produces large amounts of data traffic across the network and can be slow. Also, great care must be taken to enforce rules of access so that data is not corrupted as multiple users tie directly into the stored tables. Examples include popular database products like dBASE and Paradox, which have language-level commands that implement access rules for shared datafiles and records within them.

Client/Server NDBMS: In a client/server network, users do not access the records directly. Instead, they pass instructions to the file server, which performs operations on the stored data and passes the results of those operations back to the user. This process is more complicated, and thus more difficult to implement and maintain, but it is also faster and more efficient. Because data is handled by separate servers, the process of access and modification can take place locally at the server level, reducing network data traffic and speeding up the process overall. Also, the databases on the servers can deploy their own safeguards that keep multiple users from simultaneously accessing the same records, and accidentally corrupting them. Examples include products like Access, Oracle, and SyBASE.

To further complicate matters, related tables can be stored at various locations throughout the network. Consider an accounting table stored on a hard disk in the accounting department, which keeps records of customer payments against invoices, the details for which are stored in a separate table stored on a hard disk in the shipping/receiving department. The networked DBMS is responsible for accessing and relating information in tables that can be far-flung throughout the enterprise. Fortunately, many database product vendors provide utilities for accessing such *distributed databases*.

One important tool for accessing information in distributed databases is a language called SQL (Structured Query Language). This language is a standard for networked databases, and is supported by most, if not all, client/server database products. It is a rich and robust language, and you can sample how it works in Chapter 14.

Data Locking

If more than one user were allowed to access the same data at the same time, only the last user to save the data would actually record the changes. The previous user's changes would be overwritten. This would cause data to become unreliable. To prevent this, an NDBMS needs a system for preventing access to data by more than one user at a time. If only one user can access the data, then subsequent users will see what changes have been made to date and make correct decisions about further modifications.

Locking is a term used to describe a standard system for preventing simultaneous access to data by more than one user. Databases can lock fields, records, or entire tables.

To enable locking, the fields, records, and tables in a networked database are equipped with headers that can store an "either/or" symbol (often expressed as a 1 or 0; or a logical True or False) that indicates whether a field, record, or file has been accessed. When any user accesses the field, record, or file, this header code is set to True and the data is considered "locked" for the duration. Once the lock has been set, other users are prevented from accessing the data until the original user saves the modifications and releases the "lock."

The system is simple enough and works well enough most of the time, but there can be problems if the network malfunctions (a power failure or hard disk crash, for example). If the locking codes are not reset normally, data can become permanently locked. This is why most networks allow the system administrator the ability to access the data whenever necessary, and remove erroneous lock codes.

Data Table File Formats

So far, we have been talking about the logical arrangement of data in a relational database; that is, data broken down into fields, records, and sets of related tables. This concept is well established in the desktop database market. However, different database product developers choose to implement different file formats for their tables. Each vendor, as you might expect, touts their own file format as the best for fast and easy access to data, as well as suitability for use on a network. Some common database file formats are: Oracle, SyBASE, InterBASE, Paradox, Access, and xBASE-dialect files (which includes dBASE, FoxPro, and Clipper).

It is fairly common for users to want to share tables, and if these tables are in different formats, the data may be unusable. Fortunately, many products come with utilities that translate tables from one format into another. When you are evaluating the merits of a particular database product, one important criterion to keep in mind is how well this product can translate its file format into others' formats.

Working with the Database

The usefulness of your database depends on two important skills, *network database design* and *network database programming,* described below.

Designing the Network Database

We touched upon the basic principles of database design when we described the simple order-entry database in the previous section of this chapter. In a nutshell, database design is the process of deciding what kinds of fields to include in your tables, which fields to use to sort the records, how to access the records and display their contents, on what basis to relate different tables to each other,

Programming without Code

As you might expect, database product developers are hard at work trying to simplify their DBMS languages, thereby adding to their commercial appeal. The job is daunting. Databases that use graphical user interfaces (GUIs) require specialized programming that add complexity to the language for the sake of making things easier for the end-user. And DBMS product developers also compete on the basis of power and features. More power and more features in the product mean more functionality (and vocabulary and syntax) that must be added to the language.

Lately, the trend in programming is toward special design utilities that permit the programmer to assemble user interfaces by arranging predefined interface objects (such as windows, push buttons, and drop-down menus, among others) on the screen. The programmer links these interface objects to specific data processes (modifying the contents of a file, producing a report, and so on). When the programmer is finished arranging and linking, a built-in utility analyzes the screen information and writes code to produce the interface and the linked processes.

This kind of programming is called object-oriented because it is based on the concept of specific screen objects (windows, buttons, menus, and the like) linked to data processes that the end-user can access by pointing with a mouse or pressing special keyboard key combinations. The results can be spectacular, but the development time, especially in the beginning stages, can be slow.

In object-oriented programming, the goal of the programmer is to produce an end-user interface for those who will manipulate the database. This interface, if programmed reasonably well, will be easy for end-users to understand and use, and shield those users from the arcane and difficult details of direct database manipulation.

However, while on-screen object-oriented programming is a great leap forward, it does not altogether eliminate the need to learn the vocabulary and syntax of the database programming language. Often the programmer will find that some direct manipulation of the program code is still necessary to produce exactly the desired results. But great progress has been made in this area; and simplified, object-oriented database languages have great market potential.

and how you will store these tables on your network. The goals of good database design are to make the best use of disk space, keep network traffic to a minimum, and thereby speed up the process of adding, deleting, modifying, and reporting the data.

Since your business records are bound to have certain unique qualities, a DBMS must allow you to define whatever fields you need, and to arrange them in records to your liking, and to set any number of relationships between tables based on whatever criteria suit you.

Database design is a broad subject, and an in-depth discussion is beyond the scope of this book. Fortunately, if you are new to databases and want to learn, there are plenty of training venues available just about everywhere—try calling your local vendors and computer stores, ask them about training resources in your area. The vendors themselves may run training sessions of their own; usually at moderate cost. There are also plenty of consultants and on-site trainers who will be happy to do the job for you—at a price, of course.

Programming the Database

Most database products offer a number of preprogrammed utilities that permit you to access and process the data in specific, fairly fundamental ways. These utilities often come in the form of sample programs using the database's control language; others might be executable programs designed to automate the process of creating tables or of changing their structure. You may be able to get along by using those utility programs, supplied by the manufacturer as "standard equipment." It is also quite possible that you will have unique needs—based on personal preference, requirements of those with whom you do business, or unique aspects of the information you use, that will be beyond the scope of those generic utilities that come "out of the box."

A useful database product therefore includes some form of a programming language that allows you to manipulate the data in a more customized fashion. Some of these languages are little more than *macro languages*; in other words, a method for stringing built-in functions together so that the DBMS can execute them in order, in effect automating the steps of a particular task.

Other database languages rival high-level programming languages, complete with functions that allow you to access your computer's storage devices and RAM at the level of individual bits. (In other words, they give you the power to wreak total havoc if that's what you want.) The more powerful database products can be programmed to perform highly complex processes, and in the hands of a skilled programmer, they can easily justify their cost. But programming, like database design, takes time to learn—an investment that is sometimes difficult to justify in a world where deadlines have come to be measured in days, if not hours or minutes.

Many business people settle for a compromise, a blend of canned utilities that came with the product, third-party add-on programs that amplify the power of the database, and perhaps some in-house programming by a dedicated employee.

Electronic Messaging

LECTRONIC MESSAGING is a process that has expanded rapidly, from its beginnings as simple e-mail messages passed from one workstation to another, to an application that combines secretarial, mailing, translation, formatting, and storage service for communications across your network, or between different networks, or around the world.

In Chapter 8, you looked at simple message systems that some vendors of network operating systems provide with their products. These systems are useful for sending messages across a single installed network, but to access a larger base of recipients, a more complex product may be necessary.

A fully-featured electronic messaging application (for example, Novell's MHS, or Microsoft's MAPI) is based on a central database that contains electronic addresses of message senders and recipients (sometimes called a *post office*). A good messaging application also includes sets of instructions for formatting complex messages—messages that may contain not only text, but control information that formats the text with character fonts, integrates picture displays, and broadcasts sound. The messaging application must include instructions for collecting, storing, and retrieving these messages at any time from any user running any type of workstation over any type of connection allowed by the network.

Messaging Standards

If a user sends a message across a local network to another user running the same message system, the process is relatively simple. But if you want to send a message to a user running a different messaging program, some translation may be necessary. Because of the complexity involved in having many different systems send and receive messages in many different formats, the issue of standards arises once again.

Any number of vendors may attempt to develop and market their idea of a superior messaging system, using proprietary systems for sending, receiving, and storing messages. It would be impossible for all vendors to provide support

Digital Dialog

The process of sending and receiving messages has evolved quickly into highly auto-mated systems. For example, very little of the editing of this book was done on paper. Manuscripts, revisions, additions, and editorial comments were exchanged using a messaging system that connected author and editors, living many miles apart.

Memos, in the form of plain text files, were linked with binary-based document files. Once a package of information was complete, the message system was invoked and an automatic "address book" linked the message with its destination information. The address book feature allowed author and editors to exchange messages using familiar names rather than arcane addressing schemes. When a file was completed and sent, the recipient could expect to receive it in a matter of several minutes (or sometimes an hour or two, if the system was loaded with other messages.)

In addition to saving paper, the messaging system allowed the editing and publishing process to proceed more efficiently; the digital dialog cut hours off the project that would have been spent printing repeated revisions of the text, as well as days that might have been spent waiting for traditional delivery services to send paper manuscripts back and forth.

The final result is the paper-based document you hold, born of a digital dialog.

for all other vendor's messaging specifications. Instead, vendors have tried to support a limited set of standard specifications, translating messages between their own message system and the accepted standards.

There are a few message formats that have evolved into *de facto* standards, and most messaging products include support for them. These include Lotus's cc:MAIL, Novell's Message Handling System (MHS), and Microsoft Mail. In addition, there are shared standards for message storage and retrieval systems, including Novell's Standard Message Format (SMF), Microsoft's Messaging Application Programmer's Interface (MAPI) and Lotus's Vendor Independent Messaging (VIM).

X.400

The messaging standard with the greatest international impact is called *X.400*. This standard was developed by the International Consultative Committee of Telephony and Telegraphy, a body of international experts headquartered in France. X.400 is a monumental specification. It attempts to lay down standards for all electronic messaging systems in the world.

Large-scale messaging services (such as CompuServe and America OnLine) use the X.400 specification. If you send a message to an electronic address over one of these services, the service converts the message to comply with the X.400 specifications, and then sends it on to its destination, where it is converted again, into the message format the receiving program uses to make the message understandable to the receiving party.

Message Addresses

In order to send a message, you must specify a destination, or *address*. This address can be simple or quite complex, depending on the destination and how remote it is. Within a messaging database, the address can be simple: *Bthomas* would be enough of an address for a message to another workstation on the same local network with "Bthomas" as its identifying name.

To send a message to another messaging database (for example, on a separate network with a connection to yours) the addresses would consist of a user name in the remote messaging database plus the messaging database's identifying name. For example, a messaging database on my network is identified as "TEL". Someone using another messaging database on the network could send a message to me addressed as: *Bthomas@TEL*.

This example is but one of many possible addressing formats, with varying degrees of complexity, allowing you to send messages to destinations just about anywhere. For example, to send a message to me over the Internet, try *72261,3260@compuserve.com*, which is my messaging address at CompuServe.

Messaging System Functions

At a minimum, what should a message system do for you? The following features can be considered a minimum standard for a usable message system:

Composition: The product should include a basic text editing mechanism (though not full-fledged word processing), plus a system for importing documents you create using other word-processing and text-editing software, directly into messages you intend to send, and converting those documents to the product's message format. In addition, since much communication centers around the exchange of data files, the message system should provide a means of attaching binary files to messages, so that text messages related to the binary information can be sent together with the file as a single message.

Messages Plus

Messages can include all kinds of slick, non-text information. For example, messages can include raster images, instructions to your computer to display a picture on the screen by arranging color light points, called pixels, within a specified area. Messages can also include embedded sound files, stored digital representations of recorded sounds, or custom sounds created using specialized software.

The combination of text, graphics, and sound is called multimedia, not long ago a hot topic throughout the industry but lately revolving around new software applications for home use, such as games and entertainment software.

If your message system supports these features, and you need them in your business operations, fine; but if you don't need them, consider a less expensive system that does not support them. The critical issue is whether the system actually expedites and facilitates real business communication between employees and work teams, and thus makes or saves money.

Addressing: The system should store frequently-used addresses, access them by means of a user directory, and offer optional reply-receipt services when the message is picked up by the recipient. A good messaging product should include *directory aliasing*, a feature that allows you to store complex electronic addresses under more readable names. You can use a directory of alias names to send a message to "Bob Thomas," which is far easier to remember and recognize than some cryptic network node address on some far-off commercial access provider.

Mailbox: The system should store incoming messages, display them in any order, and offer a mechanism for immediate reply. Sequences of back-and-forth messages (*e-conversations*) should be stored as such and replayed in order when necessary.

Forwarding: The system should include, when desired, the ability to forward messages received at the local address to an alternate address. (Good for people who travel from one network to another.)

Status Reports: The system should be able to display the results of sending, receiving, forwarding, and replying (Did the message go through? If not, why not? Was it picked up at the destination?)

Translation: The system should support mechanisms for handling messages between different vendor's messaging products (usually by support—either direct or through translation—for a common standard).

Filing: The system should allow for filing or disposal of messages as required, and default storage and disposal systems if no specific instructions are given (for example, unless otherwise instructed, the system may delete messages after a given number of days).

Background Processing: The system should run smoothly while the user performs other tasks. It should include an alarm system for messages tagged as urgent, and be able to display urgent messages while other applications are running.

Groupware

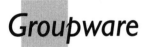

G ROUPWARE IS SPECIAL software that allows members of a work team to coordinate their activities and communications around specific shared projects. To some extent, groupware encompasses features of electronic messaging, but it does more, facilitating activities as well as communication. Groupware products provide the following kinds of services:

Scheduling: This is a distinguishing feature of groupware. All members of a work group have access to public-access portions of their schedules, and work group members can review each other's schedules, request appointments, or arrange meetings of the entire group or select members of the group.

E-mail: Usually incorporated into groupware products as a basic electronic messaging service, this feature tracks sequences of messages and allows you to replay them. It also sends and tracks the flow of shared data.

Shared Databases: This feature allows group members to store and retrieve project data, as needs require, in a centralized location. The database functions as a kind of bulletin board and history book containing project-related information.

Workflow Transfer: Simply put, this feature allows individual group members to work on a particular aspect of a project and pass the result along to other users as necessary, supporting the transfer of data between different applications. To use a simple example: a team member in accounting can draw up budget figures for a project using a spreadsheet, and deposit the spreadsheet containing the results into the shared database. Later, another team member in the word processing department can access the data from the shared database and incorporate it directly into a narrative proposal for the client. As the proposal is reviewed, the new budget figures can go back to accounting in spreadsheet format, and so on, until the final proposal is hammered out.

There are many groupware products on the market. Some, like Lotus's Notes, are complex and require good administrative skills to operate effectively (but offer significant cost- and time-saving benefits to users who invest the effort). Others, like Microsoft's Schedule+, are far easier to use, but are more limited in their application.

Even a simple scheduling system like Schedule+ will be a boon in business where a simple meeting takes forever to set up because everyone is out of their office running hither and yon (always on behalf of the business, of course). Fast communications and instant access to individuals' appointments and calendars make meetings far easier to arrange, and keep everyone informed regarding when and where meetings will take place.

Finding Out about Applications

THIS CHAPTER HAS COVERED a specific category of application: those that are specially designed to take advantage of networks. Undoubtedly you will use other applications on your network; word processors, spreadsheets, graphic image processors, and programming languages, for example. How do you go about selecting which of these are the best for your network?

There are dozens of network-aware applications written to perform all manner of business tasks, and the process of choosing the correct one may seem daunting at first. In fact, the process of selecting application software has become fairly standard, and vendors have adapted themselves to it. You begin by collecting printed information from software dealers and manufacturers. Next, whenever possible, acquire demonstration versions, or have your dealer demonstrate the software you are considering.

Computer magazines regularly publish reviews and comparisons of competing software products. The problem is often one of timing: the reviews don't usually appear just at the time when you are evaluating software. However, your public library has an important resource that can help you locate software reviews: the *Index to Periodicals*. You can use this index to identify which issues of computer magazines have reviews of software that you are considering. If the issue isn't in the library, most magazine publishers have back-issue services through which you can purchase old issues for a reasonable fee. Check the "reader services" section of a current issue for back-issue ordering information. This is an underutilized and very valuable resource.

Most importantly, whenever you can, talk to people who use the product, getting them to open up about its flaws as well as strengths. This is not always easy; there exists an all-too-human tendency to downplay mistakes. Few users will say to a stranger, "This product's a dog; I never should have bought it, but now I'm stuck with it because there's no more money in the software budget for a replacement." But a lot of us have had those thoughts on occasion.

Investigate the possibility of user groups in your area, or if you have a modem, consider online services such as CompuServe or America Online, which have support forums for an extensive variety of applications. In addition, people can be more forthcoming on forums such as these, and it's easy to get a diverse range of opinions.

Take your time; you are buying not only for yourself, but for the other users on your network as well. With patience and gentle persistence, you will find the right applications for your business.

In the next chapter, you will look at how your network and its applications are integrated into a smooth-running system: the network design.

Network Design and Management

Planning the
Network

PREVIOUS CHAPTERS have introduced you to the various hardware and software components that make up a local area network. It is important to understand these technologies, in order to inform your decision-making about the type of network that might be best for your business. However, a successful network is as much the result of good planning as of good selection of hardware and software. This chapter will introduce you to the steps required to plan and design your network.

Every business has certain unique characteristics. The everyday logistics of running your business are based on careful planning of business rules. The rules you plan evolve over time into further levels of refinement depending on the type of business you are in as well as various human issues, such as personnel management and customer relations.

Some people mistakenly believe that the acquisition of computer technology will automatically turn a poorly organized business into a well organized one. (Advertisers are notorious for capitalizing on this dangerous notion.) Actually, computers are likely to make a well-organized business better, but they can also make a badly organized business even worse; and connecting computers into a network can amplify this effect. Remember that a local area network increases both the amount of data you will handle and the speed at which you will handle it. At the same time, it leaves responsibility for the quality of that data entirely in your hands.

For this reason, you should be willing to spend a lot of time analyzing how you do business and how information flows into and through your business before making any final decisions regarding network hardware and software. If you plan your network in this context, you stand a better chance of creating a useful, problem-free system.

The planning process for your local area network has two aspects worth highlighting.

- First, the process affords you the opportunity to reevaluate the manner in which your business currently manages information. It also allows you to make immediate adjustments to that management scheme, adjustments that can save or earn money and that you can implement with or without the assistance of computers.

- The second aspect of the planning process is more what you might expect: it clarifies your needs for network hardware, software, and configuration in the context of your business problems, solutions, and goals.

As the process unfolds, you may find yourself moving back and forth between these two aspects: choosing a network type, making refinements to your business rules, and then making changes to your network proposal based on changes you made in your business.

For example, if you are currently in a non-computerized or non-networked environment, installing a network can raise significant questions with regard to the physical plant: Will existing electrical outlets become overloaded? Can you save money by moving employee desks around? What changes to the physical plant might affect the network design?

Networks can produce significant changes in the ways you do business. For example, installing an e-mail system can have enormous impact, raising serious interpersonal (and sometimes legal) issues with regard to access rights, privacy, and e-mail etiquette. All these issues are best addressed earlier rather than later.

The network planning process may seem tedious and time-consuming, especially if you perceive an acute need to implement your new system as quickly as possible. Nevertheless, good planning is as important to the usefulness and reliability of your system as the hardware and software you intend to purchase; do not neglect it.

The Planning Process

PLANNING YOUR NETWORK is accomplished in a series of steps, each of which is described in this chapter. You may find, depending on the type of business you are in, that some steps have more importance than others. You will have to reckon with each along the way, though, so be prepared to spend at least some time with each.

Murphy's Law applies especially well to networking. One of the many corollaries to Murphy's Law is worth mentioning here: Every project takes longer than you expect. There is actually a reason projects almost always take longer than planned: No one can anticipate surprises (if we anticipated them, after all, they would not be surprises). So, why not plan equal amounts of time to deal with both the planned processes and the surprises? If you expect the unexpected, chances are you will start sooner, move forward more carefully, and have time to prevent surprises from becoming crises. I know, I know; this is far easier said than done, but you're planning a local area network here. I had to warn you.

This chapter describes an eight-step planning process for networks. The steps, explained in detail in the following sections, are:

- needs analysis

- site analysis

- equipment matching

- configuration plan

- server directory structure

- configuration lists

- installation schedule

- the system log

Bear in mind that this description is not intended to be a forced march through some rigid formula; instead, be prepared to shift back and forth through the process as your network plan takes shape. Some of these steps influence each other, and it is not unusual to revise your previous decisions based on discoveries you make later.

Also remember that this chapter describes a general network planning process, which could apply to just about any reader. Your business may have unique aspects that are not accounted for here. Feel free, therefore, to approach the process described here as you might any textbook sample business plan— use it as a foundation framework only; alter it and customize it to whatever extent your unique situation requires.

Needs Analysis

Because you are reading this book, it's safe to say that you have already identified one or two organizational issues in your business that you believe a network can effectively address. For example, you may want to centralize your data to improve its accuracy throughout your enterprise, or you may wish to share expensive peripherals, or automate workgroup scheduling and communications.

The first step in developing a needs analysis is identifying and writing down your business problems. In this context, a business problem is not some kind of puzzle to be solved. It is a situation that either costs too much for you to allow to continue, or is a block to additional income that you perceive could be flowing into the business. In other words, your effective needs analysis should revolve around saving or making money. There are any number of ways a network (or for that matter, a stand-alone computer) can help you do business faster or more profitably, but this does not necessarily mean that you can quantify those gains in terms of money saved or earned. Still, it is a good idea to be on the lookout for circumstances in which the addition of technology can be related to your bottom line. For example, you may be able to show that network communications between the order-entry and shipping departments can increase shipping volume. You can then build incentives into the ordering process that encourage customers to order larger quantities of merchandise. Although the relationship between networking and increased orders may not be immediately apparent, it is nonetheless real. Throughout the planning process, strive to avoid even the appearance of introducing new technology merely for its own sake.

Some business bottlenecks are frighteningly complex. It is always a good idea to break a large, complicated problem down into a set of smaller problems. For example, you might notice that the shipping department takes two days to get a package out the door, and this is unacceptably slow, because the competition ships the same day. Stated in this general way, there is no way to know what kinds of solutions are appropriate; "we must ship our orders faster" is too general a solution to be of any use.

However, suppose the problem was that your business rules require the order entry department to record all incoming orders and verify the client's credit before sending the order to shipping. Back when the business was small, order entry and shipping were in the same room, and it wasn't a problem. You've grown bigger now, and order entry is in another room down the hall. The delay occurs because someone in Order Entry has to pick up the confirmed orders and send them down the hall to shipping (using paper, or floppy disk, or whatever). This movement is taking place near the end of Order Entry's work day. So Shipping is always sending orders out the day after your business receives them.

In addition to breaking down the problem into quantifiable smaller problems, you now have a basis for proposing a solution: allow shipping to receive a verified order nearly instantly by sending order confirmations to Shipping through the network.

Following are some examples of other common business problems that you may be able to address by networking:

Need for Data Centralization: If many users address the same data, errors can creep in unless that data is stored in a central location that all users access. This not only applies to business records like customer information, shipping and inventory, and accounting; it can also apply to internal information like boilerplate language and business memos. This type of information is less prone to error when stored, accessed, and updated at a single location. Fewer errors mean less time wasted correcting them, better customer and employee relations, and greater productivity.

Need for Automation: You can automate work flow by sending files across a network. This makes the flow of information faster and less prone to error. As mentioned before, reducing errors can save your business money. Speed is important, but less so than accuracy and reliability. If a speeded-up work flow means that you can handle more information, and this increase in volume translates to greater profits, then you can use "more speed" as a justifiable reason to network.

Need for Communication: Often, you can increase production by making communication easier, both between employees and between employee and customer. Communication, when viewed as a means to save or make money, is a competitiveness issue. For example, if you can service customers more promptly than the other guy, you have a distinct competitive advantage.

Need for Security: No amount of insurance can adequately compensate you for a significant data loss. If your business cannot survive a large-scale loss of data, you may want to use a network to automate the backup procedures; for example, an automated routine can kick in every night and make certain that the day's records are safe from accidental deletions. (See Chapter 12 for further discussion of security, data backups, and other network management issues.)

The next step in developing a needs analysis is to translate your business problems into goals. For example, if you cannot afford a separate high-speed color pen plotter for each stand-alone computer in your business, your goal becomes "implement a system for sharing a single, high-speed color pen plotter."

Restating a problem as a goal gives you an opportunity to quantify the results. For example, you could say that "sharing a single pen plotter will save us thousands of dollars, compared to the cost of purchasing multiple copies of the same device for each desktop."

Similarly, you can establish a goal of "centralizing the order entry and shipping records." You can justify this goal by stating, "This will save us half the cost of our current system (storing paper-based records in a single place rather than two) by consolidating the information on a server disk, and allow us to cut our shipping turnaround time from two days to one day. It will promote additional sales for ourselves on the basis of improved, faster customer service."

The important thing to remember about this step is to write down whatever may be preventing your business from being as profitable as possible, and restate those problems as goals. After that, consider whether a computer network is the appropriate tool for implementing those goals.

Site Analysis

A network has to be installed in a suitable location. The best way to determine your site's suitability for networking is to draw out a site plan. In the case of large networks—the kind that can be spread out all over a building, or between buildings—the site plan can be complex, even incorporated into the architectural renderings. In the case of small local networks, the site plan need only be a simple floor plan.

A good site plan is a drawing that includes the following information:

- The dimensions of the work spaces for each employee on the proposed network (important for determining the installation of the network workstations and servers);

- The locations of electrical outlets, including the devices that are currently using them (important for determining the electrical load distribution throughout the proposed network);

- The location of all immovable objects (support posts, dividing walls, or built-in wall cabinetry, for example);

- The current location of all furniture (important for determining overall network layout, as well as locations for shared devices);

- The current location of all computer equipment (for example, current desktop PCs, also peripheral devices such as printers);

- The locations of doors and windows (important for installing cable);

- The location of ventilation ducts and current electrical wiring (important for cabling very large installations).

A sample site plan is shown in Figure 11.1.

It can be especially useful to draw your site plan to some kind of scale. This does not have to be a strict architectural drawing, but if you apply a consistent scale to your plan, you can use it to make reasonably accurate estimates of the length of cable runs, thus avoiding the strenuous (and occasionally embarrassing) process of running around your plant (over doorways, under desks) with measuring tape. To make your life a little easier, consider investing in one of the many inexpensive software programs that are available for do-it-yourself home remodelers. These products, for very little money, can create scaled floor plans quickly and easily.

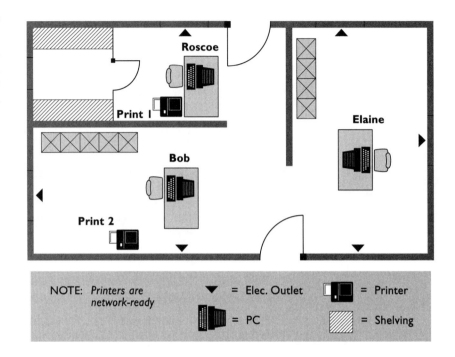

Inventorying Your Equipment

Notice that, as you draw up your site plan, you are also creating an inventory of existing business equipment. This inventory is extremely useful because it will allow you to identify which equipment has enough capability to be incorporated into the proposed network, with or without some degree of modification, and which equipment is likely to become obsolete once the network is installed. This kind of information can reduce your start-up costs and get maximum value from your existing equipment.

Depending on your network, you may be able to extend the life of some of your older workstations by using them as print servers. They may have sufficient memory and hard disk space to handle incoming print jobs intelligently and direct those jobs to printers that are not network-ready. Other older workstations may be able to handle remote access via modem.

As you inventory each piece of your current equipment, you should create a list of each item's features. This information will be immensely valuable throughout the networking process. For example, the feature list for a stand-alone desktop computer would include such information as:

Processor (for example, Intel 80486DX, 100MHz)

Hard disk (for example, Connor 1.2GB)

Monitor (for example, Hitachi 15" VGA)

Floppy Disks if any (for example, one 3.5", 1.44MB)

Also, because you will be incorporating this information into your network system log (as discussed later in this chapter), it would be a good idea to make note of all serial numbers and warranty information for any device that carries an unexpired warranty. You (or your network administrator) may well need this information in the future.

Equipment Matching

Once you have completed your needs analysis and site analysis, you are ready to begin the process of matching the kinds of equipment you need to the goals you have identified. If you have pre-existing equipment that you intend to incorporate into your network, or if your business requires that you adhere to specific technology standards (say, for example, you are required to purchase only Macintosh- or IBM-compatible workstations and printers, to fit as easily as possible into an existing setup), your choices may be limited enough that this step practically takes care of itself. On the other hand, if you are starting completely from scratch, your job is harder; although you have an opportunity to create a system that is a more precise match with your proposed solutions, you also have a larger field of possibilities from which to choose. At this stage, the information in the previous chapters can help you narrow the spectrum of choices. If you still aren't sure, a qualified consultant can help you clarify your options. (Refer to Appendix A for tips on choosing a networking consultant.)

This step in the process will overlap somewhat with the following step, the configuration plan. The configuration plan will be affected to some extent by whatever equipment you select, as will your selection of equipment be influenced by your planned network configuration. Keep everything flexible until you have worked out a good balance of configuration and equipment.

You can also clarify your options by taking your needs analysis and site plan to several vendors, soliciting their recommendations for hardware and software that meets your needs.

Some vendors might be shocked by your level of preparation, even at this stage; many are used to clients who walk in the door with only a vague understanding of how a network will help them. Use this to your advantage. Of course, tell them you are comparison shopping. Encourage them to make competitive bids and get everything they promise in writing.

The recommendations from vendors should be specific, identifying the brands and versions of hardware and software they propose, and also specifying prices, including proposed installation and maintenance services. Also, be certain that the vendor addresses any compatibility issues regarding your current equipment. Be sure to elicit a guarantee from the vendor that all the new and existing hardware you intend to use—especially NICs—is compatible with the exact version of any proposed network operating system.

Take the time to consider the amount of electrical load any proposed system will require. This issue can be especially urgent if you are installing your network in an older building. Ask your vendor for electrical specifications for the equipment you are considering, and try to make a reasonable estimate of power consumption for your existing equipment. Consult your building's owner or builder for electrical specifications; or if necessary, you can hire an electrician to analyze the power capacity and consumption at your site. Do this if you have any doubts whatever about your site's power capacity. An overloaded circuit is a fire hazard and a legal liability, not to mention a golden opportunity to dispatch your spanking-new network into sudden oblivion.

In addition, be sure to talk with your vendor about cabling issues. Using your site plan, you should be able to make reasonably good estimates of how you intend to run the cable throughout your site and how long cable segments will be. A good vendor should be able to tell you if your choices are constrained by cabling requirements.

Use a comparison chart similar to the one shown in Figure 11.2 to list the recommendations of the various vendors you contact. It is extremely helpful to establish a simplified overview of the various recommended products and their price. In addition, preparing the chart will give you an opportunity to find out how much you know about the proposals. You can call the vendors back with additional questions as you complete the comparison chart.

Configuration Plan

Your network configuration plan is based on your site plan and includes the newly added and relocated equipment. Most importantly, you can use the site plan to draw up your cable runs and determine what cable lengths you will need to connect your network. Figure 11.3 shows how the site plan is modified into a configuration plan.

FIGURE 11.2

A sample comparison
chart for establishing an
overview of competing
proposals.

	Vendor A			Vendor B			Vendor C		
	Quantity	Model	Price	Quantity	Model	Price	Quantity	Model	Price
Server:									
Workstation:									
NIC:									
Cabling:									
Kits:									
NOS:									
Apps:									
Connection Hardware:									
Accessories:									
Total Cost:									

FIGURE 11.3

The sample site plan is
modified to include cabling
and relocated equipment.

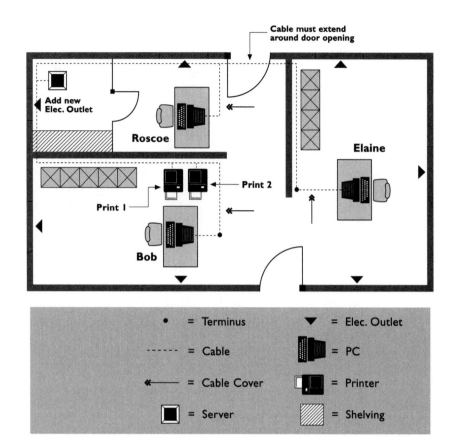

*Cable safety is an important issue. When you draw up your configuration plan, make note
of places where cable might be exposed. Do whatever you can to hide cable, out of sight
(because dangling cables are just plain ugly) but especially out from underfoot. Tripping over
cable leads to significant loss of productivity because of expensive injuries, cooked adapter
cards, and workstations flying off desktops, among other unpleasantness. If you have to run
a cable across an area that is subject to foot traffic, install a cable cover over it. A cable
cover is a piece of hard rubber that looks something like a speed bump. It's very hard to
trip over, impossible not to notice, and will prove that you really are safety-minded, should
you ever need to prove that.*

Server Directory Structure

A server directory structure is a set of named logical addresses on your server's
hard disk, which organize related disk files into logical groups and make
them easier to find. The directory structure begins with a root directory, which

normally holds other directories, which in turn can hold disk files or still more directories, and so on, to whatever depth of organization your system requires. Figure 11.4 shows a fairly typical network directory structure. It is a good idea to set up an initial server directory scheme during your network's planning stages.

The structure of the directories on your servers' hard disks is largely a personal issue. You do have to stay within some fairly broad requirements regarding the directory structure for your network operating system's files, but beyond that, you can set up virtually any directory scheme you like. However, the experience of many network users has shown that some directory structures are more efficient than others. The following general guidelines—and they are only guidelines, not hard-and-fast laws—can help you organize your server's files into an efficient directory structure.

There are certain types of files that can be found on a great many servers. These include:

- network operating system files

- client system files

- application files

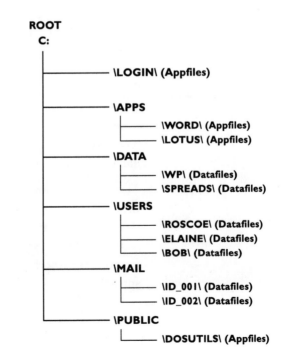

FIGURE 11.4

A typical network directory structure, such as might be found in a NetWare file server.

ROOT
C:

\LOGIN\ (Appfiles)

\APPS
    \WORD\ (Appfiles)
    \LOTUS\ (Appfiles)
\DATA
    \WP\ (Datafiles)
    \SPREADS\ (Datafiles)
\USERS
    \ROSCOE\ (Datafiles)
    \ELAINE\ (Datafiles)
    \BOB\ (Datafiles)
\MAIL
    \ID_001\ (Datafiles)
    \ID_002\ (Datafiles)
\PUBLIC
    \DOSUTILS\ (Appfiles)

- user data files

- shared data files

- e-mail files

Your directory structure should accommodate all of these types.

A modern network operating system comes complete with an automated installation process that will ask you questions about your system and how you intend to use it, and then set up a predesigned directory structure for its operating system files. Unless you have a compelling need to do so, do not make changes to this automated setup. Much of your network's operation will depend on locating the correct operating system files when the time comes, and if you have improperly deviated from your operating system's default directory structure, you can bring the system to a resounding halt.

Certain directory names have become common in the network world, and if you use them properly and keep an accurate system log, other concerned individuals (for example, third-party technical support) will be able to make sense of how your network files are organized. Here are some examples of common directory names:

APPS   This is a fairly standard directory name for software applications that are to be run across the network, or accessed remotely and run locally. Typically, the APPS directory frequently contains no files, but instead contains more directories, each one holding a separate application and its related system files. These applications are frequently installed by means of automated installation software, which will create additional directories below that of the individual application name. If you have no compelling reason to switch the application system files and change the application's directory structure, leave it alone.

DATA   This directory normally holds other directories, containing data files that are unique to a particular application. For example, there could be a subdirectory named WP within the DATA directory, holding document files for a particular word processing program. Another subdirectory, named SPREADS, can hold spreadsheets.

LOGIN — This directory, which appears in NetWare (among other operating systems), is the directory that the client first logs into when accessing the network system. Once the user has made the initial connection, he or she can traverse the directory structure at will—provided he or she has sufficient access rights.

MAIL — This directory holds a database of messages sent and received on the network's communications or e-mail system.

PUBLIC — As the name implies, this directory holds files and other directories that can be accessed from just about anywhere on the network. Although this directory is often assigned a read-only restriction, this is not the place to store secured data. For example, under PUBLIC, you may want to create a subdirectory that holds utilities for a particular operating system used on various client workstations. By storing the utilities in this location, you make them accessible to anyone on the network who needs them.

USERS — This is a common directory name for data files that are the exclusive property of individual users on the network. The USER directory frequently contains no files, but instead contains private directories for users of the system.

As a rule of thumb when organizing directories, remember that the closer you are to the root directory, the closer you are to system-wide organization. In other words, the first level below the root directory is going to be occupied mostly by other directories, which apply to the system as a whole (APPS, USERS). The next level below that will apply to categories within the system-level directories (APPS\WP, USERS\ROSCOE). The next level below that will apply to specifics within each category (APPS\WP\WINWORD); and below that, to files, or still more directories, increasing levels of hair-splitting and possibly diminishing returns.

Bad directory structures are possible. Here are some general principles regarding what to avoid:

Directories that are too shallow: You could conceivably create all your file directories one level below the root. While easy to set up, this structure is woefully inefficient because the network and your users have to battle through a long list of unrelated directories in order to find any given one.

Directories that are too deep: It's not a good idea to go overboard nesting subdirectories below one another. No one wants to log onto a long series of directories like \USERS\ELAINE\WP\MEMOS\INTEROFF to find Elaine's interoffice memos. With the exception of directory structures that are created by automated software installation routines, try to keep your subdirectories nested no deeper than three or four levels.

Duplicate user names: Although it is possible to have a user directory named USERS\ROSCOE and another directory named APPS\WORD\ROSCOE, this kind of design usually points to bad organization. If two or more directories reference the same user, try to redesign the structure so that all user data files are arranged under a single user directory. Figure 11.5 illustrates this problem and one possible solution.

FIGURE 11.5

An example of a bad directory structure and one possible way to correct it. The advantage of the second structure is that all of Roscoe's or Elaine's different data files can be found by logging onto a single USERS subdirectory. This is usually a more efficient means of organizing user files.

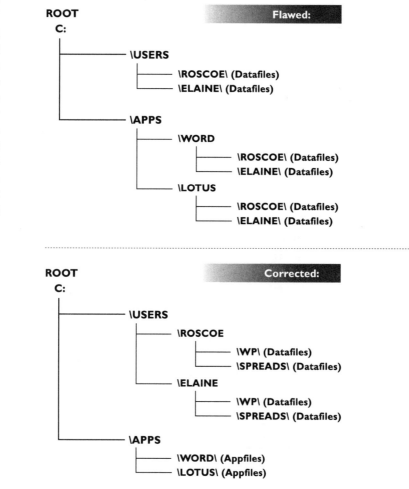

Directory names should make their contents apparent; for example, APPS could suggest a directory containing application files, but a cryptic name like TSD001_C suggests very little. Above all, bear in mind when creating your sub-directory structure that your most efficient solution is likely to be the one that is as shallow and simple as you can make it.

Configuration Lists

After you have drawn up your configuration plan, you will draw up a few important lists. You should make these lists carefully, because the information will go into your network system log:

Machine Name List: You will give each workstation and server on the network a unique name. The choice of name is usually easy to make. Usually machines are named for the user or their function within the network. Keep in mind that machine names are not passwords, and generally are not part of the security system. So, for example, if the machine on the programming desk is being used by Elaine, either "Elaine" or "Programming" would be appropriate names. The list of machine names should also include each machine's location and function: Is the machine a client only, a server only, or both client and server? If it is a server, what responsibilities does it have—for example, it may be a file server (if so, which files?), print server (which printers?), or backup storage (for whom?).

Server Directory List: This is a listing of the directory structure for each server on the network. In its simplest form, this list could be a simple print-out of the directory tree. Many network operating systems have utilities for producing this printout. A hard copy of the directory structure can come in handy, for example, in case of server failure. A hard copy of the system setup can speed up the rebuilding process.

Server Users List: It can be useful to draw up a list, for each server, of machine names with access to that server. Besides the machine names, the list should include such information as the login schedule (days and times when access is permitted), access rights, login expiration date (if any), and password renewal schedule.

Printer List: This list should include configuration information for each printer on the network. Include the name of the printer, its communication port on the print server (for example, LPT1: or COM1:), baud rate (if applicable), and its default configuration. This list can save time and guesswork if you need to replace the printer for any reason.

Bear in mind that, even though this process of assembling lists and documenting your network design is tedious, the information you record now can be a lifesaver when problems crop up. Take the time to record any information, even if it seems trivial. As Roscoe says, "Better to have it and not need it than to need it and not have it."

Installation Schedule

Networks take time to install, and as Murphy's Corollary states, usually more time than planned. Still, creating an installation schedule is important because it allows you an opportunity to get an overview of the process of physically installing the network into your business. You can go over the schedule with co-workers and create a timetable that can anticipate conflicts with work that must be done, conflicts with deadlines, and the like. In addition, an installation schedule will help your co-workers breathe a little easier, because they can prepare for the planned disruptions, while looking forward to a scheduled end of the process.

By all means, and if at all possible, elicit the advice of someone who has installed a system like yours before, and allow extra time for the unexpected. Here are the installation steps you should allow time for:

Step 1—Equipment Purchase: Be ready for shipping delays. If all your equipment does not arrive on schedule, it is probably better to move the entire installation schedule back until all the necessary equipment arrives. In practical terms, you want to avoid a long stretch of downtime during which the network is partially installed and you must wait for a crucial part (a printer, for example, or a segment of cable) to arrive.

When equipment arrives, check it thoroughly for signs of damage, and check the equipment in the carton against the packing list. Do not assume that the packing list is accurate; if there is a mistake, rectify it now, to avoid warranty problems in the future.

Step 2—Read the Manuals: Arrgh! All this neat stuff to play with, and you have to read a bunch of books—sorry, life's like that sometimes. At least read the portions of the manuals that deal with installation and configuration options. Computer equipment changes quickly, and you may find that the configuration you had anticipated has been updated.

Step 3—Prepare the Site: This means moving furniture, taking out obsolete equipment, installing new electrical outlets, and the like. (Maybe you have a co-worker who can help out with this while you're reading all those manuals.)

Get the Users on Your Side

Remember that training is a twofold process. You must do more than acquaint your users with their system's features. You must also enlist them as allies in your trouble-shooting efforts.

This part of the training process is extremely important. One key to quick problem-solving is psychological preparation of your users. Inform them from the beginning that problems are not unusual in the early stages of the network's operation (say this even if, in your heart of hearts, you believe you've got the system set up perfectly). Emphasize to your users that they should avoid, if at all possible, high-pressure situations during this transition period, as those are the times when problems are most likely to appear.

It can be extremely frustrating and anxiety-provoking for a user to experience a work-station shutdown and not have any idea what to do about it, beyond uttering a some-times-embarrassing cry for help. The object of this aspect of training is to give your users permission to experience problems and report them promptly without fear of losing face, regardless of the problem's actual cause.

Train your users to follow a definite procedure for reporting problems to you, and make sure each user is familiar with it and can find it if a problem occurs. Make this procedure quick and easy. A user's response to technical problems can be as basic as referring to a simple problem report form, such as the one shown in Figure 11.6, as they talk to you on the telephone.

The existence of a preplanned response to problems is often more important than the procedure itself. When confronted with an unexplainable problem, the user is more likely to remain calm and communicative if there is a simple, definite plan of action to fall back upon, one that the user feels is easy to follow.

Step 4—Back Up Your Data: A dull step, but vitally important. The last thing you need is an unexpected glitch that destroys files, and you caught without a backup. Think of it as installation insurance. No one has ever felt bad because they made an unused backup.

Step 5—Set Up the Hardware: Now at last you can begin to work with all that new equipment. The most important thing to remember about this phase of the process is to take your time. Careless handling at this stage can ruin a network. Specifically, double-check all switch settings and jumper pin settings (if any), even if you are using the default settings you were told were already set on the shipping product.

| PROBLEM REPORT |

Date _____

Machine Name _____

Reported by _____

Application in Use _____
(When error occurred)

Other Apps in RAM _____
(if known)

_____

Problem Description ··

Please be as specific as you can regarding the sequence of steps that caused the problem, and the exact results.
If any messages were displayed, include them in the space below:

_____

_____

_____

_____

_____

_____

Error Messages _____
(or Error Code Numbers)

_____

_____

Step 6—Install the Software: This could easily be the most time-consuming phase of the project. Again, take your time and double-check all configuration settings. Mistakes are common at this stage; take them in stride and make the necessary corrections. Don't allow your focus to be undermined by pressure to complete the project. Send onlookers and kibitzers away with a confident smile and a polite but firm reminder that they must have work of their own to complete.

Step 7—Test, Test, Test: Chances are you can't do too much testing. Especially test the printer services. Network problems and delays are often related to printing. The goal is to find and eliminate system bugs before the first user logs on. In the real world, this is nearly impossible because users have personal work habits and idiosyncrasies that will reveal problems you never anticipated. However, the next step can help.

Step 8—Training: There are two levels of training. On the first level, you must acquaint users with the network's features and supervise their initial practice until they are comfortable with what is expected of them. On the second level, you should train them in procedures to follow if problems occur. As with every other stage of this process, you should allow plenty of time, and schedule additional time if your users request it.

The System Log

PREVIOUS SECTIONS of this chapter have referred to the *system log*. A system log can be as simple as sheets of paper in a file folder, or as complicated as an entire file cabinet, depending on the size and complexity of your network.

The system log is, in effect, your network's documentation. The purpose of the system log is to provide a detailed history of all your network's hardware, software, and configuration features. It is your most valuable resource when troubleshooting problems.

The only way to keep an accurate system log is to start at the very beginning, writing down any and all system information as your design and install your system. There is very little likelihood that you will find the time to go back and document a system that has been up and running for some time, and that has undergone any number of changes and revisions during that time.

If you are the system manager for your network, do not neglect this important part of your job. Here are some of the items you may wish to include in your system log:

Hardware Warranties: Keep a separate section for warranty agreements for your hardware. Sort them by type: monitors, network interface cards, hard disks, and so on. If the equipment is part of a workstation or server, add the machine name to the warranty and file it according to the machine name.

Equipment Information: For each piece of hardware attached to each machine, store the serial number, make, configuration settings, vendor name and telephone number.

Current Setup Diary: Store the current directory structure and operating system configuration details in a separate section. Be sure to include the date the configuration was installed. Add new, updated configuration information in front of the old—keep the old configurations on file.

Backup Plan: Good network management includes a detailed backup plan, which will be discussed in more detail in the next chapter. Your backup plan should be dated, written down, and stored in the system log. Add new dated updates to the backup plan as necessary, but keep the old plans for reference.

Backup Logs: You should keep a record of when backups are done and who is responsible for doing them. If your backup procedure is automated, the server responsible for backups can print a report, which you can file here.

You can use your computer to assist you in maintaining your system log. A little flat-file database can be handy, or if your budget can cover it, you can purchase one of the many fully featured network management software programs available. However you create it, do not keep your system log stored exclusively on a hard disk. You should have an up-to-date log printed on paper and filed securely, just in case the network goes down and the hard-disk version is inaccessible.

All this planning and writing and filling out of forms is tedious work. If your network is very small (say, a peer-to-peer network with only three or four workstations) it may seem unnecessary. However, it is always necessary. Networks have a tendency to grow more complicated over time. Hardware can fail. Vendors can keep bad records and have short memories when it comes to warranties and promises they made in the heat of trying to make a sale. Some part of your written log, sooner or later, will save you time and money. The only question is how much.

In the next chapter, we move on from this discussion of the system log to a discussion of network management in general.

Network Management

12

LMOST EVERYONE WHO uses a computer must spend some time on management duties. For example, stand-alone PC users are responsible for making sure that their data is properly backed up in the event the PC (or the power company) fails them. In addition, users manage their stand-alone PCs whenever they install software, configure an application, optimize their system's memory usage, or attempt to "tweak" the system for better performance.

As you can surmise from the previous chapters, network management is more complex and demanding than managing a stand-alone PC. Network managers must master a large amount of technical knowledge and must also have human-relations skills to succeed at the job. If the network is large enough, the management responsibilities may be divided between members of a management team; still, whether these duties are carried out by a single person or a team, a computer network is only as good as those who manage it.

Good network managers carry out the following fundamental responsibilities with regard to the network. They must:

- understand the system

- maintain backups

- maintain security

- maintain the system log

- manage printing

- monitor all network functions for maximum efficiency

- evaluate and maintain applications

- keep abreast of changes and updates in the industry

This chapter describes these aspects of a network manager's job.

Understanding the System

I F YOU ARE RESPONSIBLE for hiring the network manager, do so if you can at the beginning of the network planning process, before choosing the network you want to install. The involvement of the manager in all phases of initial planning will help installation and configuration go that much more smoothly. The knowledge acquired during the planning process provides your manager with an invaluable base of information to help with the troubleshooting and upgrade processes that generally occur over the life of your network.

If you are planning to hire a new manager for an existing network, expect that the new manager will need a significant amount of time to become acquainted with your system. Do not assume that previous experience with a similar system means that a new manager can step in without missing a beat. Every network has unique features and idiosyncrasies, and a unique set of users. To understand your system, a good manager requires two things: knowledge of its technical features (which comes from formal training), and knowledge of its real-world performance, which comes only from day-to-day practice. Putting it another way, the longer the manager works with your system, the more valuable he or she becomes.

For example, one of the trickier aspects of network management is installing application software on your network, so that it runs with maximum efficiency. In many cases, the manager will want to place a copy of an application on the hard disk of each workstation that will run the application. This is not the most efficient storage method, but each workstation can then access and run the application locally, reducing network traffic and increasing performance efficiency. This can be the case with traditionally stand-alone applications such as word processors and spreadsheets, where frequent access to overlay files across the network would hamper the network's overall performance, and thus your business's productivity. However, suppose a particular application is not likely to be accessed by more than one user at a time; or the sum of its files is too large for an older model workstation's hard disk; or it is of a type that can be loaded completely into a workstation's memory and then run all day from there (like some simpler spreadsheet software). In these cases, the manager may elect to keep it on the server and let the individual user run it across the network.

With regards to some types of network-specific applications, the manager may find it more efficient, perhaps even required, to store the application on the server. This can be the case with applications such as SQL database server software, which works directly with a shared database on the server and transmits the results of its processing to the workstation. There is simply no increased performance to be gained from running this kind of software locally. Yet, a front-end database (an application that formats the results of a SQL query) may or may not run most efficiently from a local hard disk; the manager may simply have to test different configurations to find out how best to run it on a given system.

You can take the above examples as a basis for a general rule-of-thumb on network software (stand-alone applications tend to work best locally, and network-specific applications tend to work from the server) but exceptions abound. You must be prepared to make necessary changes and improvements to your system, and gain valuable experience.

With regard to data files, the subject can get even thornier, as individual user preferences and work styles influence how data files are to be stored on the network. As before, a consistent rule-of-thumb is hard to come by, but you may be able to start with this: Whenever possible, store client/server data files on the server, to make backups more efficient and backup routines more reliable. However, encourage users to make separate backups of their most critical files.

On peer-to-peer systems, data file integrity can be a more complex issue. If there is little need for sharing centralized data files, as may be the case on many peer-to-peer systems, you may consider allowing individual users to take local responsibility for the integrity of their own data files and use a specialized node for storing backups. As mentioned before, be prepared to make changes to your system as needs evolve, and as you gain more experience and learn what is desirable and possible.

Backing Up the Data

MAKING RELIABLE DATA backups is arguably the most important job a network administrator has. You can replace hardware and software, you can move to a new location, you can hire new employees, your company can start over with a new manager if it must. But if you lose your data and have no backup, you are either out of business or starting over from scratch.

Data on a network tends to be massive. It is stored either in a centralized server, or distributed among multiple servers throughout the network. In either case, the process of making reliable backups is far more complicated than it was in the days of stand-alone desktop PCs, where individual users took responsibility for making their own backups.

A network manager has to make careful decisions about what to back up, when to back it up, and where to store the backed-up data. This section provides some general guidelines for making those decisions.

Most local area networks use an automated system to make backups at regularly scheduled intervals. It makes sense to use an automated system because of the large amounts of data that are typically stored on networks, the added convenience of programming backups to occur during off-peak times, when data traffic is minimal, and the freedom to impose a disciplined backup schedule on the computer rather than on yourself.

There are several types of automated backup systems. For example, Chapter 6 described a particularly rigid form of data backup: RAID systems, which make backup copies of the data on separate hard disks as it is being created or modified. Other networks use dedicated servers to retrieve and store backup data.

Software vendors, recognizing our anxiety over data loss and our demand for reliable backups, have responded with dozens of programs for automating backups of data distributed across networks. Examples of such programs are: ArcSolo Backup (Cheyenne Software); Backup Exec for Windows NT (Arcada software); and Norton Backup (Symantec). These are just examples, not recommendations. You should evaluate as many different backup software and hardware systems as you can before making a final selection of an automated system that's right for you.

Tape cartridges are a common storage medium for backup data. To use a tape-based backup system, you install special tape-handling hardware in one or more servers; these devices use high-speed copying technology to reproduce data on the tapes from the server's disk. Tape backup systems come with software that you can program to log onto the computer after hours, perform the backup, and log off automatically.

After-hours backups are convenient, but you should take care that your automated tape backup system has access to your network during times when it would be the most difficult for others to enter your building and acquire access to the servers. (When an automated backup is in process, a determined hacker would find it far easier to access the system.) You might have the backup procedure take place when trusted employees are still at hand to keep an eye on things. Assign limited read-only and copy-only rights to your automated backup system, and make sure you program it to log off quickly when the backups are complete.

Tape is especially useful as a backup medium because the cartridges can be carried off-site and stored in a secure separate location, such as a bank safe deposit box. Off-site storage is an effective and frequently employed strategy for insuring against loss from disasters such as floods or fires. Tape backup systems can have their disadvantages, though; in particular, they can be somewhat rigid if you want to restore just one or two files. You may need to restore whole groups of files just to get the ones you want, or muddle through a complex user interface to mark specific files for restoration. Nevertheless, for many users, the advantages (speed and built-in scheduling) outweigh the disadvantages (rigidity).

Whether or not you employ a tape backup system, individual users on the network would be wise to make personal backups of critical data files onto floppies. It is far easier to make the restoration of single files from floppies. It may be possible to create batch files or scripts that start an application and upon exiting, automatically make floppy-disk backups of new or revised data files from your data subdirectory. Nothing like forcing good habits upon yourself.

What to Back Up

You need to back up application software files less often than data files. If you have master installation disks, make backups of these before installing the software. If you installed the software from a CD-ROM disk, or if the installation and configuration process was particularly complex, you may want to make a backup of the installed files off the hard disk, to avoid having to re-install the application from scratch.

Back up the configuration files for application software separately. Make a new backup of the configuration files each time you update the configuration for any reason.

Once you have one or two good backups of your application software files, you need not continue to make them. This will save you time because software application files comprise a considerable amount of the data on your hard disks, and there is no need to back up files continually if they rarely change.

If you have a well-organized directory structure, you will store your data files in directories that are separate from your software application files. Automated backup software allows you to specify exactly which directories (and which files within those directories) you need to back up on a regular basis.

One structure I've had success with is to place all repeatedly backed-up files in directories under a single \USERDATA directory, and give \USERDATA a virtual drive letter. Users (and the backup software) see something like G:\BOB, when on the server it's actually C:\USERDATA\BOB, or whatever. A directory structure like this can get complicated, but it's possible to hide the directory's complexities from the user.

In addition to everyday data files, you must also make regular backups of your network system data. Different networks manage their system data in different ways, but some examples of the types of system files you should back up include:

- security files (such as access-rights information files)
- directory structures
- login script files
- user information files
- workgroup information files
- workstation configuration files

It is the manager's responsibility to understand the system well enough to make careful note of network-specific data files that must be backed up on a regular basis.

Do not back up your passwords. If you must, be certain they are encrypted. Passwords are always rigorously memorized, never written down, and never backed up. You'll learn more about passwords later in this chapter.

Once you have used your automated backup software to mark your critical data files, you are ready to make scheduled backups. You have taken your first steps toward data security. However, you must still determine your backup schedule.

When to Back Up

Data backup schedules answer a central question that the network manager must reckon with: How much data can your business afford to restore from scratch? Of course, no one wants to lose any data at all, but if a loss does strike, how much loss is too much—a day's worth? An hour's worth? The less you can afford to lose, the more time you will spend making and maintaining backup data.

Most experienced managers use some form of a staggered backup system. For example, they may make a fresh set of backup tapes daily, reusing old backup tapes after a specific period of time (a week to a month is fairly common). This method is based on the idea that backup data becomes obsolete after it reaches a certain age, and therefore can be overwritten by more recent data. Using a series of backup tapes also provides an extra level of insurance: Should errors creep into the most recent backup, you could fall back on the next most recent, and with luck would lose only slightly more time bringing the older backup data current.

Some managers, in addition to daily backups, make complete backups at regular intervals (perhaps once a week, or once or twice a month). These backups are stored both for archival purposes and for emergency restorations when other backups are lost. They are permanent, never overwritten.

There is a curious irony with regard to backups: the most experienced and professional managers are fanatical about backups, and keep multiple sets in one form or another. Also because of their experience and professionalism, they tend to have fewer problems with their systems and have less need to actually use the backups they so fanatically maintain. Nevertheless, you should emulate those managers; they sleep better at night.

Types of Backups

There are three basic strategies for maintaining multiple backup sets:

Full Backup: In a full backup, all your critical data is backed up. As you would expect, this has the disadvantage of taking the most time and requiring the largest amount of backup storage space. It has a distinct advantage, however, if you need to restore the data. All the most recent versions of your data files are conveniently stored together in a single, albeit large, package. At a minimum, you must make a full backup at least the first time you back up your data.

Incremental Backup: This backup system reads file attributes to determine which files were added or modified since the last backup. Only the modified files are actually backed up. This is the fastest backup process, since it copies the fewest files, but restoration can be a chore. To get a failed system back to normal, you must restore your most recent full backup, followed by each incremental backup made since the full backup. If you have not made a full backup in a while, this type of restoration can be tedious.

Differential Backup: This system falls in between the first two. It reads the data file date attributes, and backs up only those files that were added or changed after the last *full* backup. This often takes a little longer than the incremental backup, but it makes restoration more predictable. To bring a failed system back to normal, you have to restore the last full backup, followed by the last incremental backup.

It is impossible to overemphasize the importance of making regular and reliable backups. Once you have settled on a backup procedure, test it from time to time to make sure that the backups are both complete and reliable. If you are a network manager, you simply cannot afford surprises when it comes to the quality of your backup data.

Maintaining the System Log

In the previous chapter, you learned about starting your system log during the network's planning process. This section examines the elements of a network system log in more detail. Bear in mind that your network may have special features not described here, but which you should document in the system log nonetheless. In general, a good system log is your best evidence that you understand your system, and your business's best insurance against system-wide failure or your temporary unavailability (for example, it would be a shame to have to come back early from your well-deserved vacation in Tahiti because some simple glitch popped up in the system while you were away).

Many modern network operating systems come with worksheets and forms that you can fill out to maintain your system log. Take these forms seriously. They are a time-saver. You can find many automated network management software packages that help you maintain an up-to-date system log. However, do not assume that prepackaged forms and management software will take care of your system log completely. Certainly add your own information. The subtitle of your system log should be "No Surprises."

Here are some of the fundamental ingredients of a system log:

Hardware Specifications: Keep lists of specifications for all your server and workstation hardware. These lists should include make and model names, serial numbers, internal network numbers, warranty information, as well as the names of the manufacturer, vendor, and installer. Include such hardware devices as disk drives, network interface cards, monitors, printers, and any peripheral devices such as modems. Also remember to store information about add-on equipment such as routers and transceivers. Finally, remember to keep files of your purchase records and payment receipts.

Boot Files: Keep printouts of all your server and workstation boot files; for example AUTOEXEC.BAT and CONFIG.SYS, for DOS-based workstations and servers.

Directory Structure: Keep dated printouts of the directory structure. Add a new printout each time you update the structure. Include volume and directory names, attributes, and access rights. Most network operating systems include a utility for producing a printout showing how directories are organized and nested below one another; for example, NetWare uses a command called LISTDIR to produce such a printout.

User Profiles: As a minimum, keep a printout of each user's machine name, given name, groups to which they belong, login script, and access rights.

System Login Scripts: If your network uses a system login script, keep a dated copy on file. Keep a copy of default login scripts that users without individual scripts may need to use.

Configuration Diary: These records represent a history of your server and workstation configuration changes. Be sure to include configuration records of installed hardware such as network interface cards. When you update a configuration, store a dated printout of the new version along with the old. It helps to keep a copy of previous configurations; you may find it necessary to go back to an old configuration someday.

Pay special attention to the configuration of workstation and server RAM. For example, make notes of how RAM has been allocated for such features as file cache buffers and memory-resident utilities. Also keep track of how various devices, such as printers and modems, use communications ports and internal interrupts. This information is especially useful for tracking down and troubleshooting network conflicts.

Software Diary: Keep version numbers, licensing information, and locations of your installed software applications. Keep the names of valid users and who originally installed the software. As you did with hardware, keep purchase, warranty, and payment records on file as well.

Hardware and Software Standards: Keep (and distribute) a list of standard hardware types and software applications that you have approved for use on your network. This amounts to a policy statement regarding the types of hardware and software for which you will furnish support. Users love to add their own personal items to their workstations (screen savers are a notorious example), and sometimes these items interfere with the network. If you have a support policy in place, you are in a better position to exert some small measure of control and expertise with regard to what the network will tolerate.

Backup Schedules: Keep records of how data backups are made and what files are backed up. If you are using an automated backup system, your backup software may print a log of the files you backed up, when the backup took place, and if any errors occurred during the process. If you are backing up manually, keep a checklist showing when you made the backup and what type it was (full, incremental, or differential).

Printing Configuration: Keep a record of printer configurations, names, internal network numbers, port and interrupts used, and printer queue information. Because printing often is a problem on a network, complete documentation regarding printers can be very important. Refer to the section on printing later in this chapter.

Security Procedures: Keep (and distribute) a written policy regarding procedures and access rights for new and current users. Include such things as when passwords must be changed, and limitations on the types of passwords that you have configured the system to accept. Refer to the section on security later in this chapter for more details.

A good system log can save you time and money when problems arise. For example, you can use the system log to look up the commands for undoing some minor configuration change without endlessly searching through thick volumes of vendor-supplied documentation. A network log gives you the power to enforce security practices and to maintain hardware and software standards consistently, which will reduce users' anxieties—even if on occasion

Remote Management

Backups, system logs, controlling access, maintaining security—it's a big job, and as you might expect, software vendors are doing their level best to create applications that they tout as tools to simplify and streamline the job. Mostly, these tools enhance utilities that you may already find supplied with your network operating system. The best of them allow you to diagnose and fix workstation and server problems across the network, rather than having to visit workstations in person. If your network is so large and complicated that you spend as much time traveling between workstations as you do actually servicing them, it's time to look into installing remote management software.

Here are some examples of software programs that offer remote management tools. Bear in mind that these are simply examples, not recommendations. Check out as many different brands as possible before you buy:

- LANDesk Management Suite (Intel Corp.)

- Norton Administrator for Networks (Symantec)

- Systems Management Server (Microsoft)

you have to deny them some cute little utility or game they just could not resist bringing in from home. You just may find that, in return for all the trouble you put into it, your network log saves your career someday.

Evaluating Applications

THE WORKSTATION REPRESENTS your network to your users. It is important to keep the workstation interface as consistent and easy to use as possible. A network manager can accomplish this by loading applications that are used by everyone, but allow for some degree of customization to individual user preferences. Modern, well-written applications for networks have these features built in, but it is the network manager's responsibility to evaluate software before it goes on the network, to be certain that it implements those features in a manner consistent with the network configuration and other applications you have already installed. Also, if you find that pressing needs for a specific application require you to adjust your users' interface, you will need to understand those adjustments well enough to explain them to your users and provide some training, thereby keeping your users interested in the network and productive while they are using it.

Of course, the network-readiness discussed here is not the only consideration in evaluating application software. The network manager also needs to consult with knowledgeable users and department managers about the performance and application features of the software being evaluated. Will it meet the users' needs as a word processor, or spreadsheet, or whatever?

Here are some features to look for when evaluating applications for possible installation on your network:

Compatibility: Most software vendors will assure you that their application is compatible with your network. Do not take these claims at face value, however. Some networks have features that may conflict with a software application. Obtain a guarantee from your vendor that, should the application prove incompatible with your network, you can return it within a reasonable time for a full refund.

An Installer's Work Is Never Done

Even after you install a software application on your network and it appears to be running properly, keep an eye on its performance for a while. You may have to make some additional changes to the application's standard configuration in order to get reliable performance on your network. Some things to look out for:

Setting File Attributes: After installation, check the file attributes for the application files you have just installed. Normally, you would mark application software files as shared and read-only, but there may be exceptions; for example, some applications need to make changes to some of their system files while they are running. Also, you will normally mark an application's data files as read/write, but you may want to mark some files as read-only; for example, files that contain default information you do not want the user to change.

Setting User Rights: After installing, check to be certain that newly created directories have the appropriate access rights. Normally, Read and File Scan rights are enough for directories of application files, but a specific application may require a different directory setup. Also, you may have to configure an application to find its data files in different user directories, depending on the access workstation or the name of the user launching the application.

Changing Workstation Configuration: Automated installation routines sometimes make changes to workstation configuration files (for example, CONFIG.SYS and AUTOEXEC.BAT on DOS-based systems, or WIN.INI and SYSTEM.INI in Windows-based systems). A good automated installation program will notify you of the changes it intends to make and give you the option of making them right away, or creating copies of the configuration files for you to edit manually. You must understand your system well enough to know how these automated configuration changes may impact your network's performance. The information in your system log can be a helpful reference during these times.

Temporary Files: Many applications create temporary files on disk while they are running. If the application attempts to write these files to a directory where it does not have read/write access, it may lock up or fail without warning or error messages.

Support for Simultaneous Users: Beware of installing applications that are designed for a stand-alone environment. Although you can usually get such applications to run on a network, you must take special care to configure your network to allow only one user at a time to operate these programs.

- For example, you may have to install the application on a single user's subdirectory, or launch the application with a special script or batch file that changes other users' access rights to the data files while the application is in use, and restores the original access rights when the user exits the application. These are fairly complicated configuration issues, and difficult to set up and maintain.

- In addition, when you install stand-alone software on your network, you may be required to take special action with regard to licensing fees, or pay a separate fee for each user of the application.

- When you can, avoid installing stand-alone applications on your network altogether. Fortunately, most major software programs are available in network-aware versions.

Directory Organization: An automated installation routine is standard for any modern software product, as is the ability to install the software in a default directory, or one of your own choosing. Still, you may encounter an application that will not allow you complete flexibility with regard to the directory locations for its files. Be certain that you can install the software in a directory configuration that will fit comfortably within your current directory structure. Otherwise, you may be introducing a complicated exception to your painstakingly planned directory structure, which may have an adverse impact on your network's overall ease of use. For example, it could complicate your automated backup procedures.

Security

N ETWORK SECURITY is a balancing act for the system manager. Data on local area networks can be distributed throughout the system on different servers, and users who legitimately need the data must have flexible access to it. On the other hand, flexible access for legitimate users is an obstacle to security. How can you keep the data accessible and keep it away from unauthorized users at the same time?

Breaches of network security can come from malicious sources (disgruntled employees, competitors stealing trade secrets, immature thrill-seeking hackers, or computer viruses, to mention a few), but just as often your network data can be damaged because of simple mistakes. In practice, the latter problem is more common, and harder to ward off than the former, because it is difficult to predict how someone might unintentionally corrupt data. This means that reliable data backups are just as much a security measure as anything you read about in this section.

There are two overall aspects to computer security: first, granting particular users permission to access the network on any level; and second, after allowing access to an authorized user, granting permission to access particular data in restricted ways. The first level of security involves programming your network to identify legitimate users and lock out those it does not recognize. The second level involves granting authorized users specific sets of *access rights* to files as well as attaching certain attributes to files that restrict what users may do with them.

Global Network Access Security

There are three ways your network can identify users and grant them permission to access it:

Permission based on who you are: This is the most secure system, because it identifies users based on unique physical attributes: Examples of who-you-are systems include finger and palm print readers, among other expensive and sophisticated identification devices. You can find examples of them near the entrances to restricted areas in airports.

Permission based on what you have: This is a frequently used system. It recognizes authorized users and grants access if they have a key to insert into a lock, or a magnetic card to slide through a card reader. The weakness of these devices is that they can be stolen or replicated and thus fall into the wrong hands.

Permission based on what you know: This is a common access system, but it has certain glaring weaknesses. Examples include secret passwords, lock combinations, or personal identification numbers (PINs). The most prominent weakness of this system is its requirement that the identifying knowledge (for example, a secret password) must be memorized. Passwords must be chosen carefully; the password must be at the same time unique, impossible to guess, and easy to remember. Passwords and lock combinations can be forgotten, or if written down somewhere, found and "stolen" by others, without leaving evidence that a theft has taken place.

Password access is also subject to accidental abuse; for example, a legitimate user can log into the network and then walk away from the workstation without logging out, leaving the workstation vulnerable to anyone who happens along.

You can create a good security system using a combination of the second two levels of permission. Systems like these require that you combine some item the user must have (for example, a card with a magnetic stripe that you insert in a reader) with something the user must know (a password or PIN). Bank teller machines use this type of security system and have good results most of the time. If your network has extremely sensitive data that must be kept from unauthorized access, your vendor can supply you with magnetic card readers that will secure your workstations and servers in a manner similar to bank ATMs.

Another frequently used level of security is to lock away the file server behind a physical barricade (in a locked room, for example). Only those with the key to the room can get access to the server. Servers are often locked away because competent hackers can be very successful at bypassing network security systems if they are allowed direct physical access to the file server.

If locking a file server in a separate room is impractical or impossible (for example, if there is no good ventilation or air-conditioning in that storage closet), consider the simple expedient of using a machine with a security lock. This lock prevents access to the machine using the keyboard or other input device. A locked machine will at least force a determined hacker to carry a set of tools to open up the server and bypass the keyboard lock; with any luck it will slow down the whole process enough to discourage the would-be hacker altogether.

Many local-area networks that do not have especially sensitive information will settle for a network access system based on passwords. You have read about how passwords are used in network operating systems (Chapter 8) and client software (Chapter 9). The following are principles for selecting, storing, using, and updating passwords, to achieve maximum levels of security and effectiveness:

- Use passwords that are at least six characters long. (Eight characters, or even ten character are exponentially even better.) The longer the password, the longer it takes to guess it. The longer it will take someone to break into your system, the less likely they will want to attempt it. For example, automatic password-guessing software can find a four-letter password in a matter of minutes; a five-letter password may take hours; a six-letter password can take many hours, even days.

- Use passwords that combine letters and numbers. These are much harder to guess than simple names or ordinary words. Even if you simply insert a single number somewhere within an ordinary eight-character password, you significantly complicate things for a hacker.

- Most network operating systems can lock out a user altogether after a certain number of incorrect password attempts. Use this feature if you can. This will discourage someone who attempts to enter your system using automated password-guessing software.

- Change passwords regularly. How regularly is a matter of how often it takes for you to feel comfortable. Change the password daily if your data is especially sensitive, and likely to attract unauthorized access by talented hackers (an example of such data would be student grade records). You can change passwords less often if your data is less sensitive or not very valuable to unauthorized outsiders (for example, business records that do not involve trade secrets).

- The users with the most extensive access rights and most power to make changes to the system (for example, the network supervisor) must change their password most often. Those with fewer access rights can change their password less often.

- Although it usually seems an extreme measure, you might want to update passwords for everyone in the system when an employee who is particularly computer-savvy—and particularly angry or malicious—leaves the company.

- If you think you can get away with it, pick passwords for your users instead of allowing them to pick their own. They will not like it, but unsophisticated users tend to settle for easily-hacked passwords (phone numbers, family names, pets, and the like).

- Finally, it's been said before in this book but it bears repeating here: Never store your password anywhere in written form, or anywhere on the network unless encrypted by the system. Do not tell others your password, or if you must, change it shortly thereafter. In short, do not allow it to be appropriated by curious eyes and ears.

Access Rights

All networks allow you to establish access rights to the network data. They differ in their degree of sophistication and complexity. For example, NetWare has a complete and thorough system of access rights. It allows you to set up specific restrictions on what kinds of modifications are allowed to directories and the files they contain, by attaching a letter-coded attribute to files and directories. In addition, you can limit the file-creating and file-modifying abilities of certain types of users, and limit those rights to specific files and directories as well. As a more detailed example, here are the common file access rights of NetWare users, which the system manager can grant in any combination:

RIGHT	LETTER	EFFECT
Access Control	A	User can change other's access rights
Create	C	User can create new files and directories
Erase	E	User can delete files and directories
File Scan	F	User can view the contents of file directories
Modify	M	User can change file names and file attributes
Read	R	User can only read contents of files
Write	W	User can modify files
Supervisor	S	Combines all rights listed above

The system manager assigns these rights using utilities provided with the network operating system. Of course, the utilities themselves are secured, and access rights to them are usually limited to the system manager alone.

Depending on your network operating system and hardware, you may have other techniques at your disposal for securing your system. For example, some networks allow you to restrict access to certain regularly-scheduled periods of time, on a user-by-user basis. You could use a feature like this to keep individuals off the system after hours. Your network may allow you to force users to log out of the system at closing time. Your network may use workstations that do not have floppy disks, to prevent copying of files; or you may be able to configure your servers to boot only from a hard disk, thereby preventing someone from gaining access to the hard disk by booting from a floppy.

Your most important allies in your quest for perfect network security are your users. Impress upon them the importance of network security and seek their assistance in designing the sort of security system that you and they can feel comfortable using.

Firewalls

With the increasing demand for remote access to networks over the Internet, security becomes more complicated. You may want to make your Internet host site available twenty-four hours a day to Internet users. The object of firewall security is to allow public access to some parts of your system and prevent access to other parts. The software that accomplishes this task is called a *firewall*. Simply put, a firewall is a security system that selectively denies all access to designated portions of your network, based on how the network is accessed. For example, if someone were to access a workstation by modem, only designated files and directories would be visible. From the remote user's point of view, no other network features would exist. A local user at the same workstation, however, might be able to access more services (such as a printer, or additional file servers).

Reliable, commercially available firewall software is just coming onto market; it tends to be expensive (for example, Gauntlet, a firewall product from Trusted Information Systems, requires on-site installation and training at high cost). Tool kits are available to build your own firewall systems, if you like. You can find one such tool kit on the Internet at

```
ftp://ftp.tis.com/pub/firewalls/toolkit
```

Printing

THE PAPERLESS OFFICE remains an elusive ideal of enterprise computing. In the real world, a significant amount of the network manager's time will be spent maintaining the network's ability to produce printed information for users.

Network printers have become quite flexible. They can be attached to special *print servers*, workstations whose function is to receive data from other workstations and direct it to printers. Printers can be attached to workstations using one of the available *communications ports*.

A communication port is a hardware device; that is, a receptacle into which you plug the printer cable. These receptacles have addresses that are recognized by the operating system. Ports with addresses LPT1, LPT2, and LPT3 handle parallel communications; that is, data that is sent in 8-bit chunks. Ports COM1, COM2, COM3, and COM4 handle serial communications; that is, data that is sent in a continuous stream of bits.

Any workstation can be a print server, as long as it has a communications port to which a printer's cable can be attached. The network manager configures the network operating system to recognize the workstation address and communications port as a local printing device, and in certain cases may choose to assign specific access rights to that printer.

Many modern printers are now *network-aware,* meaning that they come equipped with their own network interface cards and can be attached directly to the network cable. These printers act like network nodes; the network operating system can handle the printer server tasks and direct data to them as if they were other workstations on the network.

You can connect the printer to a communication port on the file server if you like. In this setup, the file server must allocate some of its processing time to act as a print server. Since this increases server overhead, it is only a possible configuration, not a preferred one.

The Print Queue

Network printers receive requests to print information from all over the network. Printer management revolves around the maintenance of the *print queue,* a utility that stores the print job requests and directs them to the print server in order.

Print queues use directories on the server's hard disk to store print jobs as data files to be sent to the printer. These data files contain both the information to be printed and instructions to the printer regarding how the information is to be formatted on the page.

In their simplest form, print queues simply hold onto the jobs and direct them to the printer in the order received. However, if you were to leave it simply at that, you would probably find yourself dealing with unfortunate printing bottlenecks: Imagine that you have to print a one-page letter and get it in the mail right away, but you cannot because the network printer is in the middle of printing a 500-page report. To avoid unpleasant situations like this, the network manager (or a designated print server manager) relies on software utilities to control the flow of print job information to print queues and from print queues to the various printers on the network.

The network manager uses a print queue management utility to access these print job files and direct them to specific printers on the network, to assign priority to one job over another, and to temporarily suspend a current print job and allow another to be printed. The network manager can automate the printing schedule, allowing print jobs to be stored and sent to the printer after hours, when there is no other network traffic on the system to slow down the printing process.

The network manager can also assign more than one print queue to a printer. This is done to allow high-priority documents to go to high-priority queues, while lower-priority documents go to lower-priority queues. The network manager or network operating system can monitor all the queues for a printer and allow those waiting in the high-priority queues first access to the printer, regardless of the order in which the print jobs were received from the network.

The network manager can also assign multiple printers to a single print queue. You might do this on networks where large amounts of data are printed, and fast output is more important than any attempt to prioritize the print jobs. In this case, the print queue keeps track of printers that are idle and ready to receive data, and it directs waiting print jobs to the next available printer.

If you choose to assign multiple printers to a single print queue, be sure that all the assigned printers are of the same type and configuration. You must do this because a print queue normally has no intelligence of its own about which one of multiple printers might end up receiving information stored in the queue. Since the print job file contains formatting instructions, it's important that the receiving printer understand those instructions. If all the printers are the same model and configuration, the problem never arises.

Solving Common Printer Problems

Efficient printing is a challenge for most network managers, who can expect to spend some time troubleshooting problems. This section offers some suggestions on how to deal with printing problems.

Many printing problems are the result of faulty hardware. The first thing to check when a problem occurs is the printer cable. Printing cables can come loose, and need only be tightened to restore the system to normal again. If a printer cable is cut or shows signs of damage, it should be replaced.

Before you play with a printer cable, be sure to turn off the printer power. If you can, turn the printer server's power off as well. Pressing a loose cable back into place, or even wiggling a printer cable with the power on can cause your network to suffer severe and permanent damage.

Sometimes a printer has simply gone off line, or paper has jammed inside the printer in a spot that is hard to see. The printer may simply have run out of paper. Sometimes the simplest solutions are the easiest to overlook.

Another common cause of printing problems is a corrupted print queue. If necessary, use your network's print queue management utilities to clear all print jobs and send them again, or if necessary, delete the print queue altogether and reinstall it.

Check the print server's setup and be certain that the interrupts used by the printer port do not conflict with interrupts used by the network or other peripheral devices connected to the printer server. (For more information on system interrupts, refer to Chapter 4.) If you find an interrupt conflict, you must take the time to reconfigure your hardware.

If a printer fails to respond at all, check the printer configuration and be sure it is connected to the correct port and that the network is configured to recognize a printer at this port address.

If the printout is garbled, the user may be using an application that is configured to format documents for a different printer. Be sure that the application is using the correct printer driver, and that the job is being sent to the correct printer.

Keeping Up

THE NETWORKING INDUSTRY is growing and maturing at a rapid rate. Networks tend to grow larger and more complicated over time. Over the life of your system, you can expect that you will be called upon to upgrade and expand it several times. To maintain and upgrade your system at maximum efficiency, stay abreast of the developments in the field; your knowledge of the latest resources and techniques is a valuable asset for your business, your users, and yourself. Although this takes time, it is not difficult.

Good information is available from a number of periodicals that deal with LAN management issues. Of course, you should pay a visit to the computer-magazine section of your local bookstore or newsstand to find periodicals whose style and content appeal to you, and subscribe. For starters, here are two periodicals to look for that deal in depth with LAN management issues:

LAN Times, 151 East 1700 South, Suite 100, Provo, UT 84606, 801/379-5850

Info World, 155 Bovet Road, Suite 800, San Mateo, CA 94402, 800/227-8365

In the next chapter, we will look closely at the manager's biggest single responsibility: the network databases.

Networking the Database—and Beyond

PART

5

Client/Server
Databases

A S YOU'VE PROGRESSED through this book, you have learned that the most important reason networks exist is to provide shared access to data. It is important that you organize your shared data as efficiently as possible. If the data on your network is scattered about in a disorganized way, the network's performance suffers.

Ideally, shared data should be stored in a format that makes it quickly accessible to all users and allows those users to view and work with the data using different applications. While users are accessing that data in individual ways, they must be assured of its continual reliability and accuracy.

A computer can maintain data, and keep it flexible, accessible, and reliable by storing it in a *database*. We've looked at databases briefly before: In Chapter 6, we looked at their relationship with file servers. In Chapter 10, we looked at them as network applications. This chapter focuses in a more detailed way on their organization and structure, the rules of information storage and access that are unique to relational databases and give them their central importance in the world of client/server networks.

We'll begin with a definition: *a database is a set of raw data elements organized into tables of rows and columns, which define common features of the data, and can be accessed and modified by one or more users to produce useful information.*

There are plenty of examples of databases in the everyday world of work, many of them not found on computers. For example, a database can be:

- a Rolodex file

- an address book

- a desk calendar

- a case of floppy disks

- a pencil holder

- a file cabinet

- some baseball cards stuffed in a shoebox

In each case above, an organizing entity contains items or information that are in some way related to each other. By grouping related items together, you make access to those items easier.

In the networking world, you have a situation in which several users are looking to access the same set of raw data. Each user has a particular purpose in mind when working with that data, and they will all access it in individual ways using unique applications. The purpose of a client/server database is to make the stored data available to different users at different times and for different purposes, while keeping its underlying organizational structure intact.

Advantages to Using Databases

YOU CAN STORE your business information just about any way you want, and businesses have discovered many different means of doing so. Some of these are clearly more efficient than others. Using a computerized database to store your business's information has certain obvious advantages.

Reducing Data Redundancy

Ideally, you will attempt to store each item of raw data in the database only once. When a data item is stored only once in the system, it can be modified quickly and reliably—rather than having to modify the same item of information that may be duplicated in several locations in different formats throughout your system, you need only modify it once in a single location. Then, any user or program can immediately access the updated data from different remote locations. It is up to the computer to make this access possible, and manipulate all the raw data items, assembling and reassembling them into meaningful information.

However, as a practical matter, some duplication of the raw data does occur within an enterprise-wide database. This duplication is allowed when the performance advantages outweigh the problems inherent in duplication. For example, it may be faster to access copies of certain subsets of data off local servers rather than a single distant one, since access via local servers can reduce data traffic across the network as a whole. (You can easily visualize this principle: Imagine what life would be like in a big city if it had only one supermarket, instead of several.) Still, database designers spend as much time as possible trying to avoid data redundancy.

Access to a Common Storage Pool

One way in which a database manipulates its raw data is by presenting it in different formats, depending on how it is being used. A database may produce output that is text-based, such as a report of earnings and expenses, to format using a word processor. Or it may produce output that is table-based, such as a budget comparison, for importing into a spreadsheet and performing what-if analysis. In both cases, the computer acts as an intermediate mechanism to access the same data. The underlying repository of data is stored in a given physical structure, and presented in different logical formats for the sake of the different users.

In addition, by maintaining data in a stored format that is independent of its displayed format, you have a degree of freedom to make changes to its underlying structure while making few, if any, changes to the presentation formats.

Enhanced Security

In Chapter 12, you saw how data can be secured from the system-wide level down through the individual data file level. A database can take this security system further. Most shared database systems provide mechanisms that can control users' access to groups of records, columns, or even individual data elements within a table. These mechanisms are somewhat like the write-protecting mechanisms for rows and columns in spreadsheet programs, with the added ability to shield selected units of data from users' view altogether.

Simultaneous Access to Information

A database can allow more than one user to access different parts of its stored records simultaneously. Databases protect their data by implementing a system of *locks*. As you saw in Chapter 10, a lock is simply an electronic mark associated with a data element (or group of elements, such as a record, or series of records) that acts as a signal to alert other users that one user has accessed the data, has possession of it, and may be making changes to it. The computer prevents further changes to locked data until the first user has finished processing. When the user finishes, the database releases the lock and another user may have access to the data.

Normally the placing and releasing of locks is transparent to the user. The only time the user becomes aware of the system is when he or she attempts to access a locked record, at which point the computer displays a message to that effect, and the database either denies access altogether or allows the user only to view the current data element without making changes. Later in this chapter we'll take a closer look at the SQL programming language's facilities for data locking.

Increased Data Reliability

A database product will include tools for creating and updating tables on your network's servers. Your chosen database also will include tools to help you keep the data in those tables as reliable and accurate as possible. Obviously, a database cannot prevent you from certain human mistakes, such as misspelling someone's name or street address, but there are some surprisingly powerful techniques at your disposal for maintaining the integrity of your data:

Constraints: A database is normally equipped with tools that disallow obviously improper data entry; for example, not allowing letters in fields reserved for numbers only. Other constraints can be more sophisticated: allowing only a valid range of acceptable values, forcing data to be displayed in certain meaningful formats, or using custom-programmed functions to test the validity of data against your own business rules. (For example, you might want to add a function to your database that disallows ZIP codes that fall outside a given shipping region, or disallows telephone numbers without proper area codes.)

Referential Integrity: A database also includes tools that check for the validity of the relationships between data elements. For example, suppose you were entering records of purchases by a customer. The database could check to see if there is a customer record on file, check to be sure that inventory items exist and are available for shipment, calculate the total cost of the order, apply rules regarding a customer's eligibility for credit, and add shipping instructions based on the quantity and nature of the items ordered.

Transaction Processing: A database can include tables whose sole purpose is to keep records of changes made to the stored data. These tables are called *transaction tables*. If a user makes (or discovers, after the fact) a serious error, or if a database instruction fails for any reason, the computer can step backward through the transaction table, reversing the changes that caused the mistake. This process is commonly called a *rollback*.

- On the other hand, if a series of instructions is carried to a successful completion, the database can be instructed to *commit* the changes, meaning that they are made permanent, and a rollback of this series of instructions is no longer possible. This is done to prevent the transaction table from becoming overly large.

Automated Information Processing

Databases normally are equipped with various software tools for creating programs that allow as much fully automated data access and manipulation as possible. The consistent structure of the database allows access to the data using standard stored functions that can be combined to create very sophisticated information processing. The tasks of sorting, finding, and retrieving data, which formerly had to be programmed almost from scratch, can be accomplished by stringing together a database's stored procedures and objects, sharply reducing the time it would take to produce highly polished output.

Relational Databases

YOU LEARNED in Chapter 10 that there are several different types of databases, including flat-file, hierarchical, object-oriented, and relational databases. The relational database is the most commonly used database in local area networks, and so we'll look at it in some detail here. A relational database is one that breaks data down into its most fundamental units, organizes those units into *tables*, and then forms associations between different tables.

A table consists of one or more *columns* (also known as *fields*) that define a common aspect of the stored data. For example, a table representing a mailing list would have columns that correspond to first and last names, street addresses, cities, states, and zip codes. A single set of stored data elements, one element for each column, combines to form a *row* (also called a *record*). Figure 13.1 illustrates such a table.

It is possible (and actually fairly common) that some elements will remain blank in the table. Part of the fun of designing databases is coming up with tables that are as efficient as possible; database designers work hard at designing tables in which as many as possible of the row and column intersections will contain data.

Other Types of Databases

Besides the relational database model, there are other types of databases, which are generally not found in computer networks (in their pure form, at least). These other types of databases are listed below for your interest:

Flat-File Databases: A flat-file database is simply a database composed of a single table. A simple mailing list, composed only of names and addresses, is an example of a flat-file database. So is a spreadsheet that does not link any of its cells to another spreadsheet. Flat-file databases are easy to work with and are generally very fast, but their usefulness is limited because they are inherently rather inflexible.

Hierarchical Databases: A hierarchical database is a set of tables linked together in a series of one-directional relationships. An example of a hierarchical database would be a file directory structure in which a single root directory contains files and subdirectories that in turn contain other files and subdirectories, and so on.

Network Databases: A network database is one in which the relationship between the tables is more free-flowing. For example, imagine a directory structure in which a single file or subdirectory can be referenced in more than one "parent" directory. Notice that in this context, the term "network" refers to the way two or more tables can "point" to each other, rather than to the kinds of computer networks that are the subject of this book. Network databases can be extremely complicated and difficult to maintain. A relational database is a tightly controlled type of network database; it keeps complexity to a minimum by enforcing strict rules regarding how relationships between data elements are established and maintained.

Object-Oriented Database: This more modern type of database is an extension of the relational database model. While the traditional database stores only data, the object-oriented database links instruction code with the data. This instruction code may execute when the user accesses the data. The instruction code linked to the data is called a method. A combination of data and method is called an object.

You will notice that there is some overlap in the definitions of these database types. For example, a hierarchical database can be used like a relational database; an object-oriented database can have relations between various tables. As computer-based databases evolve, the term relational seems to get less and less precise. As a practical businessperson, however, your first concern should be whether your database makes or saves you money, not whether it agrees with someone's definition of "relational."

FIGURE 13.1

A single database table. A table such as this is also an example of a flat-file database, in which there are no relations made to any other table.

First Name	Last Name	Address	City	State	ZIP Code

In a relational database, several tables may be related to each other by using certain *key fields* to establish linkages between them.

For example, suppose you were to expand your mailing list into a membership list, and wanted to keep track of periodic voluntary contributions made by your members. Each member could make any number of contributions. While you could add a contribution column to the original table, and add a new record each time a member makes a new contribution, this would result in many duplications of name and address data each time a contribution was made.

A more efficient solution is to give each member a unique membership number and add a column for that number to the mailing list database. Then, you would create a second table consisting of membership numbers and contribution amounts, as illustrated in Figure 13.2. This would allow any number of contribution records to be related to individual members, while keeping duplication to a minimum.

FIGURE 13.2

A membership table is related, by means of a key field (the membership number), to a contribution table.

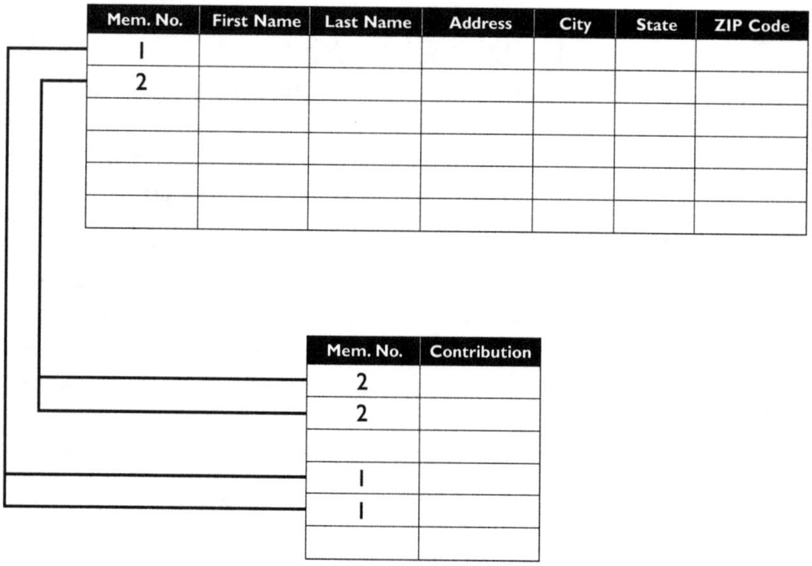

Mem. No.	First Name	Last Name	Address	City	State	ZIP Code
1						
2						

Mem. No.	Contribution
2	
2	
1	
1	

In the example shown in Figure 13.2, the records in the contribution table derive solely from the records in the membership table. This is an example of a hierarchical database, in which every "child" contribution record must be related to a "parent" membership record to have meaning. This is also an example of a "one-to-many" relationship, in which a single membership record may be related to any number of contribution records. Although the database is not, strictly speaking, "relational," there are clear relationships between the records, nonetheless.

For an example of many-to-many relationships, consider a basic general ledger system for businesses. A general ledger is a series of numbered accounts that correspond to different areas of income and expense for the business. Each account number can be subdivided into one or more departments, which allows for a more precise accounting of income and expenses. In addition, however, each department can be found under various account numbers. Figure 13.3 shows the table structure of a basic general ledger system.

In the example in Figure 13.3, there are three tables: one that holds account numbers, the type of account (income or expense), and a lengthy description of

FIGURE 13.3

Tables in a basic general ledger.

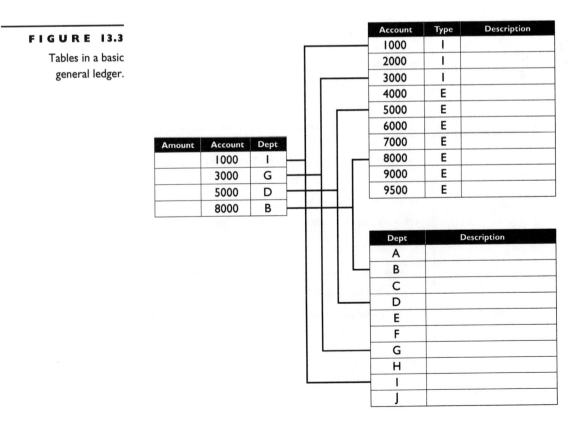

each; a second for account departments, also with a description of each; and a third table that joins account numbers and department numbers with amounts of income and expenses.

In this general ledger, lengthy descriptions can be applied to account and department numbers, but only the numbers themselves are repeated to create income and expense records. Income and expense records can be created in any order and any time during the day-to-day operations of the business. Later, the database can extract and combine specific records into a complete, formatted financial statement.

Besides the ability to produce a variety of financial statements in different formats, this type of data organization permits you to isolate and analyze various aspects of your business's finances and make important financial decisions (for example, allocating budget figures to specific areas of expense), based on your own analysis of the financial information.

How Relational Is Relational?

Trying to establish a standard for the structure of a relational database, an IBM researcher named Edgar F. Codd defined a set of rules, numbered from zero to twelve, for designing a relational database management system (RDBMS). As time goes on, these rules are happily ignored by many vendors, who have found that they can increase sales of their product simply by touting their database software as "relational." Many people are unaware of these rules and still manage to produce useful databases.

On the other hand, remember that you will evaluate a relational database management system primarily by the results it gets and its capacity to maintain high-quality output over time. A database that can qualify as "relational" by Codd's rules probably has a better chance of doing that.

0. An RDBMS must use only relational techniques to manage stored information (in other words, no bending of the other rules).

1. All data elements in the RDBMS must be stored in tables of rows and columns.

2. Every data element can be explicitly referenced using its table name, column name, and the primary key field of its row.

3. An RDBMS must have a consistent means of identifying empty data elements. In other words, if the column-and-row intersection allotted for a data element is empty, there must be a unique and consistent way to identify that empty condition, other than simply zero for number-based data and blanks for character-based data.

(continued on next page)

4. An RDBMS must store its data in a standard format that allows the data to be accessed in standard ways. In other words, the RDBMS should not use a unique, proprietary storage system.

5. An RDBMS must allow the use of at least one controlling database language, which must use ordinary character strings as commands to define and modify tables, access the data, and secure its reliability. (An example is Structured Query Language [SQL], discussed later in this chapter.)

6. The database software must be able to update any view of the data whenever changes are made in the underlying data tables.

7. Command operands that query data should be applicable as well to those that modify data. In other words, the database access language must have a consistent syntax.

8. The underlying physical structure of the database must be flexible; that is, able to be changed without requiring changes to its controlling language.

9. Database tables must be similarly flexible; that is, changeable without requiring changes to the database language.

10. Only the controlling database language should be able to place limits on what types of data are permitted in columns and rows. In other words, application software, which may use the data, is not permitted to place constraints on the type of data stored in the underlying database.

11. The controlling database language must be able to access data distributed between any number of tables, in any set of separate physical locations, without forcing changes to software applications that use the data.

12. The database must prevent application software from bypassing the limits it places on what types of data it allows to be stored.

Designing Databases

DATABASES ARE BY NATURE quite flexible and can apply to any number of record-keeping situations. Designing a good database is a skill that you can develop with experience and knowledge of a few generally accepted design principles.

Defining the Results First

Databases don't exist for their own sake—they must have a purpose. The purpose of most databases is to produce customized, meaningful information. The first step in database design is to lay out, as specifically as you possibly can, what you intend the database to produce. If the database will produce certain reports, for example, you should create mock copies of the reports you want to see. If the database will display information on the computer screen, you should draw diagrams of how those displays will look and the types of information they will present.

Although your database probably will evolve over time, and although it may eventually produce reports that you cannot envision at the outset, you must still develop the clearest possible idea of your results before you delve into the more technical aspects of database design. Many a database has failed simply because its purposes were only vaguely articulated at first.

Data Modeling

Once you have clearly defined your database's intended purpose, you are ready to analyze and chart the information-handling structures and procedures that will produce the results you intend. This process is called *data modeling*.

There are two aspects to data modeling. First, you must describe the features of the various entities in your business that you will use to produce your intended result. For example, if you intend to produce a regular report of cash balances for your business, you will need to define the business entities that produce income and expenses: customer and purchase records to show how the money flows in; creditor and expense records to show how the money flows out.

In the real world, the number of business entities can be quite large and the relationships between them quite complex. If you find that your data modeling scheme is beginning to look like a large platter of mushroom linguini, you may need to simplify your goals. You can always model a specific, limited aspect of your business (for example, a simple purchase order system) rather than some larger scheme involving expense accounting. If you have a

well-organized, simple foundation, a natural progress of evolution will be possible. Besides, simplifying to a foundation level is a good way to get past the bane of many a business: endless planning.

After you have defined the entities in your business, you must then define the relationships between them. For example, customers should be related to purchases; creditors to expenses. Figure 13.4 shows a chart of some simple business entities—customers and purchases from inventory—and how relations might be defined between them.

Defining Tables

If you have done a good job of defining your business entities, you will be able to use them as a basis for defining the tables in your database. From the previous example, you can see that a record of customer purchases would require at least three tables: one for customer records, one for purchase records, and one for inventory. Each of these tables require certain columns.

You would expect that the customer table would require customer names. It also might require shipping addresses and credit information. You would very likely want to include a customer identification number to use as a key field for relating the customer record to purchase records.

FIGURE 13.4

Modeling customer and purchase entities.

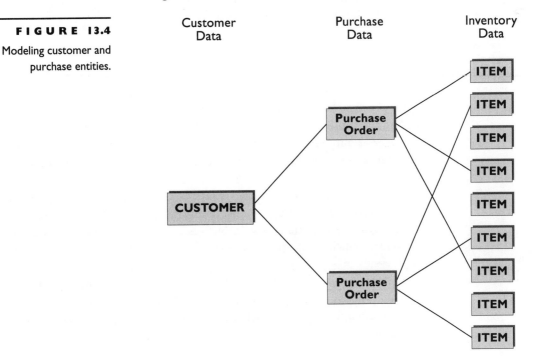

The purchase table would include key fields for customers and inventory items. The inventory table probably would include a key field plus a description of the item, various relevant features for each item, and the price.

An initial listing of your table columns for your customer purchase database might look something like this:

CUSTOMERS	PURCHASES	INVENTORY
Customer ID	Customer ID	Inventory ID
First Name	Purchase Order No.	Description
Last Name	Inventory ID	Model
Address		Color
City		Price
State		
Zip Code		
Phone		
Credit Card		
Credit Rating		

Normalization

After you have listed the tables in your database, your next step is to *normalize* it. Normalization is simply a process of going over the columns you have laid out in your initial listing and eliminating any unnecessary redundancies and accounting for problems that may have surfaced during the process of defining the tables.

For example, in the customer purchase database as it is designed so far, there is a problem with the purchase order numbers. A system of numbered purchase orders could be important to your business, but the current purchase table introduces much repetition of customer ID and purchase order numbers, one set for each inventory item ordered.

One way to overcome this is to create a separate purchase order table, which will match a customer ID number with a purchase order number. Then you can revise the purchase table to include only a purchase order number with each inventory item.

PURCHASE ORDERS	PURCHASES
Customer ID	Purchase Order No.
Purchase Order No.	Inventory ID

Although adding a new table may seem at first to add a new level of complexity to the database, it actually makes the database more efficient by reducing redundancy. Remember that the process of accessing data from multiple tables is largely automated by a controlling database language, so that multiple tables, which appear complicated to humans, can be handled very quickly and reliably by computers.

It is a fairly commonplace occurrence that, as you seek to reduce redundancy in your database tables, you will create additional tables.

Normal Forms

Over time, as database designers have acquired experience designing efficient databases, certain rules have evolved regarding the normalization process. These rules are called *normal forms*, and they describe the structure of an efficient set of database tables. There are five normal forms, of which the first three are the most frequently used:

First Normal Form: No repeating columns. A table contains only single instances of each column element. For example, you should not add several columns for purchases to the customer table—this would limit the maximum number of purchases to the number of columns. If a customer exceeded the limit, your only recourse would be to add more columns, creating a bloated table structure. Creating a separate purchase table solves this problem.

Second Normal Form: Columns depend on all key fields. If a table has two or more key fields (called a *composite key*), additional columns must be associated with the complete composite key, not just a portion of it. For example, in our original customer purchase system, the inventory ID was matched with a composite key: the customer ID and purchase order number. This was a violation of the second normal form, since the inventory ID needed only to be matched with the purchase order number. Creating a separate purchase order table solved the problem.

Third Normal Form: Non-key fields do not depend on each other. All the columns in a table that are not used as the key field do not have dependencies upon each other. For example, suppose you have established certain ratings of credit-worthiness among your customers. You would violate the third normal form if you put both a credit rating column and a credit limit column in the same customer table. It would be more efficient to create yet another table, of credit ratings and limits, and keep only a credit rating column in the customer table.

The last two normal forms apply only to the largest and most complex databases:

Fourth Normal Form: Key fields do not form interdependencies with each other. In some tables containing more than one key field, one or more of the key fields may form a dependent relationship to another, leading to a situation in which key fields must be repeated within the table. For example, suppose your customer table included a column for credit-worthiness, which indicated a variable level of credit based on the total amount of each purchase. (In technical database terms, such a state of affairs is called a *multivalued dependency*.) In such a case, it would be more efficient to create a table for credit rating codes based on purchase amounts, and relate those codes to the purchase order table, based on the total of the purchases in the purchase table.

Fifth Normal Form: Multiple key fields do not form implicit selective dependencies. This is an extension of the fourth normal form. It is possible that a multivalued dependency can imply additional dependent relationships that affect some key fields. For example, certain levels of credit may be allowed based on purchase amounts, while certain customers, based on their payment history, may have limited eligibility for credit. To track this type of interdependence efficiently, you create three tables: one for credit ratings based on total purchase amounts, as described previously, another for customer credit categories based on payment history, and a third to track the payment histories of customers.

Bear in mind that these five normal forms are guidelines for creating efficient databases. Exceptions to the rules abound, but you can justify them based on database performance and efficiency. In other words, go ahead and bend the rules of normalization, provided you can show that by doing so your database will save or make money for your business.

Charting the Relationships

The last step of the design process is vital and should not be overlooked, despite any temptation you may have to do so: Draw a picture of your tables and how they relate to each other. Figure 13.5 shows such a picture of the simple purchase system.

Drawing a chart of relationships is important not only because it may reveal weaknesses in your design (and better now than later), but also because it is the first step toward documenting your database. You will almost certainly want to refine and enhance the database as time goes by, to give it more features and power. To do this, you will need to know just how the various relations work between the database tables. A picture of your database is the best means to understand how it all fits together, weeks or months down the road when you come back to it to add those nifty enhancements.

Distributed Databases

A *distributed database* IS ONE whose tables are divided between two or more servers. It also can refer to two or more databases with tables that are linked in controlled ways.

Distributing a database can yield some significant benefits. For example, consider the customer purchase database. The shipping department may access the customer information and purchase order tables more frequently than any other department, while the inventory department may access only the inventory table

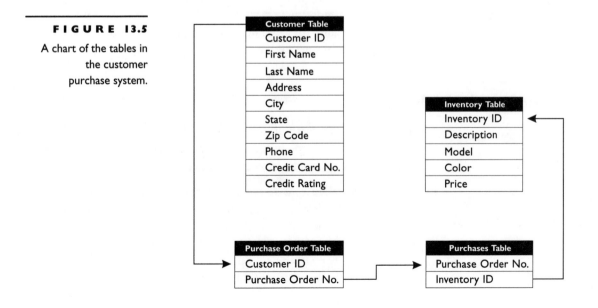

FIGURE 13.5

A chart of the tables in the customer purchase system.

regularly, as it receives incoming shipments and updates the table. If the two departments are not located very close to each other, it may make sense to have the inventory table on a server that is local to the inventory department, and the purchase order tables on a server local to the shipping department. Meanwhile, the accounting department, which needs to access the records less often, can access both tables remotely across the network.

Often, if you can place data tables on different local servers so that users who need them most often have local access to them, you will derive faster and more efficient performance. The performance gains come from reducing traffic across the network to a single server with all the tables. Fortunately, client/ server databases are equipped with tools to go out over the network and assemble relationships between far-flung data tables when necessary.

Every business has unique ways of handling information. A database manager must carefully analyze who uses the information and how often, and strike a balance in the networked database. On the one hand, you want all the performance gains you can get using local access to data tables. On the other hand, if your database becomes too widely distributed, you may lose performance because of all the network overhead required to assemble information from widely distributed sets of data tables.

Some distributed databases are created by default. The data is already stored in various locations throughout the network, and a client/server database system is brought in to tie it together. This type of installation often requires many compromises involving system performance, access to data, and the amount of meaningful information you may be able to extract. In short, you must weigh the time and effort of designing a completely new data-handling system from scratch against the compromises that come from tying separate, pre-existing data files together. Again, these are decisions you must make based on careful analysis of how your business works.

Distribution Methods

There are three common methods for managing data in a distributed database. Each method has its own strengths and weaknesses, and usually a distributed database will use some combination of the three. They are:

Extraction: Also called *data downloading,* this is the process of copying some portion of the database to another location. You can copy an entire table, a set of tables, just a portion of a single table, or the entire database, to the second location. This approach can be efficient in situations where the user receiving the copy of the data does not have to modify it at all. For example, you may elect to copy a table of prices for inventory items to the order-entry department, which needs frequent access to the information, but only references the table and never updates it.

Replication: This is also a process of copying some portion of the database to a different location, but here the user who receives the copy is also allowed to modify it. When data tables are replicated in this manner, the database system software must keep track of all modifications that are made to all the copies, and update the original as soon as possible, if not immediately. If the database software does not keep modifications current throughout the system, the database is considered out of synchronization, and destructive errors can creep in.

- For example, suppose the order entry department can make spot changes to inventory prices on its copy of the inventory department's data table. If the inventory department is not made aware of these changes, it might prepare inaccurate reports of the sale value of the inventory for the accounting department, which in turn might produce inaccurate financial statements.

- Good distributed database software includes tools that you can use to automate the process of updating copies of data tables in a distributed database. However, you can expect that this process may involve some fairly complicated system design and programming, and there is virtually no way you can have a replicated database completely in synchronization all of the time. Replication is recommended on systems where the need for the best possible performance justifies the risks involved and the extra work required to configure, program, and debug such a system.

Fragmentation: This is a process of splitting a single table up and storing it in two or more locations. As with the other distribution systems, the goal is to enhance performance by providing local access to certain types of data. For example, on a wide-area network, it may make sense to split a single customer database table between different servers in different regional areas, so that local names and addresses appear on a server located where the customer calls.

- It is also possible to split a table by columns between two different servers, although this is done far less often.

- If you find that you need to split a table between servers, be sure that your controlling database software can reassemble a split table. A good database software system can access both locations and make the table appear as a single unified table, without the user having to know the actual physical location of the data records.

Getting to the Data

ONCE YOU HAVE DESIGNED your database storage layout and either placed all your data tables on a centralized server or distributed them to different servers throughout your network, your users must be able to get to that data as easily as possible.

Users normally access data using different kinds of application software. Their software retrieves the data, perhaps does additional processing on it, and then formats the results so that the information is useful.

However, it is common on a network to have many different types of applications, and they also may be running on different local operating systems. This makes access to a single database more difficult. For example, you may have users that come into your organization already familiar with a specific database front end: dBASE, Visual Basic, Delphi, or other similar product. Can you get different products to access the same data tables? Also, you may find that, as your network evolves, you have reason to add a Macintosh machine to a PC-based network. In addition to the technical issues involved in making such a connection (see Chapter 9), you must find a way to allow the Mac to access the PC-based tables.

Fortunately, there is a mechanism that allows all these different applications to access the same database, called an *application programming interface* (API). The API is a standard feature on every popular application designed to access network databases. Very simply put, this software mechanism operates as a type of translation device that receives instructions from the application and converts them into instructions that can be understood by the database's controlling software. The API does this by passing the application's instructions to a software driver that is programmed to do the translation.

If necessary, the application's API can pass the instructions to one of several different software drivers, because it is possible to have more than one vendor's database attached to the network. If there is more than one type of database on the network, the application's API will need a separate driver for each. The API must be programmed to recognize which database should receive which instruction, and route each instruction to the correct driver.

The network database's controlling software recognizes the incoming instructions, accesses the data, and returns the requested results back to the application. The application's API then receives the resulting data and presents it in a meaningful way to the end user.

Front-end application vendors, understanding the importance of enabling their front-end products to access any underlying network database, continually update and expand their available API drivers. Of course, different vendors, in competition with each other, have developed different methods of carrying out this process of moving data between applications and databases. Some standards have emerged, however, making it easier for different application software vendors to supply reliable client/server access features with their products.

For example, one such *de facto* standard is Microsoft's *Open DataBase Connectivity* (ODBC) standard, which conforms to the model described above. If your chosen database product is ODBC-compatible, and your chosen applications are also ODBC-compatible, then you have a reasonable assurance that they will work together.

Another *de facto* standard is IBM's Distributed Relational Database Architecture (DRDA) standard. IBM developed this standard to define a means by which different application products could successfully access its mainframe database product, DB2. However, this standard has now been supported by several different network database products.

The DRDA standard governs the behavior of instructions that are sent to distributed databases from applications, and how the receiving database should handle them. It defines four levels of access to distributed databases, with increasing levels of complexity:

Level 1: Remote Requests. On this level, individual instructions access a network database on a single server. Each instruction either succeeds or fails, and the application is notified—no additional processing is required.

Level 2: Remote Transactions. On this level, a series of instructions, called a *transaction*, accesses a database on a single server. The database software is programmed to handle the transactions as a group, and it can undo them if any one of the instructions in the group should fail.

Level 3: Distributed Transactions. On this level, a transaction can access more than one database on more than one server, but each instruction within the transaction references only one database. Each database's controlling software must be able to undo the entire transaction should any individual instruction fail.

Level 4: Distributed Requests. On this level, transactions access more than one database on more than one server, and each instruction can reference more than one database. This requires very complex controlling software, in which data from different servers is joined for processing and multiple updates throughout the system are tracked and recorded. Commands to commit or roll back the transactions must be included in every database's software.

Client/server databases are one area of networking in which standards can be extremely helpful to network administrators and users. Fortunately, there is a standard language for controlling a network database. Most network-aware applications that access databases include support for this language, called *Structured Query Language,* or SQL. The next section presents an overview of this standard database language.

SQL

THE STANDARD CONTROLLING language for accessing client/server databases is called SQL. (The letters stand for *Structured Query Language,* and are pronounced either "Sequel" or sometimes "Ess-Cue-El.") IBM researchers originally designed SQL in the 1970s (Edgar Codd, whom you met earlier, was highly influential in its initial development). SQL quickly developed into a standard language for making queries in relational databases because it used a remarkably compact, English-like set of statements to perform complex sets of data access functions. SQL became a standard because its objectives are narrow, meaning that the language is used mostly for data queries and query-related processes. Simply put, you can use SQL to:

1. Create database tables

2. Define the relationships between them

3. Insert data into them

4. Extract the data in meaningful ways, based on the tables' defined relationships.

Originally, SQL's developers intended to make complex database manipulation easy for end users. However, its developers were a bit too clever in condensing the language into a few powerful command operators, and in the end, undermined their own objective. SQL is so compact, it has become rigid. It is difficult for an average, nontechnical user to master completely. In addition, it has only a few built-in functions for analyzing the data it extracts by queries.

Because of this, client/server database products use their own, more fully featured programming languages or interactive graphics-based interfaces as "front ends" for SQL. These languages execute SQL statements on the underlying database tables, and then analyze and format the data returned by the

SQL query statements. Unless you are a professional programmer, you need only be familiar with the conceptual fundamentals of SQL, rather than possess an in-depth understanding of its technical details.

SQL has great power to perform complex, sophisticated queries. It uses techniques such as nesting statements within each other, grouping key fields together, and applying built-in functions to narrow the range of records returned.

Locks

Multiuser access is the soul of client/server data processing, but allowing more than one user to access the data can allow errors to creep in. Database management software like SQL provide tools for securing data when it is available to more than one user. A standard device for doing this is a system of *locks* to prevent more than one user at a time from making changes to rows in tables.

Here are some examples of problems that can develop if you don't use locks:

Unrepeatable Reads: Suppose two users access the same data, one right after the other. The first user makes a change and issues a COMMIT statement. The second user has no idea that the data has been changed. What is worse is that the second user is now working with incorrect data and doesn't know it. If this user reads the data a second time, it will be different. A database error (or at the very least, confusion in the mind of the user) may be the result.

Lost updates: A lost update occurs when two or more users access data in a row and both make changes. Simply put, the last user to record the change with a COMMIT statement "wins." The other changes are overwritten and permanently lost.

Access to Uncommitted Data: Suppose a user accesses some data and updates it, but has not yet verified the update using a COMMIT statement. Suppose further that a second user accesses the changed, uncommitted data. If the first user backs out of the changes by issuing a ROLLBACK statement, the second user is suddenly working with incorrect data, and as before, does not realize it. This can lead to bad business decisions based on bad data.

For example, to help prevent these problems, SQL places a lock on an entire row when a user accesses a field. SQL can issue two types of record locks:

Exclusive: An exclusive lock prevents other users from reading or updating data until the lock is released. When your database program detects an exclusive lock on a row, it displays a message indicating that the data is not accessible at this time, and the user should try again later.

Shared: A shared lock prevents other users from making changes to the data but allows those users to read it. When your database program detects a shared lock on a row, it displays some form of warning message. For example, the locked data might be displayed in a different color, or a special symbol might be added, warning the user that someone else has the data and may be updating it.

Deadlocks

SQL locks are effective, but they have problems of their own. One problem that may occur with SQL locks is called a *deadlock condition*.

Suppose a user accesses some data and places an exclusive lock on the row. Then, while the lock is still in place, the first user attempts to access another row.

However, another user has already accessed data in this second row and placed an exclusive lock on it. So far, so good; the system is working as it should. The first user must now wait until the second user releases the lock before accessing this second row.

However, the second user, while keeping the lock in place, attempts to access the original row, which still has the lock on it that the first user issued!

Now the second user must also wait for the first user to unlock the original row. Unfortunately neither user can unlock the rows, because their simultaneous locks and unfortunate timing have suspended them both in a perpetual state of waiting. They are waiting for each other to remove the locks on their rows, but neither can do this, because both need the other to unlock their rows first—deadlock. Figure 13.6 shows how this deadlock condition comes about.

Fortunately, client/server database products include mechanisms that detect such a condition, and can override the users' locks and release them by sheer "brute force," and then roll back any changes that were not committed when the deadlock occurred. Both users can start over, and hopefully not bump into each other again.

SQL and Applications

If you manage a client/server database, you should expect that from time to time you will encounter SQL. For example, if you are evaluating competing

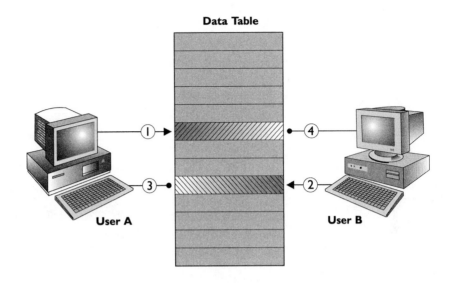

Creating a deadlock with locked files. Step 1: User A selects a row and locks it. Step 2: User B selects a row and locks it. Step 3: User A attempts to select User B's locked row, and begins waiting. Step 4: User B attempts to select User A's locked row, and begins waiting. They are both "locked out," each waiting for the other to release a row before they can continue.

database applications products, the manufacturer will undoubtedly tout the advantages of their product as a SQL front-end, and tell you how they implement SQL access for faster, more efficient, or more complete access to client/ server data than provided by their competitors. They may demonstrate to you how well SQL is integrated into their product. Hopefully, this sampling of SQL will give you a frame of reference for a better understanding of what they are talking about, and for asking questions.

Where Do I Go from Here?

14

THIS BRINGS YOU to the end of your bird's-eye overview of the networking landscape. You began by looking at the types of hardware used to connect computers; then you looked at the software that drives the systems, followed by network-specific applications: e-mail, groupware, and databases. Finally, you took a close look at networked databases, because they are a key component in most business computer networks, and the technology on top of which you will manage your business data.

Where do you go from here? The time has come to move ahead and begin the process of planning and designing your network system, or modifying your existing system to make your business work better. The information in this book is a frame of reference, a foundation for further inquiry, to help you understand the information that is out there, to cope with the rapidly evolving technology, to help you seek out the most able helpers, ask the right questions, and understand their answers.

Making the Right Choice

THE NETWORKING INDUSTRY will continue to evolve at a rapid rate. You have every right to expect that networks will become easier to use, even as their inner workings become more complicated. This has been the general trend of the industry from the beginning; there is every reason to expect that trend to continue for both hardware and software.

This book has attempted to focus on the underlying principles of networking. The most important of these is that hardware and software work together to make the technical details of network data transfer as transparent as possible—just as an automobile engine generally runs with only basic maintenance on the part of the driver, who probably isn't thoroughly versed in its inner workings. Your job is to purchase the appropriate system, drive and maintain it properly, and keep up with the changes in the industry.

This book is intended to focus your attention on a comparison of features and capabilities between different types of systems. As you have learned about different types of hardware and software, you may find that you have developed more of an interest in one type of system over another, that a particular system appears more likely to be effective for your style of doing business. For example, you may lean toward a Macintosh-based system, for its relatively easier installation and maintenance. Or you may be leaning toward a NetWare or Windows NT system, for their rich feature set and greater emphasis on data control and security. You may be leaning toward a peer-to-peer system, because communications and file sharing are most important for your business, or you may be leaning toward a client/server system, because your business requires shared access to a large-scale, centralized database.

In all cases, the process of choosing the appropriate type of networking system depends on your clear understanding of how you do business, and how you need to manage your information, rather than on any flashy features, or the latest, greatest, gee-whiz technology. The next step, therefore, is to examine how you do business. This is where you must begin.

Analyzing Your Business

A theme stressed throughout this book has been that the network you choose should lend support to—and reflect—the way you do business. Despite all our desire that the network run our business for us, while we happily push a mouse around the desktop, it will not do that. *You* still must run your business, using the network to help you.

Keep the information you have learned from this book in the back of your mind as you review and analyze how your business manages information, seek to improve your management processes, and visualize how your network will support those improvements. By all means, get your users involved in the analysis as early as possible. Encourage them to make suggestions about how your business can work better, not just about their software and hardware preferences.

Getting More Information

Once you have clarified your business goals and the rules you use to attain them, you will want to obtain more detailed information about which system seems to be best for you. There are traditional avenues through which you can obtain detailed information about network hardware and software.

User Groups

All over the world, there are groups of people who meet to exchange information and advice on popular (or even not-so-popular) hardware and software. You can obtain information about these groups by visiting local computer stores and picking up a copy of computer magazines and newsweeklies printed in your area. Most user groups run classified advertisements in these local periodicals (along with a plethora of vendor advertising). Also, your local library may have information and access to periodicals.

Even if you don't have access to these types of periodicals, you can find a wealth of information by joining an on-line service provider such as GENIE, CompuServe, or America Online. The user forums on these commercial information services function as a world-wide user group, and can yield much valuable information. Fees are variable and can be quite reasonable. They all provide access software to make it quick and easy for you to establish an account, and they usually provide some amount of free introductory usage so you can evaluate their usefulness before having to pay any service fees.

For example, imagine posting a question like this on a forum for any popular networking product: "I have a small contracting business with 12 employees and I am looking to network the desktop computers in my business. My employees need shared access to computer-based drawing plans as well as customer billing services and project scheduling. On the basis of my own data modeling, I am inclined to believe that (Windows NT, NetWare, LANtastic, or whatever product) is right for me. Has anyone had experience using this product under similar circumstances?" Questions like this have been posted before, will be posted again, and the response is nearly always helpful.

There is every likelihood that your networking questions have been asked before, so the first thing you should do when you join an online support forum is read previously posted messages. Most messages have subject headers that offer some idea of their subject matter, so at least browse those before posting any of your own. You may get the answers you are looking for without going any further. When browsing online messages, look for the acronym FAQ. This stands for "Frequently Asked Questions." Many system operators create FAQ files with answers to such questions, which you can download and read at your leisure off-line. These files can be sources of much valuable information.

Advertising

As long as you take the information found there with a large grain of salt, you can learn about product features in manufacturers' and vendors' promotional material. Of course, they will all say that they have the perfect solution for you; be skeptical and make them prove their claims before you spend any money. Many software vendors and developers offer demonstration disks, and there is nothing wrong with collecting these demos from as many vendors as will offer them to you; the more software you've evaluated, the better informed your decisions will be.

Vendors and Consultants

It's always best to obtain as much reliable information as you can on your own before talking to vendors about your needs. This is good for both you and the vendor; they are in the business of selling systems, after all, and it is appropriate that they save time and money by steering absolute beginners toward classes, promotional seminars, or books like this one.

However, it is also a fortunate aspect of this industry that many vendors are willing to offer solid, objective advice, to users of all levels. This is good business practice as it builds customer loyalty. Look for a vendor that can explain different alternatives to you and does not talk down to you, rather than one who promotes a single solution as a cure-all for every customer's problem.

Consultants are paid to offer a beginner objective and up-to-date advice. In addition, you can hire them to help you with your needs analysis, planning, scheduling, and system design. A good consultant can save you money if you hire and use them well. Refer to Appendix A for more details about hiring a network consultant.

Move Slowly

Make your moves slowly. This is classic financial investment advice, and a computer network certainly qualifies as a financial investment. There is an art to looking carefully at your alternatives, and making your commitment to a chosen system at just the right moment.

There is no compelling reason to rush into buying a system. Those beginners who are too impatient to get started with some system—any system—are more likely to be stuck with a system that doesn't fit their business model. Those who rush in too quickly are prey to cure-all salesmen who tout the advantages of one particular system, make their money on the sale, and won't follow up with service and support when the problems arise.

On the other hand, there are good reasons to go slowly: the technology is constantly improving, meaning that networks will get easier to use as time goes by, and prices on existing systems tend to fall as newer, flashier systems move to market.

One Last Word of Encouragement

I F THERE IS NO NEED to rush into networking, there is no need to be too timid either. Remember that you don't need to be a complete technical expert to get started, just someone who has taken the time to learn the basics. There are great rewards to be gained from implementing a network system that's exactly right for your business. The introductory material in this book has given you solid information to use as you pick your way through the dense mix of technical facts and marketing hype that has always characterized this relatively new industry. Go forward bravely. Never be shy about asking a question. And happy networking!

APPENDICES

Hiring a
Network
Consultant

APPENDIX

A

AFTER READING THIS BOOK, you may decide that, in order to get the best possible system, you want to contract for the services of an experienced outsider. This is a common practice that can yield significant benefits. One of the purposes of this book is to give you a common reference language for discussing your needs and possible solutions with an outside networking consultant.

If you take the time to find the right consulting services for your business, you can save a great deal of money in the long run. However, to make and keep the consultancy cost-effective, you should spend a lot of time at the outset interviewing as many different individuals and firms as possible, and negotiating hard regarding schedules and fees. Do this before you bring your chosen consultant on board and pay money. Above all else, you will be looking for an individual, work team, or firm that is compatible with the type of business you run, and your unique style of doing business. This appendix offers some advice on selecting the right networking consultant.

What Kinds of Consultants Are There?

THERE ARE MANY different types of consultants available. The market is crowded because of the great demand for their services from companies who have discovered that computer networking is more complicated than simply buying computers and stringing them together.

For larger companies, there are large consulting firms, like Andersen Consulting or Hewlett-Packard, who employ thousands of consultants and are available nationwide. On the other hand, a small business could easily get by with the services of a smaller, one- or two-person shop, found by scanning the advertisements in local computer newsweeklies and the Yellow Pages. Many of these smaller companies provide surprising value, as long as you are persistent and patient in your search, evaluating them and comparing what they offer according to the criteria described in this appendix.

Different kinds of consultants provide specific types of services. Although the terms used to describe consulting services are imprecise, they generally fall within one of the following categories:

Consultants are your advisors. They provide needs analysis (as discussed in Chapter 11) and make recommendations for solutions. They can also perform data modeling and network systems design.

Systems Integrators are hardware and software installers. They can set up new systems, or work with existing systems to upgrade, optimize performance, or add new features. They can provide management training, but they are generally not called upon to do day-to-day management and maintenance themselves.

Outsourcers are third-party managers. They control a network and manage it on a day-to-day basis. They are called *outsourcers* because they do not work from within your company. They may manage several different systems within a given locale, or license a particular system that they own and maintain.

There can be some overlap between the descriptions given above. It is important only that you be familiar with how these terms are generally used as you interview and evaluate different consulting service providers.

Making the Choice

YOU CAN LOCATE possible consultants by looking for them using the traditional channels of information: recommendations from colleagues, as well as advertisements in locally available media (for example, business journals, professional directories, chambers of commerce, and the Yellow Pages).

You solicit a consultant by calling them and arranging for an initial interview. You should be prepared to interview several before selecting one and paying any fees for services.

Following is some advice for selecting and hiring a consultant. Although some of it is pure common sense, you may find a suggestion or two here that you haven't thought of before:

Spend the most time in the planning stages. If you plan well, the implementation will go a lot more smoothly. If you plan hurriedly or sloppily, you will pay dearly in the implementation phase.

Check references. Look for an individual or firm that has done this type of project before. Be realistic about what you can afford, and be prepared to negotiate project costs and fees individually with the consultant.

Have clear, concrete, and detailed goals. If your stated goal is "installing a network to handle the records for the Marketing, Retail Sales, Customer Fulfillment, and After-Sale Support Departments," it is not specific enough. A good consultant would consider such a goal a *mission statement*, a reference point for working with you to discover the concrete, real-world results you are looking for: How do the various departments work together right now? How will the system facilitate that, or should it change the way you do business? What does the final output look like? Who sees it first? Who sees it next? What evidence is there that the new system will save or make you money? Answers to questions like these are the basis for the all-important (and all-too-often neglected) data modeling process.

Get a concrete, detailed proposal. This is the flip side of the previous advice. Perhaps you have no idea what you want; you may need the consultant to analyze your business and tell you. A good consultant will provide you with a proposal that offers alternatives, breaks the project down into a series of steps, includes a timeline for implementation of each step, describes each step's methodology, and estimates each step's cost.

The relationship is more important than the cost. Installing or upgrading a network is a long-term project. You need a productive and reliable business relationship with your hired help. Of course, you need to stay within a budget, but if you focus only on dollar costs at every step of the project, you run the risk of entering into a business relationship that is not really right for you; the result could be a bad system, more costly in the long run.

Get everything in writing. A written contract should include incentives for meeting intermediate goals, or penalties for not meeting them. Incentives work better.

Keep schedules flexible, costs firm. There are plenty of unforeseen pitfalls down the road. You will get a better system if you can allow time to react to unexpected events. You don't necessarily have to build such time into the contract; if you keep it quietly in reserve, you will sleep better at night. On the other hand, be firm regarding the dollar costs that you have negotiated. Once the cost estimate is given in writing, insist that you stick to it.

Don't throw good money after bad. There is always the possibility that things might not work out as planned. Build an *escape clause* (a basis for ending the relationship) into the initial contract. Good consultants work under contracts with such escape clauses for themselves—and so should you. Second-guessing your consultant during the project is a sure sign that you have hired one that is wrong for you, or that you could have done the job without one in the first place. Don't stay in such a relationship; if the consultant doesn't recognize the unworkable situation and bow out, invoke the escape clause and bow out yourself. You will be doing both the consultant and yourself a favor.

Hiring a consultant does not have to be a daunting task. As the client, you are in control of the process; you have the most control, however, during the selection and interview phase, so take your time and negotiate firmly. A satisfactory long-term relationship with a reliable consultant will require the least supervision and, in the long run, may well turn out to be the best networking bargain you can make.

A Glossary of
Networking
Acronyms and
Jargon

THE FOLLOWING is an alphabetical listing of the acronyms and technical terms used in this book, with a brief explanation of each.

10BASE 10 Megabits per second **Base**band. A common cable designation that indicates coaxial cable capable of handling 10 megabits data transmission per second. *See also* 10BASET.

10BASET 10 Megabits per second **Base**band Twisted-Pair. A common cable designation that indicates twisted-pair cable capable of 10 megabits data transmission per second. *See also* 10BASE.

3COM **C**omputers, **C**ommunications, **C**ompatibility. Logo of the 3COM Corporation in Santa Clara, California, makers of networking hardware.

access rights The limitations placed by a network administrator on the ability of users to locate, read, and modify data files on the network.

active hub A device that accepts, amplifies, and forwards data transmissions along a network. *See also* passive hub.

ADSP AppleTalk Data Stream Protocol. An AppleTalk protocol that monitors and verifies the flow of data between computers.

AFP AppleTalk File Protocol. An AppleTalk protocol that handles requests for data files and manages file security.

analog A communications method that represents signals by continually changing properties such as voltage or amplitude. *See also* digital.

AOL America Online. A commercial OSP that offers access to information databases, Internet access, and direct communications between users. *See also* CIS, OSP.

API Application Programming Interface. A set of driver files that allow various applications' instructions to be understood by the software that controls an underlying database.

ARCnet Attached Resource Computer Network. A inexpensive desktop computer networking system that uses hubs to connect workstations and printers.

ASP Appletalk Session Protocol. An AppleTalk protocol that verifies data sent across a network in sections.

asynchronous transmission A method of transmitting data using special data bits, called start bits and stop bits, to control the flow of data without regard to the time intervals involved.

ATP AppleTalk Transaction Protocol. An AppleTalk protocol that verifies the accuracy of network messages.

attribute A code attached to a data file that describes limits on the file's availability to users or its capability of being modified.

backbone A cable configuration in which workstations, servers, and even entire networks are connected to a main cable, for the purpose of minimizing the flow of network data traffic between them. Also refers to the cable itself.

bandwidth The capacity of a network to handle simultaneous data transmissions. The larger the number of simultaneous transmissions, the great the network's bandwidth.

baseband A cable that carries a single signal. *See also* broadband.

baud rate The measurement of speed of data transmissions using a modem, measured as the maximum number of bit changes (1 to 0, 0 to 1) the modem can handle per second.

BBS Bulletin Board System. A usually informal system in which a single computer with one or more modems manages communications and file sharing between callers who establish links using modems.

bit Binary Digit. The smallest unit of information that a computer can process.

BNC Bayonet Connector. A metal cylinder used to connect cables with computer network interface cards, or other nodes on the network.

bridge A hardware device used to link two or more LANs and manage the flow of communications signal between them. *See also* gateway, router.

broadband A type of cable that can carries more than one signal at a time. *See also* baseband.

bus The electronic pathway that carries signals from one component to another inside a computer.

C/S Client/Server. A network system in which one or more computers (called servers) are used to send, receive, and store data files, and also to manage the system; other computers (called clients) are used as workstations to receive and process data from servers.

CCITT Comité Consultatif Internationale de Téléphonie et de Télégraphie. An organization, based in France, that develops international standards for digital data communications. Same as ICCTT. *See also* X.400.

CD-ROM Compact Disk Read-Only Module. A hardware device used to read computer data from laser disks. Sometimes this acronym is used as a generic term for laser-readable disks.

CHAP Challenge Handshake Authentication Protocol. An Internet-standard protocol for verifying encrypted passwords.

CIS CompuServe Information Service. A commercial enterprise that offers access to huge databases of information and communications between users, including access to the Internet. *See also* AOL, OSP.

CISC Complete/Complex Instruction Set Computer. A term used to describe a chip with a fully featured internal architecture. *See also* RISC.

CLI Call Line Identification. A protocol that identifies a calling telephone number and checks against a stored list of authorized callers before making the link to a computer.

client A computer that has been configured to receive data on a network.

client/server *See* C/S.

clock rate The operating speed of a microprocessor, measured in MHz. The clock is a circuit within the microprocessor that uses a vibrating crystal to generate a timing pulse, synchronizing the flow of information within the computer.

CNA Certified NetWare Administrator. An individual who has passed a course of study in everyday management of a Novell NetWare network.

CNE Certified NetWare Engineer. An individual who has passed a course of study in the design, installation, and technical maintenance of a Novell NetWare network.

coaxial A type of communication cable that uses a single copper wire surrounded by insulation and a braided copper shield.

COM Communications Port. An acronym used to name computers' peripheral ports, which send and receive data in serial (single-bit) format.

configuration The process by which a computer component (hardware or software) is modified so as to make it work with another component.

CPU Central Processing Unit. The combination of random-access memory, storage device, and processing chip used to manage digital electronic data.

database A data processing system that breaks data down into its most fundamental units, and stores those units in tables of rows and columns. *See also* DBMS, RDBMS, OODB.

DBMS Database Management System. An application that organizes data into a structured framework, consisting of tables containing columns and rows, and uses that framework to provide access to the data and a vehicle for processing it. *See also* RDBMS, NDBMS.

DDP Datagram Delivery Protocol. The data-handling protocol at the heart of the AppleTalk protocol suite.

deadlock A situation in which two or more computers each attempt to access data (or some other resource) currently held by the other, and become completely inaccessible as each waits for the other to release the resource being sought.

differential backup A system of data backup that makes copies only of those files that have been modified since the last full backup was made. *See also* full backup, incremental backup.

digital A communications method that represents binary values by measuring electronic states. *See also* analog.

directory A means of representing related files as being grouped together on the hard disk under a unique directory name.

distributed database A set of data tables that is typically located on different servers throughout the network, and which can be accessed and controlled as a single unified system.

distributed processing A system in which different users on a network handle the separate tasks that, taken together, make up a single unified process involving shared network data.

DLC Data Link Control. A limited protocol designed for connections between LANs and IBM Mainframe computers.

DMA Direct Memory Access. Special circuits on some hardware components that allow users to bypass the microprocessor for certain data-transfer operations.

domain A group of computers that operate as a single workgroup within a larger network, and can be accessed as a group using an identifying unique name.

DOS Disk Operating System. A standard operating system for computers, originally developed by Microsoft for the IBM PC and used in most non-networked computers based on the Intel x86 family of microprocessors.

DRDA Distributed Relational Database Architecture. A standard developed by IBM Corporation that allows different applications to access IBM's mainframe database, DB2, along with other DRDA-compatible database products.

drive mapping The process of assigning drive letters to network nodes, for faster and easier access to them.

e-mail Electronic Mail. A network communication system for transferring messages between users.

EDC Error Detection and Correction. A memory feature that verifies RAM output, and resends output when memory errors occur.

EISA Extended Industry Standard Architecture. A 32-bit design that is an enhanced version of ISA. *See also* bus, ISA.

enterprise A term used to describe a group of network nodes that work together to share data and processes, in order to achieve common goals.

EP Echo Protocol. An AppleTalk protocol that repeats messages back to the sending node to verify its integrity.

Ethernet A popular, standard networking protocol and connection design that joins computers using a bus topology of node joined to a single main cable.

fiber-optic cable A cable type that uses a fiberglass core to transmit pulses of laser light that represent binary data bits.

fiber-line driver A hardware device that permits connections between fiber-optic and wire-based cables.

file server A computer on a network that stores and sends data files to other nodes. *See also* server.

firewall A security method that renders parts of a network invisible and inaccessible to users who establish remote connections with assigned remote-access workstations.

FTP File Transfer Protocol. A communications protocol used on the Internet to process complex messages and data files sent over a network, and automate message processing.

full backup A data protection method that makes copies of files on the hard disk, regardless of whether they have been modified since they were previously backed up.

gateway A hardware device with its own processor and memory that connects networks with more complex systems using different communications protocols. *See also* bridge, router.

GB Gigabytes. One billion bytes of data, used as a unit for measuring larger hard disks and RAM. *See also* MB.

GUI Graphical User Interface. Software that allows the user to control computer services by means of graphical objects displayed on the screen and selected using a digitizing device such as a mouse or tablet.

handshaking A process by which two computing devices determine a commonly supported protocol and transmission rate in order to exchange data.

hub A device that accepts signals from an attached network node and passes them along to another attached node. *See also* active hub, passive hub.

IAC Interapplication Communication. A process that allows applications to access data from other applications.

ICCTT International Consultative Committee of Telephony and Telegraphy. An organization, based in France, that develops international standards for digital data communications. Same as CCITT. *See also* X.400.

IDP Internet Datagram Protocol. The basic protocol in XNS, similar to TCP/IP. *See also* XNS, TCP/IP.

IEEE Institute of Electrical and Electronics Engineers. A body of experts that establishes electrical specification standards for just about every electrical device.

Internet A world-wide, free-form network using telephone lines, satellites, microwave transmission, and other media, made up of millions of users all over the world who make connections (usually via modem) and communicate with each other on just about any subject imaginable.

interrupt A means by which a computer can temporarily suspend current processing in order to accept a request for services that must take priority.

IP Internet Protocol. A communications protocol for verifying the accuracy and address of network data. *See also* TCP/IP.

IPX Internetwork Packet Exchange. A standard set of protocols, similar to TCP/IP, that handle data verification and addressing responsibilities between NetWare and other networks.

IS Information Systems. A business workgroup with responsibility for managing communication of business information. *Also called* MIS.

ISA Industry Standard Architecture. A 16-bit standard for transmitting data inside a workstation. *See also* bus, EISA.

ISDN Integrated Services Digital Network. A set of telephone-wire technologies that allow specialized data pathways to coexist with voice pathways.

ISO International Standards Organization. A body of experts, based in Geneva, Switzerland, that define global standards for networking and data exchange.

KB Kilobyte. One thousand data bytes. A standard unit for measuring the size of floppy disks and smaller data files.

LAN Local Area Network. Two or more computers that can exchange data via cables or broadcast devices. "Local" is a relative term, meaning that the computers on the network are located within reasonable physical proximity of each other. *See also* WAN.

log in To establish a connection as a user on a network.

log out To end a connection as a user on a network.

LPT Line Printer. An acronym used to name computers' peripheral ports, which send and receive data in parallel (8-bit) format.

Mac A Macintosh computer; any of several models manufactured by Apple Computer, Inc.

mainframe A large, multiprocessor computing system designed to allow access by a large number of users and process especially large amounts of data.

map To assign a drive letter (E:, F:, G:) to a node or file directory on a network.

MAPI Messaging Application Programmer's Interface. A standard for formatting and displaying electronic messages, developed by the Microsoft Corporation.

MAU Media Attachment Unit. A device used to connect computers to a shared cable.

MB Megabyte. One million bytes of data, used as the unit for measuring the size of hard disks and random-access memory.

MCA Micro Channel Architecture. A 32-bit design for transmitting data within a workstation, developed by IBM. *See also* bus.

MHS Message Handling System. A standard electronic mail and messaging system developed by Novell Corporation.

MHz Megahertz. One million cycles per second, used as the unit for measuring a microprocessor's speed. *See also* clock rate.

MIS Management Information Systems. A business workgroup with responsibility for managing communication of business information. This is an older term normally associated with mainframe systems. *Also called* IS.

MLID Multiple Link Interface Driver. Software for allowing compatible hardware to accept data using more than one protocol. *See also* ODI.

MS Millisecond. One-millionth of a second. A unit of measure of the time takes the hard disk to find data.

MSAU Multistation Access Unit. A special hub on token-ring networks used to connect workstations.

MS-DOS *See* DOS.

multiprocessing The ability of hardware or software to perform more than one process simultaneously.

multiprocessor A server with more than one processing chip, used to provide greater power and efficiency to the network.

NAC Network Adapter Card. *See* NIC (Network Interface Card).

NBP Name Binding Protocol. An AppleTalk protocol that translates user-defined network node names into network node addresses.

NCB Network Control Block. Instruction code sent by network software to a computer's network-aware operating system.

NCP NetWare Core Protocol. A NetWare protocol that manages the flow of data between NetWare clients and file servers for maximum efficiency.

NDBMS Networked Database Management System. An application that synchronizes multiple users' access to centralized databases. *See also* DBMS, RDBMS.

NDS NetWare Directory Services. A system for organizing network locations into a hierarchy, used in NetWare version 4.

NetBEUI NetBIOS Extended User Interface. A small protocol suitable for networks where all nodes establish direct links with the server. *See also* NetBIOS.

NetBIOS Network Basic Input/Output System. A standard developed by the IBM Corporation for accessing network services by means of a computer's operating system.

network administrator A person responsible for the day-to-day operation and maintenance of a computer network.

NIC Network Interface Card. A hardware device inserted into a slot inside the computer, which manages the flow of data between the computer and the rest of the network. *Also called* NAC (Network Adapter Card).

NOS Network Operating System. Software that directs data traffic throughout the network, manages security, and handles requests for network services.

NS Nanosecond. One-billionth of a second, used as the unit for measuring the speed of random-access memory chips.

object A specialized form of data in which information is stored together with code that executes when the information is accessed. *See also* OODB, OLE.

ODBC Open DataBase Connectivity. A standard developed by the Microsoft Corporation for moving data reliably between application programs and databases.

ODI Open Datalink Interface. A software standard for allowing compatible hardware to accept data using more than one protocol. *See also* MLID.

OLE Object Linking and Embedding. A protocol developed by the Microsoft Corporation that allows applications to exchange data in the form of objects that are either stored in separate files and linked to the application, or embedded as copies within applications. *See also* object.

OODB Object-Oriented Database. A database that links instruction code directly with stored data. *See also* DBMS.

OSP Online Service Provider. A large-scale enterprise that offers access to huge databases of information and communications between users. *See also* CIS, AOL.

packet A block of data sent over a network, which includes both raw information and protocol-specific code used to identify and process the block.

PAP Password Authentication Protocol. An Internet-standard protocol for verifying passwords from remote callers.

PAP Printer Access Protocol. An AppleTalk protocol that monitors the flow of data that is sent in a continuous stream instead of in sections.

passive hub A device that is used to make connections between nodes on a network, but does not act upon the signal in any way. *See also* active hub.

PCI Peripheral Component Interconnect. A bus design developed by the Intel Corporation to take advantage of the advanced processing power in systems that use 80486 or later microprocessors. *See also* bus.

PDL Page Description Language. A set of functions used by printers to control the formatting of text on paper.

peer-to-peer A form of computer networking in which workstations are permitted to act as both clients and servers. *See also* client, server, C/S.

PEP Packet Exchange Protocol. An XNS protocol that processes messages for transport along a network. *See also* XNS.

PIN Personal Identification Number. A memorized number used as a password in some security systems, such as those for bank ATM machines.

port A hardware device used to make connections between a computer and a peripheral device, such as a printer or modem.

power supply An electrical device that acts as a transformer between a computing device and a standard electrical source.

print server A computing device that handles requests for printing services across a network.

protocol A rule, or set of rules, that allow computers to transmit and receive data, maintain consistent timing, and check for errors.

query The process of extracting meaningful information from a database.

RAID Redundant Arrays of Independent/Inexpensive Disks. A system that uses more than one disk to make additional copies of the same data at the time it is being stored.

RCP Remote Courier Protocol. An XNS protocol that allows software to run services available on other network nodes. *See also* XNS.

RDBMS Relational Database Management System. An application that organizes data into a structured framework of tables containing columns and rows, and sets up linked relationships between those tables. *See also* DBMS, NDBMS.

remote access The process of making connections to a network or workstation from distant locations using common-carrier or dedicated telephone lines.

rights *See* Access Rights.

ring network A network topology in which workstations are connected to each other in a closed ring.

RIP Routing Information Protocol. An XNS protocol that establishes the best data path for messages from one network node to another. *See also* XNS.

RISC Reduced Instruction Set Computer. A term used to describe a chip with internal architecture that has been simplified and optimized for the most common types of internal operations. *See also* CISC.

router A hardware device that can send and receive data between multiple linked networks.

RPS Redundant Power Supply. A secondary computer power supply that takes over in the event that the main power supply fails.

RTMP Routing Table Maintenance Protocol. An AppleTalk protocol that monitors the location of nodes on the network and maintains a database of reliable connections between them.

SA System Administrator. A person or department that manages the day-to-day operations of a computer network. *See also* CNA.

SAP Server Advertising Protocol. A NetWare protocol that monitors the process of logging on and off the network and manages the transfer of data throughout the network.

SCSI Small Computer Systems Interface (pronounced *scuzzy*). A standard for the electronic circuitry controlling a computer's peripheral hardware such as hard disks and tape backup devices.

server A dedicated computer that stores data and processes requests to access or transmit the stored data. *See also* file server, print server.

SFS System Fault Tolerance. A set of special data storage techniques that protect the integrity of data on the NetWare network.

SMB Server Message Block. A protocol that translates computer instructions into NetBIOS instructions. *See also* NetBIOS.

SMF Standard Message Format. A standard for formatting electronic messages, developed by the Novell Corporation.

SMP Symmetrical Multiprocessing. A feature that integrates more than one processor into a single file server.

SMU Symmetric Multiprocessor Units. A file server that uses more than one central processing chip for greater speed and efficiency.

SPP Sequenced Packet Protocol. An XNS protocol that verifies transmitted network data. *See also* XNS.

SPX Sequenced Packet Exchange. A NetWare protocol that uses NetWare functions to verify the accuracy of data.

SQL Structured Query Language. A standard language for managing client/server databases. *See also* DBMS, NDBMS, RDBMS.

star network A network topology in which workstations are independently connected to a central hub or server.

STDA StreetTalk Directory Assistance. A feature of VINES that lists node names on the network.

STMP Simple Mail Transfer Protocol. A communications protocol for processing ASCII text messages sent over a network.

TI A specification for telephone cable that handles data (non-voice) transmissions only, providing 24 separate channels of communication, each channel transmitting data at a rate of 64Kb per second.

T3 A specification for telephone cable that handles data (non-voice) transmissions only, providing 672 separate channels for communication, each capable of transmitting data at 64Kb per second.

tap A device that connects a workstation cable to a main or backbone cable. *Also called* vampire tap.

TCP Transmission Control Protocol. A host protocol for processing data sent along a network and over telephone lines. *See also* TCP/IP.

TCP/IP Transmission Control Protocol/Internet Protocol. A communications protocol used as the basis for the Internet, and supported by most network operating systems.

TTS Transaction Tracking System. A NetWare system that keeps records of network processes, and can roll back, or undo, the processes in the event a system crash damages the integrity of data on the network.

telecommuting A process by which users perform day-to-day computing tasks from home via remote access rather than personally appearing at the workstation site. *See also* remote access.

thick Ethernet A coaxial network cable (approximately one centimeter thick) used to connect large networks with nodes that are up to 1000 meters apart.

thin Ethernet A coaxial network cable (approximately 5 millimeters thick) used to connect local area networks with nodes that are less than 500 feet apart.

token-ring network A network topology in which data traffic is regulated by passing a special electronic signal, called a token, between nodes. The token controls which nodes can send and receive data.

topology The layout of a network. A physical topology describes the real-world connections between network nodes. A logical topology describes the data paths used by the network operating system.

UPS Uninterruptible Power Supply. A hardware device that provides continuous electrical power to the server, usually for a short time, in the event of a external electrical power failure. (Also United Parcel Service, a commercial mailing and shipping service sometimes called upon when the network fails.)

vampire tap *See* tap.

VGA Video Graphics Array. A screen resolution standard for color monitors.

VIM Vendor-Independent Messaging. A standard for formatting electronic messages, developed by the Lotus Corporation.

VINES VIrtual NEtwork System. A file-server based network operating system designed as an extension of the UNIX, developed by Banyan Incorporated.

VLM Virtual Loadable Module. Software that controls a limited set of processes on a NetWare network.

WAN Wide Area Network. Two or more computers that can exchange data via cables or broadcast devices. "Wide" is a relative term, meaning that the computers on the network are located outside of a reasonable physical proximity of each other. *See also* LAN.

Windows NT Windows New Technology. A client/server operating system developed by Microsoft Corporation.

WTS Wireless Transport Services. Hardware for managing network connections using radio or infrared signaling devices.

X.400 An international standard, developed by the International Consultative Committee of Telephony and Telegraphy, for formatting electronic messages transferred across or between computer networks.

XNS Xerox Network System. A simplified communications protocol suite developed by the Xerox Corporation.

ZIP Zone Information Protocol. An AppleTalk protocol that analyzes the network configuration and collects device addresses into groups to establish efficient access.

Index

Note to the Reader: Throughout this index **boldface** page numbers indicate primary discussion of a topic. *Italic* page numbers indicate illustrations.

H

half duplex, 103
handshaking, 103, 266
hard disk space, for Windows for
 Workgroups, 118
hard disks
 speed of, 56
 for workstations, 48
hardware
 for NetWare, 128
 setup during network install, 191
 specifications in system log, 203
 standards in system log, 204
 warranties in system log, 193–194
hierarchical databases, 225
hierarchical structure for network,
 129
high-security environment, diskless
 terminals for, 55
hiring
 consultants, **254–257**
 network managers, 197–198
home users, remote connections for, 99
hubs, 23, **66**, 74, 266

I

IAC (interapplication communication),
 122, 266
IBM
 Distributed Relational Database
  Architecture (DRDA) standard,
  239
 Micro Channel Architecture, 54
 PowerPC processor, 49
IBM-compatible network system, 38
ICCTT (International Consultative
 Committee of Telephony and
 Telegraphy), 266
IDP (Internet Datagram Protocol),
 40, 266
IEEE (Institute of Electrical and Elec-
 tronics Engineers), 266
Immediate Compress file attribute,
 132
incremental backup, 202
Indexed file attribute, 131

Industry Standard Architecture (ISA),
 53, 267
Info World, 216
information, simultaneous access to
 database, 222–223
information management, 96
information processing, automated,
 224
Information Services Department
 (IS), 4–5, 267
 current, 6
 function of personnel, 6
information sharing, 5
installing
 applications, 207
 cable, **70–73**
 schedule for, **190–193**
 software, 192–193
 Windows NT client software, 135
 Windows for Workgroups, 118
insulation, for cabling, 73
Integrated Services Digital Network
 (ISDN) communication, 100, **107–
 108**, 110, 267
Intel Corporation, 54
interapplication communication
 (IAC), 122, 266
InterBASE, 160
International Consultative Committee of Telephony and Telegraphy,
 164–165
International Standards Organization
 (ISO), 35, 267
Internet, 29, 213, 266
 remote connections via, **108–109**
Internet Access Kit, 121
Internet Datagram Protocol (IDP),
 40, 266
Internet-in-a-Box, 29
Internet Protocol (IP), 37, 266
internetwork messages, 43
Internetwork Packet Exchange (IPX),
 43, 267
interrupt, 266
 for network interface card, 57
 for printer port, 216
inventory of equipment, 180–181
Invisible NET/30, 39
IP (Internet Protocol), 37, 266
IPX (Internetwork Packet Exchange),
 43, 267

IPX.COM, 143
IPX/SPX, 32-bit protected mode
 version of, 149
IS (Information Systems), 267
ISA (Industry Standard Architecture),
 53, 267
ISDN (Integrated Services Digital
 Network) communication, 100,
 107–108, 110, 267
ISO (International Standards Organi-
 zation), 35, 267

J

jumper block connectors, to configure NIC, *58*, 58, 59

K

KB (kilobyte), 267
key fields, 226, 232, 233, 234

L

LAN (Local Area Network), 267
 development, 6
LAN Distance software, 150
LAN Manager (Microsoft), 144
LAN Times, 216
LANDesk Management Suite (Intel),
 205
LANtastic, 39, **115–117**
 32-bit version, 121
layers in OSI model, 36
layout. *See* topologies
leaf object, 129
licenses
 for network software, 7
 user vs. site, 52
linear bus topology, 17–18, *18*
linear logical topology, 21, *22*
Local Area Network (LAN), 267
 development, 6
local install of applications, vs. on
 server, 197–198
local processing, and bandwidth, **109**
local terminal, 37–38
LocalTalk connector, 78